THE GLASS PALACE CHRONICLE
OF THE KINGS OF BURMA

AMS PRESS

NEW YORK

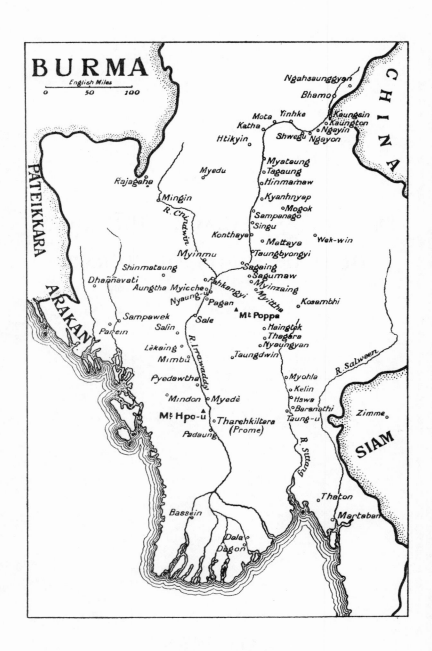

THE
GLASS PALACE CHRONICLE
OF THE
KINGS OF BURMA

TRANSLATED BY

PE MAUNG TIN

AND

G. H. LUCE

———

Issued by
The Text Publication Fund of the
Burma Research Society

———

OXFORD UNIVERSITY PRESS
LONDON: HUMPHREY MILFORD
1923

Library of Congress Cataloging in Publication Data

Hmannān maha yazawintawkyī. English
    The Glass Palace chronicle of the kings of Burma.

    Translation of Hmannān maha yazawintawkyī.
    "Issued by the Text Publication Fund of the Burma
Research Society."
    Reprint of the 1923 ed. published by Oxford
University Press, H. Milford, London.
    1. Burma—History—To 1824. 2. Burma—Kings
and rulers. I. Burma Research Society. Text
Publication Fund. II. Title.
DS529.2.H5613   1976   959.1'02   75-41137
ISBN 0-404-14555-8

Reprinted from an original copy in the collections
of the University of Chicago Library

From the edition of 1923, London
First AMS edition published in 1976
Manufactured in the United States of America

AMS PRESS INC.
NEW YORK, N. Y.

CONTENTS

PART IV

PAGE

PART V

INTRODUCTION

The Glass Palace Chronicle. In the year 1829 King Bagyidaw of Burma appointed a committee of scholars to write a chronicle of the Burmese kings. The committee consisted of 'learned monks, learned brahmans, and learned ministers', who met together and compiled a chronicle which they 'sifted and prepared in accordance with all credible records in the books'. The name of the chronicle was taken from the Palace of Glass, in the front chamber of which the compilation was made. The preface sets forth the purpose and nature of the undertaking: 'The king of the Law seeing the many discrepancies and repetitions in the former chronicles gave thought to the matter. Being convinced that a chronicle of kings should be the standard, a balance, so to speak, for all duties of the king, for all affairs of state, for all matters of religion, and not a thing full of conflicting and false statements, he assembled his ministers and ecclesiastical teachers in the front chamber of the palace, which was variegated with divers gems and a fit place for the most exalted personages, and caused the chronicle to be purified by comparing it with other chronicles and a number of inscriptions each with the other, and adopting the truth in the light of reason and the traditional books'. The compilers, in utilizing the earlier records, have made observations on various debatable points in them. These observations, which are mostly in the form of learned and lengthy disquisitions, are inserted into the body of the work and thus greatly disturb the flow of the narrative. But they are a testimony to the learning and assiduity of the compilers, who have drawn upon almost every form of literature in support of their arguments. In the present volume alone are quoted by name eleven inscriptions, eleven chronicles, ten *thamaing*, besides the Pali chronicles and the Burmese poetical literature.

When I began the translation, I followed the example of the compilers of examining all available records which bear on history,

in the hope of discovering the sources and tracing the development
of Burmese historical literature. After collecting as many materials
as I could get, I made a detailed comparative study of them,
embodying the results in the form of foot-notes and appendices to
the Glass Palace Chronicle. But this apparatus of notes with
numerous cross-references would entail a higher cost of printing
than the Burma Research Society was prepared to defray.
Besides, the materials I was able to collect were far from complete :
I failed to get copies of some of the chronicles, like the Godhavara
Chronicle mentioned on p. 112. And the uncritical edition of the
inscriptions detracts from their value as historical material. For
these reasons I have decided to print nothing but the plain
translation, divested even of explanatory notes on some words and
expressions, which might have demanded exposition. Insufficient
as my materials have been, I have attempted, however, to give
a brief sketch of them as a preliminary contribution to the literature
of Burmese history. I have not considered the Pali chronicles, such
as the Mahavamsa, and the Pali commentaries, such as the
Dhammapada Commentary, as they belong to the domain of Pali
literature, and as their authority is used by the Glass Palace
Chronicle mainly on religious grounds.

   The Inscriptions. First in indigenous literature come the inscriptions, the oldest and most trustworthy materials. They may be
studied in the six volumes issued by the Archaeological Department. (The Department is now undertaking a critical edition
and scientific study of the inscriptions in its new official organ, the
Epigraphia Birmanica.) Only the first volume has been translated
into English. It is a serious defect in the editing of most of these
volumes that the dates of some of the inscriptions are left undecided.
The confusion that arises in these dates is largely due to the
enthusiasm of king Bodawpaya (1781–1819), who, ostensibly for
reasons of scholarship, made a collection of all available inscriptions.
Of some he made true copies, called *hsin-hto,* i. e. authorized versions
of the originals. Of others he made revised versions, altering the
spelling and in some cases the contents also. These are called
sat-hto, i.e. revised versions, and may generally be recognized by
the modern spelling and the artificial style and grandiloquent
phraseology of a later and pedantic age. The original inscriptions
and the true copies, on the other hand, reflect the spirit of an earlier

age, when men were expressing their thoughts and hopes and fears
in vigorous and simple language. The crudeness of their spelling
and the quaintness of their expression make them valuable as
philological and archaeological records. There are, thus, broadly
speaking, three groups of inscriptions: the original inscriptions
which Bodawpaya did not copy, and the true copies and revised
versions which he made of the original inscriptions he collected.
In every case great care is required in consulting the inscriptions
especially as to date and orthography. With this qualification
inscriptions constitute the best records for the social and political
history of the times. Even the revised versions are, to say the
least, as reliable as any of the chronicles, for they faithfully re-
produce the subject-matter, though not the spelling and phraseology,
of the original. The earliest inscriptions belong to the Pagan
period (eleventh–thirteenth century), when the religion in its pure
form had just been introduced into Upper Burma from Thaton.
The new religion produced a general outburst of faith, manifested
in the whole-hearted devotion to works of merit, and especially the
building of sacred edifices. King and minister, rich man and poor,
queen and handmaid, vied with each other in the erection of pagodas
of various types and monasteries of every design, lavishing their
wealth on images of costly gold and sets of scriptures, on the
dedication of glebe-lands and the maintenance of ' pagoda-slaves '.
Inscriptions, in simple vernacular or polished Pali, in unaffected
prose or ambitious verse, faithfully record these ' works of merit '.
The very buildings bear silent witness to the religious spirit that
pervaded the whole land. It is significant that kings left us, not
stately palaces as monuments of their earthly greatness, but magni-
ficent pagodas as a proof of the sincerity of their faith. Their
reward is merit. Yet to say that a king built a pagoda from a
selfish desire to gain merit would be doing him an injustice.

> ' By this abundant merit I desire
> Here nor hereafter no angelic pomp
> Of Brahmas, Suras, Maras ; nor the state
> And splendours of a monarch ; nay, not even
> To be the pupil of the Conqueror.
> But I would build a causeway sheer athwart
> The river of *samsara*, and all folk
> Would speed across thereby until they reach
> The Blessed City.'

So prays Alaungsithu at the dedication of the Shwegugyi Pagoda.
An early instance of this sharing with others the merit accruing
from a work of merit is afforded by the inscription on the Wardak
Vase of 'the year 51' (*Epigraphia Indica,* vol. xii, 202). The
motive of this inscription is the same as that of most of the Pagan
inscriptions. The donor desires merit only to share it with others.
'What then, will there be loss of merit to him who thus shares
what he has attained? No. As when from a burning lamp a
thousand lamps were lit, it would not be said that the lamp was
exhausted; the light, being one with the added lights, becomes
increased, thus there is no decrease in our sharing what we have
attained; on the contrary there is an increase.' So Buddhaghosa
(fifth century A. D.) comments in his Atthasalini. The fervency of
the aspiration to gain and share merit often gives rise to a formula
of curses upon those who should in any way desecrate the work of
merit. Often in one and the same inscription the most beautiful
blessings end with the most terrible imprecations: 'Who favours
and upholds like me the gift of faith which I thus offer with all my
heart—be he my son, grandson, or any future king who comes after
me, queens, princes, royal ministers, high or low, men of wealth
and substance, bailiffs, headmen, persons of good family hereafter,
yea, all who bountifully support—may such, like me, be favoured
above others with the Wheel of treasure; may he be endued like
king Mandhata with glory, majesty, and power; may he receive
the full fruition of the boon of Buddhahood, silent Buddhahood,
the boon of apostleship, or the boon of saintship. But whoever spoils
even so much as an oil-lamp out of the glebe I have offered to the end
that the religion may last five thousand years, may he be oppressed
with the eight dangers, the ten punishments, the thirty-two results
of *karma,* the eight calamities, the ninety-six diseases. May he be
suddenly overtaken with a great affliction which a thousand doctors
may not avail to cure. Having suffered thus for long, generation
after generation, when his bodily elements dissolve, may he suffer
by going in and out among the eight chief hells [Sañjiva], Kala-
sutta, Sanghata, Roruva, Maharoruva, Tapanna, Mahatapanna, and
Avici, and likewise the twelve minor Ussaddarek hells and the forty
limbos of Yama and Lokika; may he suffer with the hosts of
Pretas, Asuras, and Lokantareks. Even if he survive all these
sufferings, may he revisit five thousand times these glebelands in

the form of a boneless and miserable creature, a Preta, a worm,
a water-leech. If he survive this, may he be born times without
number as a mad dog, a mad pig, a mad fowl, a mad man. Thus
I denounce, pouring waterdrops from this golden kettle ' (Pagan
Pahtodaw Inscription).

The Chronicles. The chronicles quoted in the present volume are
The Abridged, Arakan, Godhavara, Great, Middle, Nangyaung,
New, Old, Pagan, Tagaung, and Thaton. I have not been able
to get copies of all of them. The following is a brief sketch of those
I have studied, beginning with the earliest.

The Celebrated Chronicle. The oldest chronicle extant is the
Celebrated Chronicle by Samantapasadika Silavamsa, familiarly
known as Thilawuntha, the great poet who lived in the fifteenth
century. It is disappointing as history. It gives us less information about Burma than about the Buddhist movement in India and
Ceylon. It is not even mentioned in the present volume, which,
however, quotes from Thilawuntha's poetry as the writing of 'the
famous Maha Thilawuntha, whom a line of scholars learned in
book-lore have not forsaken, but made their prop and backbone of
authority'. Men of letters of the fifteenth century were so much
under the influence of the religion and Pali studies that com-
paratively few works on secular subjects were written in the vernacular. Thilawuntha shows the extent of that influence on
himself by writing the preface to his chronicle in Pali verse. The
Chronicle may be divided into three parts: The first part deals
with the kings of Buddhist India and Ceylon. This list of the
kings takes up a great portion of the Chronicle and is based
on the Pali chronicles of Ceylon, and gives the usual account
of the Sakiyan kings and their quarrels, the Buddha's personal
name, Bindusara and Asoka, with a rather lengthy epilogue. The
second part tells of the conquest of Ceylon as given in the Ceylon
Pali chronicle, the Mahavamsa, with a short account of the kings
of Ceylon till Buddhaghosa's visit in the fifth century A.D. The
third part is devoted to Burmese history. It lays stress on the
Buddha's visit to Lèkaing village as told by the Glass Palace
Chronicle in § 103, and argues therefrom that 'in Ceylon the
religion did not begin to arise before the year 236 A.D. But in
our land the religion arose since the time the Lord came to dwell in
the sandalwood monastery'. It is singular that no mention is

made of Tagaung. Perhaps Thilawuntha in his religious zeal does not think it worth while referring to a dynasty of kings who flourished 'long before the appearance of the Buddha'. The trend of the narrative supports this view. The Chronicle derives considerable interest also as the prose work of a poet. The style is natural and free from poetical conceits, and indicates that the author, had he chosen, might have been a model prose writer.

The Old Chronicle of Pagan. This is supposed to have been composed in the sixteenth century. The author is unknown. It opens with the usual genealogy of the Buddha. The history of Burma begins with the Buddha's prophecy on Thintwè or Tagaung, followed by the prophecy on Tharehkittara. There is no mention of the Sakiyan migrations. Only the story of the blind twins is given to account for the founding of Tharehkittara and the descent of Dwattabaung. This omission of the Sakiyan migrations suggests that the Chronicle is not one of the old chronicles on which the Glass Palace Chronicle bases its account of ' the lineage of the kings of Burma, Sakiyans of the Sun dynasty' (p. 6). Its list of the names of the seven founders of Tharehkittara is identical with the list quoted by the Glass Palace Chronicle (p. 15) from the Middle Chronicle. Thus the Chronicle does not appear to be the oft-quoted Old Chronicle. It has some points which are followed by later chronicles but not by the Glass Palace Chronicle. On the other hand, it omits many passages from the present volume, e.g. §§ 102, 113, 132, 134, 135, pp. 93, 114–18, 120–22, 128–31, 143–46, as well as portions of other passages. These omissions make it a shorter work but give it unity of composition. Its diction is simple and unambitious.

The Great Chronicle. This is the work of Maung Kala, who composed it in the early part of the eighteenth century. It quotes from other chronicles the incidents of the domination of Pagan by the Gourd, the Tiger, the Bird, the Boar, and the Squirrel. It also quotes by name the Nandamawgun, Shwezigon inscription, Kalyani inscription, *thamaing* of the Tharekhkan Five Parts. It has nothing to say about the migrations of the Sakiyan Abhiraja and Dhajaraja, and omits the whole of § 102. Apart from these points, it is practically the same as the Glass Palace Chronicle if we leave out the learned disquisitions of the latter. The language of one in the historical narrative obviously follows the language of the other.

The conclusion, therefore, is that the Glass Palace Chronicle is a copy of the Great Chronicle, with slight variations of language here and there and interpolations of disquisitions on points of difference in opinion.

The Middle Chronicle. This is a shorter and later work by Maung Kala. It is an abridgement of the Great Chronicle, with which it agrees in its points of difference from the Glass Palace Chronicle and in its omission of the Sakiyan migrations. It omits accounts of the death-omens of kings in the Glass Palace Chronicle and summarizes long passages. Thus the Pyusawhti legend is summarized in this way : ' When he slew those creatures his father was the sun-prince, his mother the naga-princess. He was born of their union, brought up by the Pyu—hence his name Pyuminhti. When he had vanquished the four enemies, the king gave him his daughter in marriage and appointed him heir'. Occasionally it puts in a note not to be found in the Great Chronicle. It is interesting to see that it quotes Thilawuntha's Celebrated Chronicle on the formation of kingdoms and provinces in Jambudipa. It quotes the Kalyani inscription as evidence that Alaungsithu was also called Narapatisithu, and the Pali Visuddhimagga and the Jinalankaratika. It does not appear to be the Middle Chronicle quoted by the Glass Palace Chronicle.

The New Pagan Chronicle. This is said to have been written in 1785. It omits the first Sakiyan migration of Abhiraja but mentions the second one of Dhajaraja. It is thus the first of the chronicles which connects the lineage of the Tagaung kings with the Sakiyan family. Some of the works it quotes are the Yazawin Mawgun on the names of Tagaung, the Yazawin Linka Thamaing on Sandamokhki the ogress, on Pyusawhti and on Kyaussaga, the Mawgun Linka on the meeting of the princes with Bedayi, the Udan Linka on Dwattabaung's warfare against the Asuras, the Linka on the nineteen villages of Pagan, on the founding of Pagan, and on the different kinds of boats, the Paukkarama Thamaing Linka on Pyusawhti's fight with the grèat bird. With this Chronicle we come to that stage in the literature of the chronicles where the chronicler, having at his disposal a large number of materials, begins to display critical powers. ' It is said in the chronicles that Peitthato was a powerful queen in Taungdwin, owning a big drum for the collection of revenue, that Dwattabaung's spies went to her

country and on a fair opportunity destroyed the drum, so that she
and her revenues became Dwattabaung's property. This is not
probable. Again, the she-mole of Mt. Hpo-u is said to be queen
Peitthato, but this is not confirmed by the chronicles. The Great
Chronicle says that the she-mole was the Pantwa queen'. The
Chronicle is based not only on the Old and Great Chronicles but
also on other sources of information. Sometimes it criticizes its
materials. Generally it reproduces from the Old Chronicle those
passages which are omitted by the Great, and thus gives more
information than either. The author possesses literary gifts and
has produced a work of no mean order as a prose composition. He
displays his literary taste in the selection, from various poetical
sources, of sumptuous passages with which he adorns his narrative.

The New Chronicle. This was written towards the end of the
eighteenth century by Twinthin Mahasithu, a scholar well known
in literary circles, and one of the men appointed by king Bodawpaya for the examination of the inscriptions he had collected.
Twinthin thus had the splendid opportunity of checking the chronicles by means of inscriptions. And as he was a scholar well versed
in other branches of learning also, his New Chronicle is a welcome
addition to the literature of the chronicles. 'Although chronicles
have been written by the wise men of old, there are in them many
things not in agreement with the inscriptions and *thamaing*. Therefore, minding the exhortation given by our king, I will compose a
brief chronicle of kings after comparing it with old inscriptions,
thamaing, egyin, and *mawgun,* and revealing what has been omitted
in former chronicles'. 'Brief' is hardly the epithet for the New
Chronicle. It criticizes the older chronicles, adducing reasons :
' Various chronicles say that Anawrahta dedicated Manuha, king of
Thaton, to the Shwezigon .... If Manuha was so dedicated, his
grandson would not have been married to Narapati's daughter ....
The Great Chronicle says that, five years after Htihlaingshin's
accession, Thambula came leading her son by the hand when he
was seven years old, and that Sawlu had reigned 26 years.
Adding 5 to 26, the son of Thambula must have been 31 years
old, which is absurd .... The Arakan chronicles show not a shadow,
a hint about the golden image, on which, however, our various
Burmese chronicles are agreed '. On many points it gives interesting details or new information, which the Glass Palace Chronicle,

more often than not, ignores to its own loss. The omission of the human touch about the two princes winning the hearts of the Pyus before the elder prince, Mahathambawa, won the heart of the Pyu queen is an instance. The New Chronicle is the first to make a serious attempt to check history by means of inscriptions. That the Glass Palace Chronicle quarrels with some of its decisions does not signify that they are wrong. The Alaungsithu *versus* Narapatisithu controversy will be decided, so far as inscriptional evidence goes, by the authenticity and correct interpretation, rather than the multiplicity, of the inscriptions. The New Chronicle vies with the New Pagan Chronicle as a work of literary merit.

The Standard Chronicles. The Chronicles: the Old, Great, New Pagan, and New, together with the Glass Palace Chronicle, which follows them in point of date, may be called the Standard Chronicles, as dealing with the whole period of Burmese history from the beginning, in contradistinction to others, like the Tagaung or Thaton Chronicle, which profess to deal with particular places or periods. The results of the study of the Standard Chronicles may be summed up as follows : There are many divergences between the Old and the Great Chronicles. If on that account we regarded them as two schools, then the New Pagan Chronicle would belong to the school of the former, and the New and Glass Palace Chronicles to that of the latter. The Glass Palace Chronicle bases itself on the Great, utilizing materials from the others wherever it thinks fit. The New Chronicle is the most critical, yet, with all its criticisms, on the whole it follows the Great Chronicle. The remarks which I have made above on the Celebrated Chronicle explain its exclusion from this summary. And the Middle Chronicle may be levelled under the Great (of which it is an abridgement by the same author). The attitude of the Standard Chronicles towards the two great events of Burmese history : the Sakiyan migrations and the introduction of Buddhism, is worthy of note. The Sakiyan migrations occur only in the New Pagan and Glass Palace Chronicles (the former omits the migration of Abhiraja and gives that of Dhajaraja). The Buddha's introduction of Buddhism by his visit to Lèkaing is mentioned by almost every one of the Chronicles. More importance thus seems to be attached to the religious side of history than to ethnological considerations.

The Tagaung Chronicle. This is quoted by the Glass Palace

Chronicle as one of the sources of information on the founding of Tagaung. The portion of the Chronicle relevant to the subject-matter of the present volume has been translated in the *Journal of the Burma Research Society*, vol. xi. It begins with the story of the twin brothers. The actual story, however, is not related till after the legend of the Naga of Tagaung and the myth of the palace-post, the births of the three queens, and the travels of king Santarit. Nothing is said about the Sakiyan migrations. It assumes, as does the Old Chronicle, the establishment of the king-dom of Tagaung without accounting for it. Of the actual history of Tagaung we thus learn nothing beyond what is legendary. So far the Chronicle bears the mark of an early age, being in the loquacious style of a story, in contrast with the finished and ornate diction of some of the Standard Chronicles. As a story it derives considerable charm from the legendary and miraculous elements. In some of the Standard Chronicles the charm of the story is often spoiled by the intrusion of logical reasoning, which is as out of place in a legend as science in nursery rhymes. The latter part of the Chronicle is incoherent. After dismissing the history of Tharehkittara and of Pagan rather abruptly, it goes back to Tagaung. The long and sometimes confusing account of the revolt of the twelve villages gives us the information that ' Tagaung became servant to the Shan '. The narrative then goes on to Anawrahta and Narapatisithu of Pagan, of which some interesting details are given. Some of the prophetic utterances have little or no connexion with the trend of the narrative and are probably interpolations. The Chronicle furnishes interesting parallels to some of the stories told by the Standard Chronicles. The story of Naganaing becoming king with Sakra's help is the same as the story told of Kunhsaw by the Glass Palace Chronicle. The signs, that foretell the coming of the Naga of Tagaung, also foretell the coming of the great bird of Pagan as related by the Old Chronicle. Htiluga, the name of the place where the crows' talk is overheard, suggests Htihlaingga, the name of the great bird of Pagan. And the story of the queens of Thamadi has many points in common with that of Bedayi.

The Rahkaing Chronicles. Further information about the Sakiyan migrations and the later history of Abhiraja and his two sons and the fall of Tagaung is supplied by the Rahkaing Chronicle.

A paper copy of this Chronicle taken from the manuscript made in 1775 and based on old writings by the minister and Royal Reader of king Sandawimala exists in the Bernard Free Library, Rangoon. A later chronicle is the New Dhaññavati by U Pandi, printed at Rangoon, 1910. Besides details about other events the Rahkaing Chronicle contains many dialogues between king and minister on questions of religion, politics, ethics, and so forth. Thus it throws sidelights on history and abounds in legendary lore. It furnishes information on the intervening period between the fall of Tagaung and the rise of Pagan, on which the Burmese chronicles do not shed much light. Both the Rahkaing and New Dhaññavati Chronicles tell us about the events in Arakan prior to and contemporary with the Pagan dynasty. This information often conflicts with the stray references given in the Standard Chronicles.

The Tharehkittara Chronicle. A short chronicle of unknown date and authorship, and of modest pretensions. It begins with the Tharehkittara hermit and the settlement of Vetthadipa and Allakappa kings at Tharehkittara. It does not always agree with the Standard Chronicles, but it is interesting and deserves study. It gives Paukkyaing as the name of the slayer of the Tagaung Naga and carries the history down to Supaññanagara.

The Hngeppyittaung Chronicle. A short chronicle on the history of the clergy at Hngeppyittaung. It gives the succession of the elders and the boundaries of the monastery, which was later almost utterly destroyed by the Talaings. It tells us of the events that took place after the fall of Pagan, such as the revolt of the Talaings and the founding of Shwebo, and ends with Sinbyushin 1773.

The Pagan Chronicle. A copy of this chronicle is the British Museum manuscript (Or. 1021) with the interesting note that it was ' presented by the Dowager Marchioness of Westminster 21 December 1869 '. It opens with the usual Buddha's genealogy, which, however, is not exactly the same as that in the Glass Palace Chronicle. The history of Burma begins with the Buddha's visit to Thindwè and to the Man stream. After giving the history of Tharehkittara dynasty it passes on to the Pagan period, with a short account of the later period of Myinzaing, Sagaing, Pinya, and Ava. The Chronicle is thus not confined to Pagan only. The author is Gunasamisirilanka, living north of Myebontha, built at the sacred spot where Sithunarapati's chaplain, Panthagu, deposited the Lord's relics in consultation with Sakra. The date unfortunately is not to be found, as the last leaves are missing.

The Pali Paukkan Chronicle. This is a chronicle of Pagan in Pali attributed to Vajirabuddhi. The date is not certain. It begins with the prophecy of the founding of Pagan and gives an account of the Pagan Period more or less on the same lines as the Burmese Chronicles. It agrees closely with the Great Chronicle and may be a Pali version of it.

The Vamsadipani. This is an exposition on the chronicles by Mèhti Sayadaw, printed at Rangoon, 1916. It confirms the introduction of Buddhism into Tharehkittara as in § 103, and into Thaton five years after the enlightenment of the Buddha through Gavampati and later through Sona and Uttara. It states that the religion did not fade, and that there was no schism as in Ceylon.

Other Chronicles. There are other chronicles like the Talaing Chronicles (which are generally translated from the Talaing), Pegu Chronicle, Tavoy Chronicle, Sasanavamsa, Zimmè Chronicle, Cetiyakatha, Cetivamsa, and so forth. But as they deal with particular periods or aspects of history I have not discussed them here. Doubtless there are yet others which might be included. But it is not my present purpose to make an exhaustive study of the chronicles. Much confusion exists with regard to these late and particular chronicles; and it seems to me premature to make a proper study of them before they are critically edited, and the question of their date and authorship definitely settled. The above sketch, however, will have given a fair idea of the nature and scope of the literature of the chronicles.

The Historical Ballads. A contribution to history is to be found in the historical ballads called the *egyin*. The twelve Old Egyin have been edited with introductory notes by Maung May Oung, Moulmein, 1912. They are poetical compositions of great beauty in praise of a prince or princess, recounting the glories and achievements of their ancestors. They thus furnish information, which, though highly coloured, is based on historical facts. As special compositions on historical subjects in honour of a king or crown-prince, they are also called Nadawthwin, i.e. 'presentations to the Royal Ear'. Thus the well-known Paleissa Egyin by Maung Hpyaw is also called the Singumin Nadawthwin. The twelve

Egyin were composed between 1338–1638 by various poets. They confirm the Sakiyan descent of Burmese kings. Their value as history, however, is often marred by the flight of their poetical imageries. The same argument more or less applies to other forms of poetical composition, such as the *yadu, linka, pyo,* and so forth. And as they do not fall within the proper scope of history, I have not dealt with them.

The Thamaing. The literature of the *thamaing* forms a mine of curious information on history. The name is generally associated with the prose-history of a pagoda. But there are also *thamaing* on other objects such as monasteries and towns. From the religious nature of their contents, *thamaing* may be said to be mainly devoted to objects which testify to the establishment of the religion. And as pagodas are the most fitting monuments which do this, each pagoda possesses a *thamaing* of its own. The *thamaing* of a pagoda (monastery or town) tells us all its history, legendary and authentic. Incidentally we learn something about the doings of a king, who is the donor of the pagoda, or about some political events with which the building of the pagoda is intimately connected. Thus the Thaton Shwezayan Hpayagyi Thamaing (printed at the Sun Press, Rangoon, 1915) says, ' In 994, year of the religion, Nawrahta went to dig up the relics at Thaton Hpayagyi (Shwezayan), built in king Thurisanda's time over the four teeth of the Lord. But he was chastised by the spirits so that he became deluded, and put on his queen's skirt. Hence the name of the place is Lèhtami'. And the Shwenattaung Thamaing (printed at the same press, 1911) says, ' The Pyu king ruled over the Shan country called Savana; the Kanyan king ruled over the seven hill-tracts on the west bank of the Irrawaddy. The Talaings were in the south in pre-Buddhistic times, when Shwedaung near Myoma was founded by king Suratapa, son of king Accima, 28th in descent from Mahasamata of Mallakusavati. The Talaings governed the Mron, i.e. Tavoyese'. A serious charge against the *thamaing* is that the information given is often vitiated by incoherent and improbable statements. And as the history is written in most cases long after the building of the pagoda, it is not always reliable. A *thamaing* sometimes professes to be based on older materials. Thus the Hpo-u Thamaing is copied from the Shwehsandaw Thamaing, which is also the source of the Zat-ngaya Thamaing. And the

Shwehsandaw Thamaing professes to be based on *mawgun* and the Pali chronicles of the relics. It is therefore no easy matter to decide the date of the *thamaing*.

A *thamaing* may also be in verse, like the Shwezigon Thamaing Linka. It begins with a short account of the Buddha's career and sings of the various historical events in poetical language of an emotional nature. The original of Anantathuriya's death-song on p. 139 of the present volume is an example of a linka.

Transliteration. The question of transliterating Burmese names is one of peculiar difficulty. The strictly literal system adopted by the Archaeological Department may serve the purposes of scientific research, but is not suitable for the general reader. The phonetic system adopted by the Government is not applicable to those early words, whose sounds we have as yet no means of ascertaining. I have therefore used, at discretion, both the systems, perhaps with some partiality for the latter. I am aware that this procedure lays itself open to the charge of inconsistency. But in the absence of a perfect system which our present knowledge of Burmese phonetics and philology has not succeeded in working out, this seems to me the only course open, especially as I have tried to satisfy both the general reader and the learned scholar. I have therefore treated phonetically many of the Pali names, which might all very easily have been written in the usual literal manner. Thus the phonetic version, Thilawuntha, makes it, I think, more familiar as a Burmese name than the literal version, Silavamsa. On the other hand I keep such words as Dhaññavati and Supañña because of their greater classical associations. Here also I have found it difficult to draw the line between the two systems. It will be noticed that I generally follow the modern transliteration of such names, e.g. Irrawaddy, as have received popular sanction, except in those names where I have assimilated two different consonants, as Kyaussè for Kyauksè, Thiripyissaya for Thiripyitsaya. Any other variation which I may not have explained will, I hope, readily explain itself. No diacritical marks other than ñ have been used.

Manuscripts and Acknowledgements. I consulted the manuscripts of the Glass Palace, Celebrated, Great, Middle, and New Chronicles belonging to the Bernard Free Library, Rangoon. My thanks are due to the Superintendent, Archaeological Survey, Burma, for a loan of the Tagaung Chronicle; to Saya Pwa of University

College, Rangoon, for lending me his manuscript of the New Pagan Chronicle; to U Tin of Pagan for letting me use his manuscripts of the Old, Pali Paukkan, Tharehkittara, Hngeppyittaung Chronicles, the Cetivamsa and the Shwezigon Thamaing Linka. The remarks I have made above on the remaining works specify the manuscripts or printed copies used.

I also thank the members of the Committee and the Text Publication sub-committee of the Burma Research Society for their permission to publish this book in the Text Publication Series; and Mr. G. H. Luce, to whose collaboration the translation owes its English style. But I wish to make it quite clear that I alone am responsible for the correctness and final form of the translation.

PE MAUNG TIN.

EXETER COLLEGE, OXFORD.
    1st November, 1922.

NOTE

THE present translation is based on the Mandalay edition of 1907. It begins with the third part of the Chronicle. The first two parts are left untranslated as they merely retell the story of Buddhism and of the Buddhist kings of Ancient India, with which the student of Pali and Buddhism is well acquainted. The third part opens with the history of the three Burmese kingdoms of Tagaung, Tharehkittara, and Pagan. The fourth and fifth parts continue the history of Pagan until the time of its fall, with which the present volume closes.

THE GLASS PALACE CHRONICLE OF THE KINGS OF BURMA

HERE endeth the second part. And we shall presently relate the full history of the kings of Burma, originally descended from the noble Sun dynasty of the Sakiyans. We shall begin with the founding of Tagaung, their first city, and add, moreover, the record of the sacred relics, the establishment of the religion, and the lineage of divers founders and rulers of cities.

102. *Of the first founding of the great kingdom of Tagaung by the Sakiyan Abhiraja of the Middle Country.*

[*The founding of Tagaung by Abhiraja.*] Tagaung was known as Thantharapura in the time of Kakusandha the Buddha, as Ratthapura in the time of Konagamana the Buddha, as Thintwè in the time of Kassapa the Buddha, and as Tagaung in the time of our Buddha Gotama. Abhiraja the Sakya Sakiyan was its first ruler. And this is the story of Abhiraja.

Once upon a time, long ago, before our Lord the Buddha unfolded the Four Truths under the Wisdom Tree at the Place of Conquest, the king of Panchala, lord of the two kingdoms of Kosala and Panchala, desired to ally himself by marriage with the king of Koliya, and sent ministers to ask the hand of a Koliyan princess. But the king of Koliya in his pride of birth answered him ill; so that a great war broke out between the two kingdoms. The king of Panchala was victorious, and the Sakiyan princes of the three kingdoms, Koliya, Devadaha, and Kapilavatthu, were isolated each from each and their empire wrecked. Later the Sakiyan princes of the three kingdoms arose again into prosperity; but when first their power was wrecked, Abhiraja, the Sakya Sakiyan king of Kapilavatthu, took all his army and left the Middle Country and ruled in the Tagaung country, called Sangassarattha, which he founded. This kingdom first founded

by Abhiraja is written Sangassanagara or Sangassarattha. There
is no difference, for both *nagara* and *rattha* being interpreted mean
a country.

[*Kanrazagyi and Kanrazangè.*] On the death of Abhiraja his
two sons, Kanrazagyi and Kanrazangè, quarrelled over the throne.
But a wise minister said, 'If ye princes fight a great fight, ye
bring ruin on all beings in the country. Wage not therefore
a war of enmity but wage a war of merit'. Then the princes
asked, 'How may this be?' And the minister made answer,
'Princes! let each of you build in the course of one night an
alms-hall on a large scale. And whoever first completeth the work,
let him take his father's place and be king'. So the princes agreed,
and each chose a hill and began to build an alms-hall on a large
scale. Kanrazagyi completed not his hall, for he built it of massive
timber and bamboo. But Kanrazangè completed his, for he built
it of small timber and bamboo and covered it with white cloth and
whitewashed it. And at dawn when the elder brother beheld the
white hall put up by the younger brother he gathered his army and
went down the Irrawaddy. Thence he passed up the Thallawadi,
and having given the name of Rajagaha to the hill Kaletaungnyo
he held court there for six months. When the Pyus, Kanyans, and
Theks of the Western Country desired a prince to reign over them,
he made his son Muducitta king of the Pyus. And he founded the
city of Kyauppadaung to the east of the river Kacchapa and reigned
for seventy-four years. And moving thence he took possession
of the old city of Dhaññavati, first built by king Marayu, and
reigned there, building a new palace and fortifications. As for the
younger brother, he ruled in Tagaung in his father's stead.

[*The kings of Tagaung.*] Thus in Tagaung, called Sangassarattha,
thirty-three kings reigned in unbroken succession, beginning with
Abhiraja the Sakya Sakiyan; his son Kanrazangè: his son
Jambudiparaja: his son Sangassaraja: his son Vippannaraja:
his son Devataraja: his son Munikaraja: his uncle Nagaraja:
his younger brother Indaraja: his son Samutiraja: his son Deva-
raja: his son Mahindaraja: his son Vimalaraja: his son Sihanuraja:
his son Manganaraja: his son Kamsaraja: his son Kalingaraja:
his son Thintwèraja: his son Sihalaraja: his younger brother
Hamsaraja: his son Vararaja: his son Alaungraja: his son
Kolakaraja: his son Suriyaraja: his son Thingyiraja: his son

Tainggyitraja: his son Maduraja: his son Minhlagyiraja: his son Samsusiharaja: his son Dhanangaraja: his son Hindaraja: his son Moriyaraja: his son Bhinnakaraja.

[*The fall of Tagaung.*] In the time of the last of these kings, Bhinnakaraja, the kingdom of Tagaung, called Sangassarattha, perished under the oppression of the Tarops and Tareks from the Sein country in the kingdom of Gandhala. And Bhinnaka, mustering what followers he might, entered the Mali stream and abode there. When he died his followers split into three divisions. One division founded the nineteen Shan States of the East and were known thenceforth as the descendants of Bhinnakaraja. Another division moved down the Irrawaddy and entered the Western Country, where dwelt Muducitta and other Sakiyan princes among the Pyus, Kanyans, and Theks. The third division abode in Mali with the chief queen Nagahsein.

[*The destruction of the Sakiyan kingdom.*] It was then that Gotama our Lord the Buddha appeared in the Middle Country; and Pasenadi, the Kosalan king of Savatthi, sought in marriage a daughter of Mahanama king of Kapilavatthu; who, desirous of preserving the purity of his race, gave him not a princess of the blood royal but gave him his daughter by a slave woman, the princess Vasabhakhattiya. And she was made queen and bore prince Vitatupa. He, when he came of age, visited Kapilavatthu. Now when he returned home, they washed with milk the place he had occupied, reviling it as the place of a man slave-born. When he came to know of it, he nursed his wrath and said, 'When I am king, I will wash in the blood of their throats!'

So when his father was no more, he remembered his wrath and marched out with his fourfold army thrice to destroy the Sakiyan princes, but the Blessed Buddha prevented him. Howbeit the fourth time the Buddha, considering the past life-history of the Sakiyans, prevented him not; and Vitatupa marched with a great army and reached Kapilavatthu and slew the whole Sakiyan race, save those who dwelt with king Mahanama, not sparing even suckling babes. Only those who being asked 'Are ye Sakiyan?' took hold of grass and answered 'Grass!' and those who took hold of reeds and answered 'Reeds!' and those who took refuge with king Mahanama, remained. There were thus three classes of Sakiyans: those who took hold of grass and escaped slaughter were called Grass-Sakiyans, those who took hold of reeds and escaped slaughter were called Reed-Sakiyans, and those who trusted in king Mahanama and escaped slaughter were called Sakiyans proper. Thereafter the Sakiyan princes took refuge in divers places, such as the cities of Moriya, Vedissagiri, and Panduraja.

Thus the great kingdom called Kapilavatthu, Devadaha, and Koliya, the Sakka land of over eighty thousand princes, having a diameter of seven *yojana*, fulfilled with all the dignities of a royal capital, wherein one man could overcome an hundred, nay a thousand men, might not escape the law of rise and fall. Albeit it was a sacred and auspicious land, it came to ruin twice, once in the time of the Koliyan prince, and once in the time of king Mahanama.

[*Dhajaraja restores Tagaung.*] When thus the Sakiyan princes perished, Dhajaraja the Sakiyan king moved with his followers from the Middle Country and first founded and reigned in Moriya. The name Moriya occurs in religious books such as the Commentary on the Dhammapada; in secular works such as Gotamapurana it is called Moranga, and Mawrin in the Arakan Chronicles; now it is Mwerin.

Thence he moved again and founded and reigned in Thintwè. Thence he moved again, and meeting queen Nagahsein who abode in Mali he espoused her, being of the same Sakiyan race, and founded and reigned in Upper Pagan. Here their son Viraga was born. Thence he moved again, and built a palace and fortifications in the country of Tagaung, called Sangassarattha, the land of the ancient Sakya Sakiyan princes and named it Panchala. The country was known as Pyinsa Tagaung.

[*His anointing and building of the palace.*] When he had founded it he took possession of the palace with the pomp of kings of exceeding majesty, opened the noble door leading to the coronation throne, assumed the title of Thado Jambudipa Dhajaraja, observed a great *thingyan* ceremony, and was anointed king. He bestowed titles first on the learned, and gave one thousand and three score title-warrants to ministers and high officials, to his minions, masters of elephants and horse, foot-soldiers, wealthy men, brahmans, astrologers, doctors of medicine, and artisans.

This is the record of the building of the golden palace by Thado Jambudipa Dhajaraja. He planned it for three years and seven months. All the central pillars of the main palace stood on golden

trays; all pillars around this row of leading pillars upon silver trays.
A jewelled jar was set on top of the great central pillar. Two
saints pronounced the love-charm to ward off evil. The upper part
of the golden palace was built by Nagas and spirits, the lower
by men of Sangassanagara. The main palace had a *pyatthad* in
the centre and nine mansions, with a double line of doors within
and without leading to the throne on all four sides. Images
congruent with the birthday-planet were placed on the four sides,
two outside and two within. Spirits brought cool waters of
Anotatta lake and the five great rivers and mixed them with the
water of the Irrawaddy against the calling of the *thingyan*. On
the day of the festival the queen and concubines and all the people
performed the ceremony of washing the head.

When the *thingyan* was completed the king ascended the palace,
with Brahma and the Naga king on the right, Sakra and Pajjunna
on the left, while eight Brahman councillors, each holding a dextral
conch in his hand, abode on the right. Attended by his generals
and ministers, a hundred thousand in all, two chief queens, seven
hundred concubines, fourscore and ten white elephants, one hundred
and fourscore Sind horses, and an host of officials, he ascended the
ground-palace. Thence ascended he the main palace ; and in honour
of his ascension he partook of food. Pots of rice and curry—of
each one hundred threescore and ten—were served in jewelled
salvers. He offered food moreover to the god of the birthday-
planet, also to Sakra and Brahma and the guardian spirits of the
umbrella, the palace, and the city. On the floor of the palace food
was scattered. It was eaten by two cats, and one hour later by two
men ; one hour later the king himself partook of it ; then the heir-
apparent, then the ministers and officials.

Spirits brought the great Einshin drum. Two great *muyo*
drums were hung near the royal umbrella, one on each side ;
moreover one great *pauccho* drum, one *kabyin* drum, one *saga*
drum, one *padauk* drum, one *kyun* drum. There were five bells,
named Nadawshauk, Nadawtin, Nadawpa, Nadawsaung, and
Nadawthwin.

[*His successors.*] In the reign of this king there befell four
showers of gems. His two chief queens had twenty sons and
twenty daughters, who intermarried. From this king to Thado
Maharaja there reigned a line of seventeen kings, each the son

or younger brother of the king before him. Their names are
these : Thado Jambudipa Dhajaraja, Thado Taingyaraja, Thado
Yahtaya, Thado Tagunya, Thado Hlanpyanya, Thado Shwe, Thado
Galonya, Thado Nagaya, Thado Naganaing, Thado Rahawla,
Thado Paungshe, Thado Kyausshe, Thado Hsinlauk, Thado Hsin-
htein, Thado Taingchit, Thado Mingyi, Thado Maharaja.

Their royal splendour was not long, for that they were oppressed
by evil spirits, demons, ogres, snakes, and dragons. In the reign
of Thado Maharaja, the last of the seventeen kings, there was
no son, and Khepaduta, younger brother of the chief queen Kinnaridevi, was made heir-apparent.

[*The Pyus.*] Meanwhile in the land of the Pyus king Tambula,
the Sakiyan, a lineal descendant of prince Muducitta, son of
Kanrazagyi, was oppressed and captured by Dhaññavati ; therefore
his queen Nanhkan and all her followers moved and dwelt in
Thagya-in.

None of these facts so far are mentioned in the Great Chronicle
or the New Chronicle. All that is worthy of belief in religious
works such as the Commentary on the Dhammapada, and in secular
works such as Gotamapurana, the Arakan Chronicle, the Tagaung
Chronicle, the *thamaing* of the building of the royal city of Tagaung,
the *thamaing* of the Arakan Mahamuni, as well as old manuscripts,
old chronicles, and tales of kings from divers sources, has been
extracted in order to set forth in time to come the foundation of
the great kingdom of Tagaung, the first to arise in Burma, and
the lineage of the kings of Burma, Sakiyans of the Sun dynasty.

103. *Of the founding of the great kingdom of Tharehkittara.*

[*The prophecy of the Buddha on Mt. Hpo-u.*] We have told the
story of the Tagaung kingdom, the first to arise in Burma, long
before the appearance of the Buddha ; and now we shall tell the
story of Tharehkittara.

The Lord, the Holy One, the Omniscient, the Chief of Con-
querors, had appeared and kept his fifth Lent, when Mahapon and
Sulapon, two brothers from Lèkaing, a village of merchants in the
Western Country, made suit to the Buddha and built a monastery
of fragrant sandalwood. And the Lord foreseeing that in time
to come his religion would be established for a long time in Burma,
came many times with five hundred flying *pyatthad* and five

hundred saints until the monastery was finished. And when it
was finished he gathered alms and for seven days enjoyed the
bliss of mystic meditation, and refreshed the people with the
ambrosia of the Law. Thereupon five hundred men and five
hundred women of the Western Country became saints, and
fourscore and four thousand people won deliverance. He preached
to Saccabandha the hermit of those parts and confirmed him in
the fruition of sanctity. Moreover, he vouchsafed two sacred
footprints as a seal impressed upon the rock, the one on the top
of Mt. Saccabandha at the suit of Saccabandha the elder, the
other near the stream of Man at the suit of Namanta, king of
the Nagas. Furthermore he prophesied and said, 'In the land
of the Burmans, the Western Country and Ceylon, my religion
shall be firmly set'. And thence he passed to divers places.

When he reached the summit of Mt. Hpo-u he beheld some
dried cow-dung floating on the surface of the ocean to the south-
east. Moreover a small mole scraped up some earth with his snout
and did obeisance therewith to the Lord Omniscient. And he
smiled at these two omens; and his cousin Ashin Ananda entreated
him saying, 'Why smilest thou?' And he said, 'Beloved Ananda,
in the 101st year of the religion after my entry into *parinirvana*
five great signs shall be manifested in this place. The earth shall
quake with a great echoing sound. At Hpo-u-maw a great lake
will appear. There will arise the rivers Samon and Samyeit.
Mt. Poppa will arise as a cone out of the earth. And the sea-
courses will dry up around the foundations of Tharehkittara.
When these signs appear, the mole will leave his present body
and become a man named Dwattabaung, who shall found a great
city and kingdom and set up a palace and umbrella and rule as
a king. Beginning from the time of this king my religion shall
long be manifest in Burma.' And this is the fulfilment of the
prophecy.

[*The great boar slain by the Tagaung heir*, 504 B.C.] In the fortieth
year of the religion after the Lord entered *parinirvana*, in the
reign of Thado Maharaja, seventeenth in descent from the Sakiyan
kings above recorded, a wild boar twelve cubits in height appeared
in Pyinsa Tagaung and so ravaged the land that the people living
in the border villages durst not venture abroad. Now when the
king of Tagaung was ware of it, he called the heir and said 'I

hear that a huge wild boar is ravaging the border villages insomuch
that men cannot work. Strike, Sir Heir, unto victory!' And
the heir answered and said, 'No foe in all Jambudipa can withstand me. The boar dieth; else will I not return unto my home!'
And he took the five weapons in his hand and gat him to where
the boar was.

It appears in some chronicles that he encountered the boar while
he was at sport in the forest. And the boar durst not withstand
a man so glorious, but fled to the Shan country of Maw, a place
of forests. The heir tracked him down by his footprints, and the
boar in fear of death entered a gap in the mountains. The place
where he entered is still known as Wekwin. In the Great Chronicle
it appears that the boar ran thence south-west and crossed the
Irrawaddy, that so vast was he in stature that in entering the
river he wetted not even the skin of his belly, and that the place
was still called Wekmasut. In the Old Chronicle it is said that
the boar which crossed the river was that slain by Pyuminhti of
Pagan. Now whereas the old *thamaing* and chronicles declare that
the height of the boar slain by the Tagaung heir was but twelve
cubits, this conflicts with the statement that in crossing the river
Irrawaddy he wetted not even the skin of his belly. Thence he
fled straight on till he reached an island near the site of Tharehkittara. And there the heir pierced the boar, and the island is
known as Wet-hto island to this day.

[*He becomes a hermit.*] And when he had conquered the boar
the heir said to himself, 'I have followed this boar to slay it. The
journey I have now made is very great. Were I to go back to
Tagaung and tell the king, "The boar is dead!" he might not
believe me. Even if I were to bring the boar as proof and present
it to him and he believed me, it would be but a present advantage.
Moreover I am now ripe in years. It were better to become a
monk and aim at bliss hereafter than to go back to Tagaung and
enjoy the pleasures of an heir'. So he became a hermit and dwelt
there. And ere long he obtained mystic powers and the higher
knowledge.

[*The birth of Bedayi.*] Now as thus he lived, it was ever his
wont to make water into a cup in the rock. And a young doe
was fain to avail herself of the water in the cup, and thereafter
she conceived, and when her time was come, gave birth to a human

girl. And the mother, the doe, being a mere animal took fright
and fled when she heard the cries of the babe. And the hermit
said, 'This place is far from the haunts of men. What meaneth
this sound of a babe's crying in mine ears?' And he looked
around and saw his little daughter; and behold! she was very
beautiful; all the signs of royalty she had, both great and small.
And the hermit thought, 'A young deer hath done this. She
hath licked up the water I have made and the seed therein, and
lo! she hath conceived and given birth to the babe.' And he
made a solemn vow and said, 'If, as I think, she hath conceived
of me, may milk flow from my first and middle fingers and suckle
the child!' And the two fingers yielded milk and the child
drank.

So the hermit took her and brought her up as his daughter.
And when she came of age he called her Bedayi. And the spirits
who ministered continually to the hermit brought meet raiment
for her to wear. Now when she was seventeen years old, the
hermit bethought him : 'It is not seemly for an hermit to live
with womankind, nor to be seen by others with them.' So he
gave her a gourd and bored no hole in it, and he caused her to
dip the gourd in water and fill a bamboo tube, so that she might
be away all day at the waterside and return at nightfall. Even
so she did, and was busy all day long. Day after day thenceforward he made his daughter Bedayi draw water in this way.

Thus far is the tale of the hermit, brother-in-law of the
Tagaung king, and how he left Tagaung and came to the site of
Tharehkittara.

104. *Of the two brothers Sulathambawa and Mahathambawa.*

[*The story of the blind twin brothers of Tagaung.*] In the fortieth
year of the religion—the year in which the heir, brother-in-law
to king Thado Maharaja, ruler of Tagaung, followed the boar to
pierce it—the queen of the Tagaung king gave birth to blind twin
brothers, Mahathambawa and Sulathambawa. And the king was
ashamed and said to the queen, 'Do away with the two children
that are born, so that none may know it!' But the queen hid
them, for they were her own blood from the breast.

Now in the fifty-ninth year of the religion the royal father, the
king of Tagaung, came to know that the queen had been hiding

them, and commanded her, saying, ' Queen! Hast thou not abased
my fame? Slay these two brothers at once!' And the queen
durst not keep them, for she feared the royal command. But
she said, ' Let not their death be sudden! Let them rather meet
their fate out of my sight!' So she had a goodly raft built,
wherein she placed with care great store of food for the journey so
as to last for a long time, and telling the princes where it was kept
she put them on the raft and set it afloat. And the royal brothers
ate of the food stored by their mother, and floated along.

[*They receive their sight from an ogress.*] When they came to Sikkaing, the raft struck an overhanging acacia, so that Sandamokhki,
the ogress of that place, boarded the raft; and whenever the royal
brothers partook of the food, she also ate. The place of that overhanging acacia is called Sikkaing to this day. But in some chronicles
it would appear that the ogress boarded the raft only when it reached
the Bilutek stream at the outskirts of Pagan. Again other chronicles would say that she boarded it only when it reached the bank at
Nyaung-u. The royal brothers said to each other : ' Our meals
were at first enough for us. Now they are not. There must be a
reason. In eating our food let us know our hands, my hand from
thine, my brother.' And as they fumbled they grasped the hand
of the ogress Sandamokhki. Thereupon they drew sword from the
scabbard and were about to strike the ogress, who struggled in vain
to escape princes so glorious, when she in fear of death cried out
' Princes, take not my life! I will do whatever my young lords
desire'. So the royal brothers made demand and said, ' Ogress!
canst thou give us our sight?' And she answered ' Yea'. So the
princes made her swear to keep her promise, and released her. And
the ogress consulted mighty spirits and ogres. And the mighty
spirits foreseeing how a line of kings beginning with these royal
brothers would uphold the religion of the Lord for ever, sent divers
kinds of medicine for the eyes. And the ogress followed the
brothers as they floated down on the raft, and applied the medicine.
The place where the medicine was first applied is still called Sagu,
and the place where sight dawned on the princes is still known as
Ywalin; and the place where receiving sight they exclaimed, ' Sky
around! Earth within!' is still known as Mobon-myedè.

The Great Chronicle says that the place where the ogress Sandamokhki first began to apply the medicine to cure the brothers'

eyes, was at the site of Sagu town, and that they received their sight when they reached Ywalin. But the New Chronicle says that she first began to apply the medicine from Sagumaw, near the town of Sagaing, and that they received their sight when they reached the site of Salin town. Now, the Prome Shwehsandaw Thamaing states that it was only after going hungry many times that they seized the ogress and made her give them their sight. It says, moreover, that when they reached the Teknwè stream she landed and made search for the herb ; that the first application was made at Sagu ; that Yalin was so called because there they received their sight ; and that because they said ' Earth within ! Sky around !' the place was called Myedè-mobon. Moreover the Old Pagan Thamaing agrees with this and says that Yalin was so called because there this name was uttered when they received their sight and obtained two rolls of spirit-medicine from the ogress. And the distance between Yalin on the outskirts of Malun town and Mobon-myedè makes this story probable. Therefore in some old chronicles it is said that sight dawned on them only when they reached Malun. And considering the statement in some chronicles that the ogress boarded the raft only at Nyaung-u, the mere distance between Sagu and Yalin makes this story probable. And considering the statement that the ogress boarded the raft only at Sagaing, at the overhanging acacia, and that she often ate of the food of the royal brothers before they seized her, it is plain that between the place where she boarded the raft and the place where they seized her the distance must be great. And so the nearness of Sagaing to Sagumaw conflicts with the statement that the ogress had often eaten of the food. And it is not plainly stated in any other chronicle that the first application of medicine was made at Sagu-maw, nor that they received their sight at Salin. This is stated only in the New Chronicle. Again, the statement that they received their sight only at Salin, and saw the sky and earth only at Mobon-myedè, is not reasonable, for the places are not near, but far apart. Moreover scholars spell Salin by the Pali word Calanga-pura. Whereas divers chronicles and *thamaing* agree in mentioning Sagu and Yalin. Therefore the statement of the New Chronicle that the first application of medicine was made at Sagumaw and that they received their sight only at Salin should be regarded as a heresy.

[*They meet Bedayi and the hermit.*]　Now when the princes had received their sight, they continued their voyage on the raft till they reached the place called Konsapyin after the flying of cranes. Here they stopped the raft, and went forth armed with the five weapons till they came to the spot where their uncle the hermit was practising piety.

Konsapyin is now known as Kontalin; and the Shwezigon Thamaing says that it takes its name from the saying of the princes, ' The rising ground is bright'. And it so befell that they followed the track of the feet of Bedayi, the daughter of the hermit their uncle, as she went to draw water. And when they met her and saw how she drew water, they said, ' O maiden, the gourd with which thou art drawing water hath no hole in it. How foolish thou art!' Then they took the gourd, cut off its face with the sword, dropped the seed out, and made her draw water and fill the tube. And aye thereafter men use the proverb ' not to bore the ear of a gourd'. So when the tube was filled, the maid Bedayi went to the cell of her father the hermit, and he said, ' How easily thou hast filled and brought water to-day!' So Bedayi told him all. And the hermit called the two young men and straitly questioned them. And they told him fully that they were the sons of Kinnaridevi, chief queen to the ruler of Tagaung : that owing to the breath of the Naga they were born blind : that the ogress Sandamokhki had cured them and given them sight : and so forth. When the hermit heard the speech of the princes he said, ' Ye twain are my nephews, my sister's own sons'. And in the sixtieth year of the religion he joined Mahathambawa and his daughter Bedayi in wedlock.

[*The troubles of the Pyus.*]　At that time Tambula, king of the Pyus, was troubled with war and captured by Dhaññavati. And the Kanyans, wishing to occupy the land where Nanhkan queen of the Pyus had settled, waged a mighty war with the Pyus. The Pyus were victorious and the Kanyans fled. By Kanyans are meant the people living in the group of seven hill-tracks beginning with Thantwè. Among the Pyus also a quarrel for the throne arose between queen Nanhkan and her brother. The sister won, and founding a village at Thagya-in lived there with her army, while her brother moved out to Hpo-u with his army and lived there. In this connexion the Great Chronicle and the New

Chronicle merely mention 'the Pyu queen'. The name, Nanhkan, of the queen of king Tambula has been added, so that men may know it, in accordance with the Old Pagan Thamaing.

[*Mahathambawa*, fl. 484–478 B. C.] Now at this time the Pyu queen and all who dwelt at Thagya-in resorted to the hermit, brother-in-law of the Tagaung king, and worshipped him as though he were the Lord. And the hermit was possessor of mystic powers and the higher knowledge, and exceeding mighty and powerful, well seen in the eighteen arts and sciences. Being shrewd in kingcraft he said to the Pyu queen one day, 'My nephew, prince Mahathambawa, is master of all kingly duties. He is adept in law. His valour in fighting an enemy is heroical. Make him king over your country, and let him rule, order, and unite you.' And the Pyu queen thought, 'I am a woman. The country will be peaceful and prosperous only when one with might and authority quells the rising of our enemies.' So she made Mahathambawa king.

[*The lineage of the Pyu queen.*] The Pyu queen was of the race of the Tagaung Sakiyans. Therefore the place where she lived is known as Thagya-in. To show that she was of the Sakiyan race : while king Kanrazagyi was holding court at Kaletaungnyo Raja-gaha, the Pyu chief Devaduta came to ask for an heir. So the king placed upon the throne in the Pyu country his son Muducitta, then sixteen years old. And this is the story of prince Muducitta. While king Abhiraja the grandfather was alive, his son Kanrazagyi was married to Thubattadevi his daughter, and their child was Muducitta, his mother dying before his birth. Thus the Pyu queen descended from the Sakiyan race of Muducitta, is always known to be of Sakya Sakiyan race, and the place where she lived is known as Thagya-in. This fact is omitted in the Great and New Chronicles, but is added here in accordance with the Old Pagan Thamaing, the Tagaung Chronicle, and the Arakan Chronicle, so as to make plain the lineage of the Burmese kings, who were descended in unbroken succession from the Sakya Sakiyan race.

In the sixtieth year of the religion Mahathambawa became king. His two queens were Bédayi and the Pyu queen. Of these the Pyu queen gave birth to a daughter and died not long after. And when prince Dwattabaung had been conceived three months in the womb of queen Bedayi, his father, king Mahathambawa, died.

Twenty years in the nether house, six years he flourished; he
passed at the age of twenty-six. When he was about to die there
was an earthquake for seven days. The day of his birth was
Monday.

[*Sulathambawa*, fl. 478–443 B.C.]   In the sixty-sixth year of the
religion his younger brother, Sulathambawa, became king. His
queen was Bedayi, his sister-in-law. When Bedayi was made
queen, the ogress Sandamokhki, who had ministered to him while
heir, was grieved, and taking Peitthano, her son by him, she built
a village in the parts about Poppa and dwelt there. The king
reigned justly and died. Twenty-six years in the nether house,
thirty-five years he flourished; he passed at the age of sixty-one.
When he was about to die it was dark like night for full seven
days. The day of his birth was Monday.

105.   *Of king Dwattabaung.*

[*The founding of Tharehkittara*, 443 B.C.]   In the 101st year
of the religion the five portents foretold on the summit of Mt.
Hpo-u came to pass all in one night. The Great Chronicle says
the five portents came to pass in the reign of Mahathambawa;
this conflicts with its own statement of the original prophecy,
namely that the five portents would come to pass in the 101st
year of the religion. At that time these Seven Exalted Ones—
Gavampati, Rishi, Sakra, Naga, Garula, Sandi, and Paramesura—
met in accordance with the Lord's prophecy and conferred together
about the founding of the city. And Sakra stood in the centre
of a piece of pleasant level ground and described a circle by means
of a rope dragged round by the Naga. And on the land thus
encircled Sakra founded the golden city of Tharehkittara, noble
and glorious as Sudassana city, his own abode; marvellously
graceful it was, having all the seven things needful for a city,
namely : main gates thirty-two, small gates thirty-two, moats,
ditches, barbicans, machicolations, four-cornered towers with
graduated roofs over the gates, turrets along the walls, and so
forth; the whole being one *yojana* in diameter and three *yojana*
in circumference.

Among the Seven Exalted Ones the Great Chronicle omits
Gavampati and includes Gumbhanda; the New Chronicle omits
Gumbhanda and includes Gavampati; the Middle Chronicle

omits both and includes Mahapeinnè; but the list in the Old Chronicle includes Gavampati together with Rishi, Sakra, Naga, Garula, Sandi, and Paramesura, and furthermore it hints that the noble Gavampati and Rishi appointed the hour when king Dwattabaung should invest the palace with an auspicious name. Thus the various authorities, the Old and the New Chronicles, *egyin* and *mawgun*, record only the Seven Exalted Ones mentioned above.

And for the date of the founding of the city: in the 101st year of the religion after the Lord made *parinirvana*, on Sunday the first waxing of Tagu, sixteenth constellation, at the first glimpse of the sun, these three works were accomplished—the golden palace, the city, and the moat. Some chronicles declare that the city of Tharehkittara was founded on Monday the eleventh waxing of Tagu; we have followed the greater number of reliable records. Three mansions with storeys seven, nine, and eleven, were built by spirits for the king's delight during the rains, the hot season, and the winter; and these together with the city were completed in seven days.

[*The glory of king Dwattabaung,* fl. 443–373 B.C.] When thus the labour of the city and the palace were fulfilled Sakra lifted king Dwattabaung by the hand to the golden throne, and he was anointed king. The two queens were the king's sister, Sandadevi, daughter of the Pyu queen whom the royal father king Maha-thambawa had made his consort, and the Naga princess, Besandi. Sakra invested king Dwattabaung with the five emblems of royalty, Thilawuntha the sword of virtue, and the rest. Moreover he gave vessels for the royal use, engines of pomp and power worthy of a universal monarch; Areindama, the lance to crush all his enemies; the bell and the big drum; the Walahaka horses that trode the sky; and the Nalagiri elephant, 15 cubits in height, 20 cubits in length, for the king to ride. He gave him also seventeen valiant spirits to be his perpetual bodyguard, and the ministers Nga Nipa, Nga Yegya, Pyissinbyu, Pyissinnyo, Atwinpinlè, Pyin-pinlè, all masters of statecraft and the eight virtues, men of glory and wisdom and authority.

He was a king majestical. At every stride he took the earth sank beneath his feet; wherefore Sakra by his power and might caused his every step to be received upon an iron plate. He accepted tribute from Jambudipa island as far as the land of the

Asuras and the Nagas, which he conquered and took. And his taking of tribute was on this manner. The king would write his message or letter and hang it on the flying lance. And he would ascend the lance-throwing mountain, and with his own hands he would throw the lance. And lo! the lance hung suspended as if to fall upon the heads of those kings. Nor did the flying lance depart until those kings had humbled themselves and done obeisance and sued for mercy in sweet and seemly words. And whenever he took tribute by means of the big bell and the big drum, at the first beat the sound reverberated as though they had been struck at the root of the ears of the kings of men and kings of Nagas. Nor did the sound cease until those kings had humbly sued for mercy. Whenever thus he took tribute, many hundred kings of Jambudipa year by year had to present him with the choicest of their virgin daughters, of their elephants and horses, rubies and treasures of gold, silver, and other precious metals, and *paso* of fur and silk, of silk and cotton, and of cotton. The pile of treasures of silver and gold thus given in tribute was 40 cubits high.

An ogre once unwittingly approached the king's palace at an unseasonable hour. And when Sakra knew of it, he said, ' Art thou worthy to tread the palace-floor of this majestic king, upholder of the religion ? ' And he cast him into an iron cage. Thereupon the king had the figure of an ogre carved in stone for future kings to know, and he kept it in a cage just as Sakra kept the ogre.

He built the outer palace and held the ceremony of warding off evil, at a time concurring with the year 167, Monday the tenth waxing of Tabodwè, Taurus being in the ascendant, the Moon in Taurus, Mars in Libra, the Sun conjunct with Mercury and Venus in Capricornus, Saturn and Rahu in Aquarius, Jupiter in Pisces. He ascended the palace at the time determined by Rishi and Gavampati, concurring with the year 168, Thursday the eleventh waxing of Wazo, Taurus being in the ascendant.

This king while he reigned had three hundred and three score white elephants, six and thirty millions of black elephants, and an innumerable number of warriors. There befell five great showers of gems. Each day the king bestowed the four priestly requisites on three thousand noble saints, sons and pupils of the Lord, whom he made his teachers. Over the relics of the Lord's body he built *zedi pahto* that all the people might worship them. Their names are these: One work of merit Thaukyamma, one Nyinyi, one Sisi, one Pawpaw, one Lyawlyaw, one Myathitin, one Hpayataung, two Hsutaungpyi, one Myinbahu enshrining the arm-relic of the Lord, one Pahtogyi built over the relics of the Lord's frontlet brought from the Kanyan country—eleven in all.

The Great Chronicle omits one work of merit Tharama, one Hpayataung, two Hsutaungpyi, and gives only eight—Thaukyamma, Nyinyi, Sisi, Pawpaw, Lyawlyaw, Myathitin, Myinbahu, Pahtogyi. The New Chronicle gives only nine: Myinbahu, Myintin, Thaukyamma, Pawpaw, Lyawlyaw, Sisi, Nyinyi, and the two Hsutaungpyi, elder and younger. The Old Chronicle gives only nine: Thaukyamma, Nyinyi, Sisi, Pawpaw, Lyawlyaw, Hpayataung, Tharama, Myinbahu, and Pahtogyi. Beside these diverse accounts the Prome Hsandaw Thamaing states that the Hsandawshin pagoda, originally built by the two merchant brothers, Ajjita and Balika, was restored by king Dwattabaung and named Myathitin, that the king also built the two Hsutaungpyi, and that the ministers built Myathitin pagoda. And this accords with our list of eleven pagodas above-mentioned, which we have obtained by comparing sundry *yadu*, *kabya*, chronicles, and *thamaing*, omitting excess and supplying defect; and it may be regarded as the truth.

Again, will not the statement about the frontlet-relic conflict with the statement made in the book Nalata-dhatuvamsa, that it reached Ceylon? It is but reasonable to hold that *unhissa* means the frontlet and that *nalata* means the forehead. But this point will not be treated in detail till we come to the reign of Anawrahta-minsaw.

During the reign of this king the religion of the Lord was manifest. In consultation with three thousand saints the king prepared the code of laws beginning with the line *Apāyagatim upayam* for the study of future kings and the welfare of all beings.

[*His fall.*] Now one day it befell that this great and powerful king seized a mere five *pè* of monastery glebeland which had been dedicated to a saint by a woman, a seller of cates. Thereupon the flying lance given by Sakra would no more do the king's errands. The big bell and drum when struck uttered no sound. The king sought counsel of certain noble saints, who meditated thereon and in their wisdom saw that it was because the king had seized the five *pè* of monastery glebeland dedicated to a saint by a young woman, a seller of cates. And they spake to the king after this wise: 'O king, all things in this world appertaining to the Three Gems are as the viper and the cobra, snakes of fatal venom. It is the nature of these snakes when touched to strike again; and when they strike no creature can escape grave calamity. Even so when objects appertaining to the Three Gems are wrongfully seized, a man may lose all his fortune, may fall into danger and calamity, may even forfeit his life. Because, O king, thou hast seized unlawful things, this has befallen thee!' So the king restored the five *pè* to the patron of the woman, the seller of cates.

Howbeit the flying lance and the big bells and drums would no more do the king's bidding, for that an unlawful and unclean object had been seized. Therefore the tribute paid of old by divers kings did not arrive. And the king was exceeding wroth, and sent one day for Pyissinbyu and Pyissinnyo and cried, 'Ho! ministers, the kings of Jambudipa Island, fiefs of mine, pay not their tribute. Begone ye and collect it!' And he sent them away. And Pyissinbyu and Pyissinnyo with their followers collected the tribute and presented it, seven years. But at last the king lost faith in them, and he put them to death by guile.

After their death there was none with might and authority to collect the tribute. Wherefore the king himself boarded the *nagakye* boat which the Nagas had presented to him, and collected tribute throughout all Jambudipa. Now once he came to the kingdom of Pantwa. And the queen of Pantwa devised evil in her heart, and she took a foul *paso* and made by sleight and subtilty a soft kerchief and offered it to the king. And he trusted her and took no heed, neither suspected he anything, but he wiped his face with the kerchief. Thereupon the live mole on the king's forehead disappeared; wherefore the Naga princess Besandi left him. And the king was sorry and he returned home. And it so befell that the king voided not his spittle into the spittoon, as was his wont, but he voided it into the ocean. When thus the *karma* of his good acts was exhausted, the Nagas became exceeding wroth and took the king and the *nagakye* boat and carried them off to the Naga country.

The New Chronicle, wishing to reject the statement of the Great Chronicle concerning the carrying off of king Dwattabaung and

the *nagakye* boat to the Naga country, points out that the *nagakye*
boat is the same as the *linzin* boat; and finds a fault in the Great
Chronicle and says that if, as it is said, the *nagakye* boat was
afterwards bricked up and buried in the reign of the king's son
Dwattaran, this tallies not with the statement that the Nagas
had already taken it away.   But the Great Chronicle merely says
that Anawrahtaminsaw dug out the *nawarat* boat which had been
bricked up and buried since the reign of king Dwattaran, and that
after he had seen it he buried it again.   It says not that he buried
either the *linzin* boat or the *nagakye* boat.   And the author of the
New Chronicle errs in supposing that the *linzin* boat is the same as
the *nagakye* boat; for it is plain from the list of the twelve kinds
of royal boats that they are different.   Here is the list: Thonlupuzaw, Thonlukya-hngan, Pyigyi-hman, Pyigyinaung, Wazira-
thinhka, Aungthatago, Mopawkyè, Swèlek-yathit, Nawarat, Pyi-
gyiwuntinyapyizon, Linzin, and Nagakye.

Of the two queens of Dwattabaung, Besandi, the Naga princess,
had no child; Sandadevi, daughter of the Pyu queen, gave birth
to Dwattaran.   His mother Sandadevi and his grandmother the
Pyu queen, being of Sakya Sakiyan race, were of pure descent.

King Dwattabaung was born on a Tuesday.   Thirty-five years
in the nether house, threescore and ten years he flourished; he was
carried off by the Nagas at the age of one hundred and five, in the
171st year of the religion.   From the story of king Dwattabaung
it is clear that kings who govern the land should seize unlawfully
not even a fruit nor a flower, nor anything appertaining to the
Three Gems, but should treat them with judgement and discretion.
Moreover, kings who rule over sea and land should mark with care
their vessels of royal use, and only when certain of their cleanliness
should they use them.

The land of Tharehkittara was known as Patthanapati in the
time of Kakusandha the Buddha, as Punnavati in the time of
Konagamana the Buddha, as Punna in the time of Kassapa the
Buddha, as Tharehkittara in the time of Gotama the Buddha.
It was known later as Yathepyi, after the turning hermit of the
brother-in-law of the Tagaung king.   Dwattabaung became king
in the year that followed the holding of the second Buddhist
Council of seven hundred noble saints, convened under the leader-
ship of Mahayasa and the patronage of king Kalasoka at Vesali

in the Middle Country, in the 100th year after the Lord made
parinirvana.

106. *Of the eight generations of kings from Dwattaran to Thiririt.*

[*Dwattaran*, fl. 373–351 B.C.] In the 171st year of the religion
the king's son Dwattaran became king. Fifty-nine years in the
nether house, twenty-two years he flourished; he passed at the age
of eighty-one. About the time of his death the thunderbolt fell
seven times in one day. He was born on a Wednesday.

[*Ranpaung*, fl. 351–301 B.C.] In the 193rd year of the religion
his son Ranpaung became king. He delighted in the good deed
of charity. He sought the company of hermits, brahmans, saints,
and learned men; his wisdom was great. He had compassion
on all the people as though they were his own womb-children.
He was master of the ten kingly duties. Forty years in the nether
house, fifty years he flourished; he passed at the age of ninety.
About the time of his death two suns appeared and fought till
noon. He was born on a Saturday. In the second year of his
reign Siridhammasoka convened the third Buddhist Council at
Pataliputta in the Middle Country.

[*Ranman*, fl. 301–251 B.C.] In the 243rd year of the religion
his son Ranman became king. He was reckless in conduct and
character. Thirty years in the nether house, fifty years he
flourished; he passed at the age of fourscore. About the time of
his death the Thursday star passed across the disc of the moon.
He was born on a Tuesday.

[*Rakhkan*, fl. 251–220 B.C.] In the 293rd year of the religion
his son Rakhkan became king. He was of fair complexion and
had many queens. He excelled in archery. Forty years in the
nether house, thirty-one years he flourished; he passed at the age
of seventy-one. About the moment of his death stars appeared in
the daytime; the shadow was reversed. He was born on a
Monday.

[*Hkanlaung*, fl. 220–182 B.C.] In the 324th year of the religion
his son Hkanlaung became king. Thirty-seven years in the nether
house, thirty-eight years he flourished; he passed at the age of
seventy-five. About the time of his death a great shell-fish dropped
from the sky. He was born on a Wednesday.

[*Lekhkaing*, fl. 182–148 B.C.] In the 362nd year of the religion his son Lekhkaing became king. Thirty-nine years in the nether house, thirty-four years he flourished; he passed at the age of seventy-three. About the moment of his death two suns appeared. He was born on a Monday.

[*Thirihkan*, fl. 148–120 B.C.] In the 396th year of the religion his son Thirihkan became king. Forty years in the nether house, twenty-eight years he flourished; he passed at the age of sixty-eight. About the time of his death the Friday star passed across the disc of the moon. He was born on a Thursday.

[*Thiririt*, fl. 120–111 B.C.] In the 424th year of the religion his son Thiririt became king. Fifty-one years in the nether house, nine years he flourished; he passed at the age of threescore. He was a man of peace and steadfastness. He kept his word, and delighted in the good deed of charity. He tried to establish a new era by annulling 403 years; but he might not annul them, for the number was not fit. He sought the company of six teachers whose names are these : Poppamani, Indriya, Kittariya, Candariya, Sakka, and Massa. With their help he made history and Vedas. He purified and set in order the Lord's religion. Many were the *gu*, monasteries, and rest-houses that he built. He was ever mindful of the glebelands that they should not perish. The ten kingly duties he thoroughly mastered, insomuch that the people of the land loved him, both laymen and saints, ministers and followers. In him was completed the ninth generation of king Dwattabaung; and the Tagaung dynasty ended. He was born on a Monday.

107. *Of king Ngataba.*

[*The story of Ngataba*, fl. 111–60 B.C.] In the 433rd year of the religion Ngataba became king. Now this is the story of Ngataba :

A dweller in that country kept his son in the charge of a saint, and let him become a novice in early youth. And the teacher took pity on him and taught him the Pitakas and Vedas. And the novice gently ministered to the teacher's wants. Now the teacher had a cock which he reared, and it came to pass one day that whenever the cock crew, he crew 'Who eats my head, becomes king Ngataba !' And the teacher took note of it, saying, 'What things for such a creature to crow !' And he called the novice, and said, 'Young man ! this cock in his crowing uttereth strange things. Cook it therefore and offer it to me.' And the novice cooked it according to the teacher's word. When he had cooked it, while he was taking it out of the pot, its head was severed and dropped onto the fireplace. And because it was unclean the novice washed and ate it. And when the teacher asked him, ' Where is the head of the cock ? ', he answered, ' When I was taking the cock out of the pot, the head fell off, and because it was unclean I did not serve it, but I ate it myself.' So the teacher thought, ' Now we shall know if the crowing of the creature come true or not.'

Therefore he taught the novice divers duties pertaining to the religion, the world and the state, and made him a layman and placed him in the charge of a minister, a captain. And the captain made the lad his son and dressed him in fitting raiment; for he had the bloom of beauty, wisdom, and glory and all the signs of royalty both great and small; wherefore the captain always took him with him wheresoever he went. One day he took him to the king's palace; and the king finding that the lad behaved wisely and possessed kingly qualities, was well pleased, and having no son he demanded him of the minister and made him his royal son. So the king relieved the minister of the guardianship. Now the lad was adept in the duties incumbent upon kings and in managing the home-affairs of state. He ministered to the royal father with great respect. Moreover, he made deep research into the Law. And the king and ministers, soldiers and people, both laymen and saints, loved him exceedingly. And the king made him his heir; some chronicles add that he married him to his daughter.

He was fifteen years old and heir-apparent when his father died, and he reigned in his stead. As king he paid reverence to the Three Gems. He sought the company of wise saints and brahmans and ever observed the Five Precepts, the Eight Precepts, and the Ten Precepts. He was master of the ten kingly duties and the four rules for extending royal favour. All people in the land he treated with kindliness and weight, as his own womb-children. He made five hundred noble saints his teachers. He possessed, moreover, the seven qualities of good men, to wit, faith, virtue, learning, self-sacrifice, the sense of shame, the fear of reproach, and wisdom.

In his reign there were seven showers of gems. Sakra saw to the building of the jewelled Pahtogyi pagoda. At its dedication the earth quaked. This king was not of the lineage of

Dwattabaung.   Because he was a king of alien stock he was known later as Ngataba.   Fifteen years in the nether house, fifty-one years he flourished; he passed at the age of sixty-six. About the moment of his death two suns appeared.   He was born on a Tuesday.

[*The writing of the Pitakas in Ceylon*, 94 B. C.]   In the seventeenth year of the reign of king Ngataba, in the 450th year of the religion, while king Vattakamani reigned in the island of Ceylon, five hundred noble saints, feeling that it was impossible to carry the three Pitakas, the word of the Lord, in memory for long, inscribed them on palm leaves and kept them after collating them an hundredfold.

108. *Of the twelve generations of kings from king Papiran to king Beizza.*

[*Papiran*, fl. 60 B. C.–6 A. D.]   In the 484th year of the religion, Papiran, son of Ngataba, became king.   He was born on a Tuesday. Twenty-seven years in the nether house, sixty-six years he flourished; he passed at the age of one hundred and three.   About the time of his death the Thursday star passed across the disc of the moon. It was in the sixth year of his reign that great questions were asked and answered between Milinda, king of Sagala, and Shin Nagasena in the Middle Country.   At that time, it is said, there were ten thousand crores of noble saints, disciples of the Lord.

[*Ranmokhka*, fl. 6–21 A. D.]   In the 550th year of the religion Ranmokhka, son of king Papiran, became king.   He was born on a Saturday.   He was a deep scholar of the Four Vedas, great in glory, power and influence, calm, steadfast, and deliberate.   He was master of the kingly duties and treated the people, both laymen and saints, with kindness as his own womb-children.   Sixty-seven years in the nether house, fifteen years he flourished, he passed at the age of eighty-two.   About the time of his death the Wednesday planet was stationary for seven whole months.

[*Rantheinhka*, fl. 21–24 A. D.]   In the 565th year of the religion his son Rantheinhka became king.   He was of a black complexion; his eyes and eyelashes were red.   He was rough and cruel and jealous of another's wife.   He regarded not nor mourned the death of another.   All the ministers and people were in exceeding fear of him and cursed him in their hearts.   In his reign there was

a famine and the people starved. He upheld not the religion of
the Lord. Sixty-five years in the nether house, three years he
flourished; he passed at the age of sixty-eight. About the time
of his death light streamed from the four points of the compass.
He was born on a Sunday.

[*Ranmonsaleinda*, fl. 24–39 A. D.] In the 568th year of the
religion his son Ranmonsaleinda became king. He was filled with
virtue, wisdom, and fixity. He had compassion on the people, both
laymen and saints, as though they were his own womb-children.
He was true to his word. Fifty years in the nether house, fifteen
years he flourished; he passed at the age of sixty-five. About the
time of his death a comet appeared. He was born on a Thursday.

[*Bereinda*, fl. 39–51 A. D.] In the 583rd year of the religion his
younger brother Bereinda became king. He went to study at
Takkasila and was deeply versed in medicine, charms, and the
Vedas. Sixty-three years in the nether house, twelve years he
flourished; he passed at the age of seventy-five. About the time
of his death it was noon at sunrise and the sun set at noon. He
was born on a Saturday.

[*Monsala*, fl. 51–56 A. D.] In the 595th year of the religion his
son Monsala became king. Fifty-eight years in the nether house,
five years he flourished; he passed at the age of sixty-three. About
the time of his death it was noon at sunrise. He was born on a
Wednesday.

[*Ponna*, fl. 56–59 A. D.] In the 600th year of the religion Ponna
his son became king. Forty-three years in the nether house, three
years he flourished; he passed at the age of forty-six. About the
time of his death there was an earthquake for seven days. He was
born on a Friday.

[*Thahka*, fl. 59–62 A. D.] In the 603rd year of the religion his
younger brother Thahka became king. Forty-four years in the
nether house, three years he flourished; he passed at the age of
forty-seven. About the time of his death ten vultures alighted on
the palace. He was born on a Monday.

[*Thathi*, fl. 62–65 A. D.] In the 606th year of the religion his
son Thathi became king. He was of ruddy complexion and an
evil-doer. He sought not the good of the people, neither respected
he the Three Gems. Twenty-nine years in the nether house, three
years he flourished; he passed at the age of thirty-two. About the

time of his death the earth quaked over all the city ; the ground
was rent into fragments ; water oozed through ; the sun and moon
was in total eclipse for one month.	He was born on a Saturday.

[*Kannu*, fl. 65–66 A. D.]	In the 609th year of the religion his
younger brother Kannu became king.	Thirty years in the nether
house, one year he flourished ; he passed at the age of thirty-one.
About the time of his death a miracle was seen in the Pahto
pagoda.	He was born on a Sunday.

[*Kantek*, fl. 66–69 A. D.]	In the 610th year of the religion his
elder brother Kantek became king.	Thirty-two years in the nether
house, three years he flourished ; he passed at the age of thirty-five.
About the time of his death the whole sky was dark like night.
He was born on a Monday.

[*Beizza*, fl. 69–73 A. D.]	In the 613th year of the religion his
elder brother Beizza became king.	Thirty-seven years in the
nether house, four years he flourished ; he passed at the age of
forty-one.	About the time of his death the Friday planet passed
across the disc of the moon.	He was born on a Monday.

109. *Of king Thumondari.*

[*Thumondari*, fl. 73–80 A. D.]	In the 617th year of the religion
Thumondari became king.	He was reckless in conduct.	Twenty-
four years in the nether house, seven years he flourished ; he passed
at the age of thirty-one.	About the time of his death the Thursday
comet appeared.	He was born on a Saturday.

[*The Short Era.*]	The year of the passing of this king, 624, is
according to the era fixed by five hundred saints under the leader-
ship of Shin Mahakassapa in consultation with king Ajatasattu, who
in the year when the Lord made *parinirvana* annulled 148 years in
order that the date might coincide with the year of the religion.
At Lokananda Kyaussaga Sakra, king of spirits, in the guise of
the brahman Mahallaka calculated on a rock the Short Era by
abolishing 622 years *dodorasa,* the number being fit.	The era
which king Thiririt sought to establish is not included in the
counting, as the number was not fit.	The number of the
long era is *dodorasa,* that of the short era is *khachapañca.*
The phrase 'year of the religion' has been used because the
religion, as we have shown, has come down in line with the
era.

110. *Of king Atitra.*

[*The crime of Atitra*, fl. 80–83 A.D.] In the second year, Short Era, Atitra, son of king Thumondari, became king. He was a doer of evil. He even visited his mother's house to sin against her. Now she had established herself in the Five Precepts and took refuge in the Lord. Moreover, she took a solemn vow and said 'If my virtue fail not, when my son cometh, may the state chamber stand as a vault about me!' Therefore the roof of the chamber stood about her as a vault. So the king her son turned back in shame. And even as he turned, his whole body was seized with an itch; and as he was going down to bathe in the four-cornered pond within the palace, his body was covered all over with monkey's hairs, and he turned straightway into a monkey, visibly, so that all might see. And the people threw bricks and spears at him that he died. And when her son became a monkey and fled, the royal mother came down from the palace and followed him. And when she saw her son she cried, 'Come, Alaung beloved!' The place is known as Laungthachaung to this day. Fifteen years in the nether house, three years he flourished; he passed at the age of eighteen. About the time of his death the Friday comet appeared. He was born on a Saturday.

111. *Of king Supaññanagarachinna.*

On the death of that king his younger brother and his son quarrelled over the throne, and the brother Supañña won. In the fifth year, Short Era, he became king. He was later known as Nagarachinna for that in his reign the line of kings at the capital came to an end. He was filled with beauty and all the signs of royalty great and small, with faith, virtue, learning, self-sacrifice, the sense of shame, the fear of reproach, and wisdom. He had compassion on the people, both laymen and saints, as though they were sons of his bosom. He was diligent in upholding the religion.

[*Supañña* (fl. 83–94 A.D.) *and the image.*] Once he marched with his fourfold army to subdue the Kanyan country, then tumultuous. And when he had conquered that country he saw therein a golden image of the Lord, eighty-eight cubits in height (judged by the forearm of an average man). And he was filled with faith transcendent as though he had seen the Lord himself, and fell down and worshipped day and night. Even so he did for three years, nor could he tear himself away from the image. It weighed tens and hundreds of crores of viss of gold, and was made in the likeness of Arimiteyya, the coming Buddha.

And the ministers spake into the royal ear and said, 'Great king! Thine elephants and horses and followers are grown stiff! May it please thee to return home straightway.' But the king answered, 'I cannot forsake this image of the Buddha. Make we a great jewelled raft, and place this image of the Buddha on the raft, and take it home to Tharehkittara by sea, fetching a compass around Mt. Nagayit.' And the ministers and followers were sad, thinking 'The king hath conceived the impossible; and while he is of this mind we shall never see our families again.' So they conferred together, and dug a pit beneath the Buddha's image. And the image, being cast of pure gold and heavy, fell. And when the king saw the image that it fell, he questioned them and said, 'Ministers, why hath the image of the Lord fallen?' And his ministers and followers made answer, 'Lo! Our Lord, the Master, hath entered *parinirvana*.' When the king heard their answer he was sad and abode in silence. And the ministers and followers thrust each a stick of firewood and a handful of coals and set fire to them. And when the king saw that there was fire, he questioned them again saying, 'Ministers, why set ye the image of the Lord on fire?' The ministers made answer, 'The Lord hath entered *parinirvana*, and lo! the spirits are holding the cremation ceremony.' And the king knew that their answer was not true, and he was sad and abode in silence. And the ministers and followers feared lest the king should be angry, and they cast twenty-eight seated images of the Lord in plated gold, one full cubit in height, and presented them to the king. Moreover, they cast images of solid gold and presented them. They also took away many for themselves. And the king returned to Tharehkittara, the homeland.

[*Fall of Tharehkittara*, 94 A.D.] But when these vessels were used by the people, this noble kingdom, albeit it was founded by the Seven Exalted Ones, became disordered and ungovernable, infested with thieves, robbers, plunderers, and cut-throats. A great whirlwind arose at that time and carried away a winnowing-tray, and the woman whose tray it was ran after it crying, 'Nga sagaw! Nga sagaw!' Thereupon the whole country was alarmed

and said, 'The Ngasagaw war is come!'; and the people split into
three divisions. And the king fell ill and died. Seventeen years
in the nether house, eleven years he flourished; he passed at the
age of twenty-eight. About the time of his death the winnowing-
tray was blown away by a whirlwind, and the people split into
three divisions. He was born on a Monday.

112. *Of the reigning of king Thamoddarit, and the dwellers in nineteen villages at Yonhlukkyun, after the Pyus, Kanyans, and Theks split
into three divisions.*

In the year 16 they were split into three divisions—Pyus,
Kanyans, and Burmans. The Pyus and the Kanyans waged war
with each other. Now they made a compact that victory should
fall to the greater number; and with that intent they built each a
pahto, the Pyus to the west of Tharehkittara, the Kanyans to the
north. And they agreed that whoever finished a large *pahto* first
should win. So the Kanyans built their large *pahto* with bricks
and could not finish it. But the Pyus thought wisely and built
bamboos in the likeness of a *pahto*, covered it with a white cloth,
and crowned it with an umbrella. And when the Kanyans saw it
they admitted defeat and fled.

[*Thamoddarit settles near Pagan*, 107 A.D.] When the Kanyans fled, the Pyus fought among themselves and split again into
three divisions. The Kyabins took one division, the Theks another.
The third made their home in the country of Taungnyo. After
three years they were attacked by the Talaings and spoiled. And
they moved thence and founded the country of Padaung Thettha
and dwelt there. After six years they were attacked and spoiled
once more by the Kanyans. Thence they moved and built Mindon
and dwelt there for three years. Thereafter Thamoddarit began to
build in the country of Yonhlukkyun in the year 29, Short Era.

In the sixteenth year after Mahallaka the brahman abolished the
old era, the kingdom of Tharehkittara perished. When the Pyus had
fought with the Kanyans and dwelt in Taungnyo, Padaung Thettha,
and Mindon, in the twenty-ninth year Short Era (including the
twelve years of interregnum), king Thamoddarit began to build a
city with the dwellers in nineteen villages at Yonhlukkyun.

This total of twelve years—three at Taungnyo, six at Padaung,
and three at Mindon—is written as thirteen years of interregnum

in the Great Chronicle; and compared with the usual reckoning in the Chronicles this figure may be regarded as reached in the following way: by subtracting 16, the year of the destruction of Tharehkittara, from 29, the year of the founding of Pagan : leaving 13 as remainder.

[*The nineteen villages at Yonhlukkyun.*] The names of the nineteen villages are these: 1. Nyaung-u. 2. Nagabo. 3. Nagakyit. 4. Magyigyi. 5. Tuti. 6. Kyaussaga. 7. Kokkèthein. 8. Nyaungwun. 9. Anurada. 10. Tazaunggun. 11. Ywamon. 12. Kyinlo. 13. Kokko. 14. Taungba. 15. Myegèdwin. 16. Tharekya. 17. Onmya. 18. Yonhlut. 19. Ywasaik. There were nineteen headmen, one to each village, and over the nineteen headmen was king Thamoddarit. Singu is also included in the Great Chronicle. But inasmuch as this conflicts with the statement that Singu is also known as Ngasingu—the place where the hunter Nga Sin lent aid to Kyanzittha—we omit it and add Onmya in its stead according to the New Chronicle.

113. [*Of Pagan, known as Arimaddana.*]

Now we shall tell the story of Pagan Arimaddana.

When the Lord revealed himself, he passed in his journeyings from the Middle Country and came to the site of that kingdom. He stood on the summit of Mt. Tangyi, and looked and saw a white heron and a black crow alight on the top of a *butea* tree on a steep bank; moreover, he saw a *preta* in the form of a monitor with a double tongue abiding within the fork of the *butea* tree, and a small frog crouching at its base. And he smiled. His cousin Shin Ananda entreated him saying, 'Why smilest thou ?' And the Lord prophesied and said, 'Beloved Ananda! In the 651st year after my *parinirvana* there shall be a great kingdom in this place. The alighting of the white heron and the black crow on the top of the *butea* tree signifies that there shall be many persons practising charity and virtue in that kingdom; there shall also be many wicked persons without virtue. The *preta* in the form of a monitor with a double tongue abiding within the fork of the *butea* tree, signifies that the people of that kingdom shall not till the land but shall live by merchandise, selling and buying, and their speech shall not be the words of truth but falsehood. The small frog crouching at the base of the *butea* tree signifies that the people shall be cool-bellied as the frog, and happy. In the reign of king Thamoddarit, the first founder of that kingdom, a great bird, a great boar, a great tiger, and a flying squirrel shall usurp dominion. And a prince full of glory, might, and dominion shall pierce the four, even the great bird, the great boar, the great tiger, and the flying squirrel.'

Thus he prophesied; and according to his word king Pyusawhti pierced his enemies, the great bird, the great boar, the great tiger, and the flying squirrel.

113 a. *Of king Pyusawhti.*

This is the story of king Pyusawhti.

Our Holy Lord, sprout and blossom of three hundred and thirty-four thousand five hundred and sixty-nine Sakya Sakiyan kings of the Sun dynasty, starting with king Mahasamata at the beginning of the world—He the crown of the three kinds of beings, had revealed himself in the reign of king Mahanama. Thereafter, as we have said, the Sakiyan kings perished in the danger of Vitatupa; and a Sakiyan king Dhajaraja fled with his followers from the Middle Country, and when he came to Mali on the upper Irrawaddy he wedded the queen Nagahsein, both being true Sakiyans of the same blood, and rebuilt and reigned in the old great kingdom of Tagaung. From him onwards in unbroken succession the Thado line of the Tagaung kings sprang and flourished, and in the seventeenth generation Thado Maharaja became king. His son, king Mahathambawa, founded Yathepyi and reigned there. Thus the royal father and the royal son ruled at the same time, king Thado Maharaja in the great kingdom of Upper Tagaung, king Mahathambawa in Yathemyo, which he founded.

Now while the country villages in Mali were still unsettled, a Sakiyan king called Thado Adeissaraza, lineally descended from the dynasty of the Tagaung kings, departed and dwelt secretly in disguise, supporting himself upon the hills by gardening and tilth. Now in his garden there was a Naga hole; and it was the custom at that time for all the people and villages to make prayers and offerings to the Naga daily, whenever they desired the gift of a son. Thus it befell one day that the queen of Thado Adeissaraza, by virtue of fair destiny and merit, conceived, and when the tale of months and days was fulfilled she gave birth to a son who had all the signs of royalty and beauty; and they named him **Sawhti**. The Naga king and queen who abode in that garden always tended him and loved him as their own son. When he was seven years old he was put in the charge of the chief hermit of that place, a master of the art of archery; moreover, he was learned in divers secular and Vedic books such as Rupanikaya, Saddanikaya, and others. And when he saw the young man's gait and stature and appearance, his royal marks and signs, he said, ' This youth is of true royal bone. He hath all the signs of royalty and beauty. Without a doubt he will gain kingship in the lower country.' So he changed his name Sawhti and called him Minhti, and throughly taught him the eighteen arts that future kings must know. When he was sixteen years old he wished to go to the country of Pagan, and asked leave of his royal father and mother. And they granted him leave, remembering the words of the chief hermit long ago that he would become king in the lower country. And the royal father gave him a bow and arrows richly fraught with gems. That bow was not a bow made by men; for it is said that Sakra, having heard the prophecy that this man would quell and conquer all his enemies in the Pagan country and become king, and that thereafter there would be a long line of sons and grandsons, all of royal bone, worthy to uphold and minister to the religion—gave him a demon bow and arrows richly fraught with gems. And the youth took the bow and arrows and went to the Pagan country, and lived dependent on an old Pyu couple. And they, having no son nor daughter of their own, tended and cherished him as a son with exceeding love and reverence.

One day, wishing to try the bow and arrows he had brought, he asked leave of the old Pyu couple to go abroad into the forest. But they, caring for him as if he were their own son, dissuaded him saying, ' Beloved, in this country in the east quarter there is a great boar followed by five hundred; in the west quarter there is a great bird followed by five hundred; in the south quarter there is a great tiger followed by five hundred; in the north quarter there is a flying squirrel followed by five hundred. Beloved, even the king, though lord of the country, cannot conquer these enemies, but daily he must give the great boar sixty lumps of rice, nine cartloads of pumpkin, and nine cartloads of bran. To the great bird he must give seven maidens once a week, one maiden

a day. It is now full twelve years since these exceeding terrible
and strange foes have oppressed the land.' But the youth trusted
in his own power and might and went searching for the dens
of his enemies ; and meeting the great tiger living in the south,
the flying squirrel living in the north, and the boar living in the
east, he pierced them and slew them by means of the bow given
him by his royal father.

Thence went he to the west where the great bird was. And
at that time he who saw to the feeding of the bird was on his way
bringing seven women to offer as food to the bird. And the young
prince met him and asked him straitly what he was about ; and he
who saw to the feeding of the bird, told him all. And he said,
' What sorry word is this thou speakest—to offer as food to a bird—
while such an one as I am liveth ? ' And he took charge of the
seven women ; and they rejoiced in hope of their deliverance from
danger and made fervent prayers and aspirations for the young
prince. Thereafter the bird came forth from his haunts, and seeing
the prince, discovered in divers ways his might and prowess. But
the prince was not afraid, for he was of nature cool and steadfast,
but he spake aloud and uttered words of challenge, and he pierced
and slew the mighty bird with the arrow barbed with Sakra's
thunderbolt.

Some say that he slew only the great bird and the boar, and
quarrel with the Great Chronicle and take their stand on the
kabya :

> The bird-ogre and the wanton boar,
> Greedy devourer of lumps of fat—
> The Sun-descendant at Arimaddana
> Pierced unto victory . . . .
> And broke the bud of enmity.

And again the *kabya* :

> Plauding, the host with ceremony upraised
> To the golden throne the lord of men
> Who slew the huge bird-elephant and the boar.

But all four enemies—the great bird, the great boar, the great
tiger, and the flying squirrel—are mentioned not only in the Great
Chronicle but also explicitly in others too, such as the Pagan
Chronicle and the Old Pagan Thamaing. Hlawgathonhtaunghmu,
it should be noted, has written in his *kabya* only the plain truth.

[*He becomes heir to Thamoddarit.*] The prince plucked one feather from the dead bird and caused the seven women to carry it on their heads. It is said that they had much ado to carry it. And he sent them away saying, 'Go ye, and offer it to your king.' And the seven women bore away the feather of the great bird, meaning to offer it to the king; but on the way they dropped it, being unable to carry it any longer, for it was heavy. That place is still known as Hngettaungpyit, and the place where the great bird was shot is still known as Hngeppyittaung. Now the seven maidens spake into the ear of king Thamoddarit, 'The great bird is dead, pierced by a young man!' And the king, hearing that the enemies he had had to feed for twelve years were conquered and killed, was exceeding glad and went with his fourfold army to where the prince was. There he saw the body of the bird, in bulk and stature like a small mountain. And he said to the prince, 'Of what race art thou, young sir, piercer of enemies so mighty? With what weapon didst thou pierce them?' And when the prince had told him all the truth, king Thamoddarit said, 'Verily he hath the glory, might and wisdom of such a bone and race'; and he married him to his daughter Thirisandadevi, and made him his heir. It is said that the number of persons offered as food to the great bird for the whole twelve years of the reign of king Thamoddarit was four thousand three hundred and twenty.

The story as above related accords with the Old Thamaing of ancient Pagan. This Thamaing was based on original texts of treatises annotated and approved by a long line of scholars famous and eminent, men learned in booklore. But other chronicles state :—

[*A different tale of the birth of Pyusawhti.*] A female Naga called Zanthi, daughter of Nagakyaung son of Kala, king of the Nagas, came to the world of men in order to practise the duties of virtue. While she lived near Mt. Mali she had intercourse with the Sun prince and became pregnant. The Sun prince deserted her; and she, when she was about to give birth, sent him a white crow; and this white crow would not return until the Sun prince wrapped up a ruby and gave it. Now it befell that some merchants, masters of ships, were taking their meal; and the crow, after the nature of crows thinking to pick up morsels of food, left the ruby bundle in the fork of a tree. And while it was picking up the morsels, the merchants found the ruby bundle which the white crow left in the tree-fork and took it, and left in its stead a bundle of dry dung. And when the white crow had eaten the morsels of food, it returned bringing the bundle and came to where the Naga was, and gave it to her. And when she saw the dry dung she was sorrowful and laid the egg-embryo on the mountain and went to the Naga country.

At that time spirits carried away a certain hunter. When they reached the place where the Naga had laid her egg, the hunter finding the egg bore it away joyfully. But while he was crossing a stream, swollen by a heavy shower of rain till it overflowed its banks, he dropped it from his hand. And one golden egg broke in the land of Mogok Kyappyin and became iron and ruby in that country. One dark egg floated down stream and reaching the Thintwè country gave birth to a jewel, a daughter, who when she came of age was made queen to the king of Thintwè. Some chronicles say that it reached the kingdom of Gandhala, others Tagaung; each has its several story. One white egg floated down the river Irrawaddy and reached Nyaung-u. And an old Pagan couple from Myegèdwin village came down to the shore at Nyaung-u and found it, and took it out of the water and showed it to the hermit practising piety at the foot of Mt. Tuywin. The hermit, being a man of wisdom and merit, prophesied saying, ' This egg is not an ordinary egg, but an exalted egg. He who will be hatched of it will have glory, wisdom, and the signs of royalty both great and small. He will quell his enemies on the surface of the whole earth. Moreover, he will uphold the Lord's religion.' And the old Pyu couple were joyful and treasured it; and when in due time it gave birth and the child was full of glory, wisdom, and the signs of royalty both great and small, they nourished him as a son born of their own bosom. And when he was of age, his father the Sun prince came and gave him a bow and arrows, richly fraught with gems, wherewith to conquer all his enemies.

[*Objections to this tale.*] So this story runs; but it is at variance with all curious and reasonable versions in the Pali commentaries and sub-commentaries. And this is how it varies:

With regard to the statement ' The female Naga called Zanthi, daughter of Nagakyaung son of Kala king of the Nagas', the books speak only of Kala king of the Nagas; he it was who took

charge of the golden cup that floated in the river Nerañjara, after
the future Buddha had eaten the boiled rice received as alms on the
day he was to become the Buddha. Not a shadow, not a hint
appears in the books of the existence of Nagakyaung son of that
Kala, king of the Nagas. This is one point of variance with
the books.

It is quite clear in the books that the Sun spirit dwells only
in the Sun mansion, ornament of the world. Not a shadow, not
a hint appears in the books of the existence of a son of the Sun
spirit. This is another point of variance with the books.

In a Vedic book it is stated as a mere opinion that the
Saturday planet is the prince of the Sunday planet. Not a shadow,
not a hint appears in any secular or Vedic book that the Saturday
planet is husband of the Naga called Zanthi. This too is a point of
variance with the secular books.

As for the statement that a human being was born from the union
of the Sun prince with the female Naga, these are the only parallel
instances in the books : in the Bhuridatta Jataka, the birth of
a human being after the father's kind from the union of a human
prince with a female Naga, and the birth of a Naga after the
father's kind from the union of Dhattharattha the Naga king with
the princess Samuddaja ; in the Mahavamsa, such tales as the birth
of prince Sihabahu after the mother's kind from the union of the
human princess, daughter of king Vangaraja, with a lion. Even if
there were real union between the Sun prince and the female Naga,
either a spirit or a Naga should have been born after the kind
either of the father or of the mother. Therefore, that a human son
was born, and not a spirit nor a Naga, is contrary to reason, and
this is a point of variance with the books.

The statement that the white crow was sent to where the Sun
prince was, is incredible, and a sort of fable.

As for the statement that one golden egg broke in the land
of Mogok Kyappyin and became stone, iron, and ruby, this land
of Mogok Kyappyin being thus singled out from among the fifty-
six places of precious stones on the surface of Jambudipa, it is
worth considering whether, in the other places also, the divers
kinds of gems, stones, iron, ruby, gold, and silver, and pearl, were
likewise the result of the breaking of a Naga egg. Not a shadow,
not a hint appears in the books that in all those fifty-six places

a Naga egg broke and became stone, iron, or ruby. This being so, it should be regarded as a figure of speech, uttered for the sake of vaunting and effect.

As for the several statements that one dark egg reached Gandhala, Tagaung, or Thintwè: it is a journey of six months from Gandhala to Burma, the distance being more than a hundred *yojana*. Furthermore, there is no stream nor river from the land of Mali to the kingdom of Gandhala. This too is utterly unreasonable.

Again, alleging that it reached Tagaung and Thintwè, kingdoms very near to Burma, and became a queen, the *thamaing* and chronicles ought to specify which queen, and who was the king then reigning, if it really became a queen. But this not being manifest, the wise like not the phrase ' oviparous bone of kings egg-born and undetermined ', as contrary to all reason.

If this be so, how comes there to be the Uhkunhwek pagoda at Pagan ? Various chronicles and *thamaing* state that the skull of the huge bird was buried at Anuradha. Hence it should be named not Uhkunhwek but Okhkunhwek.

Therefore the phrase ' Egg-born bone of kings' should be rejected. Indeed, the history of the bone and lineage of kings of the Sun dynasty, starting from Mahasamata at the beginning of the world, is found in the books on this wise : Prince Siddhattha, the future Buddha, retired into the forest and turned monk wearing the lotus robe offered by Brahma near the river Anoma, and he went to the kingdom of Rajagaha, thirty *yojana* distant from the river Anoma. King Bimbasara saw and followed him, when holding the lotus-bowl, ornament of the world, he came a-begging into the kingdom of Rajagaha, called Giribaja, encircled as a cattle yard by five dark mountains—Pandava, Gijjhakuta, Vepara, Isigili, and Vepulla. He met him in Pandava vale, and offering him his kingdom asked after his lineage. And the prince replied :

> O king, I am of the Sun race,
> A Sakiyan by birth ;
> I have left my family and become a monk,
> Desiring not the pleasures of sense.

This is told in the Pali of the Pabbajja Sutta Nipata. This stanza tells, moreover, of the unbroken line of princes of the Sun dynasty, descended without flaw in the succession down to king

Suddhodana, numbering in all three hundred and thirty-four
thousand five hundred and sixty-eight, from king Mahasamata
at the beginning of the world unto king Suddhodana. It also tells
that he is known as a scion of the Sakiyan dynasty.

Referring to the fact that the unbroken line of kings of the
true race of king Mahasamata, as supported by the Pali of the
Pabbaja Sutta above recorded, are of the Sun dynasty, kings of
the rising Sun, the Sun lineage, the Sun race, the famous
Mahathilawuntha has written :

> The Lord of the Wheel of authority,
> Heir of the Sun dynasty
> Of a line of eighty thousand kings,
> What time he should govern the three kingdoms,
> What time the day of his inheritance approached,
> Hath cruelly abandoned it
> And entered the forest.

And the famous Mahathilawuntha, whom a line of scholars learned
in booklore have not forsaken, but made their prop and backbone
of authority, has written thus because, king Mahasamata being of
the race of the Sun spirit, and being said to be of the Sun dynasty,
every true scion of his race is also said to be of the Sun dynasty.
And divers commentaries and sub-commentaries, such as Sarattha-
sangaha, have shown that he was of the Sun dynasty :

> There was a king, Mahasamata,
> Of the Sun family,
> Paragon and Potentate
> Of pure and mighty merit ;
> Eye of the world !
> His blinding radiant virtue
> Dispelled darkness, shining
> Splendid as a second Sun.

Thus it shows that king Mahasamata was of the race of the natural
Sun king, and that he was graced with virtues radiant as a second
Sun king.

Therefore some thoughtful people say that while the natural
Sun king dispels the outer darkness, king Mahasamata dispels the
inner darkness, and that being thus alike in the merit of dispelling
darkness, the very body of king Mahasamata by simile is called

the Sun Adeissa or king Nemi. The wise like not that saying; and why? In the books only the natural Sun king is known as the Sun, and the son of the Sun king is known as Manu. In religious books that same Manu is also called Mahasamata. Hence the phrase 'the family of the Sun, the Sun family' is only used in the books to indicate that king Mahasamata is literally of the family of the Sun king, of the Sun family. In the Pali 'Sun family' the word *Sun* indicates the Sun king, the word *family* king Mahasamata. Hence Ashin Mahasariputtara, who had no peer in wisdom save the Lord, preached in the book Mahaniddesa that the natural Sun king is known as the sun (*adeissa*), and that the exalted Lord who was of the race of that king is called 'kinsman of the sun' (*adeissa*). For he says, 'Adeissa is the Sun, Gotama is of the race of the Sun. And the Blessed One is Gotama. Therefore the Blessed One is by race akin to the Sun, related to the Sun. Therefore the Buddha is called kinsman of the Sun.' Because the Sun king and the Lord are by race related, this phrase means that the Lord is known as the race of the Sun king, related to the Sun king. And using the word in this sense we see that the unbroken line of kings, descended first from king Mahasamata, being identical with Gotama's lineage, is called the race of the Sun king, related to the Sun king; for the title 'king of the rising Sun, of the lineage of the Sun' is given and all is clear if we depend on documentary evidence and due and probable interpretations as above recorded, and cling to the fact that the bone and line of kings of the Sun dynasty are descended from king Mahasamata at the beginning of the world.

But other authors write as though the title 'race of the Sun' were used merely because king Pyusawhti was born by oviparous conception from the union of the son of the Sun spirit with the female Naga. And in later poems *kabya*, *linka*, *eggin*, and *mawgun*, and so forth, divers writers, each in turn passing down the expression from one to another, have vied with each other in asserting:

> The bird-ogre and the wanton boar,
> Greedy devourer of lumps of fat—
> The egg-descendant at Arimaddana
> Pierced unto victory, proving prowess,
> And brake the bud of enmity.

as though to be born of an egg were better even than to be of
the bone of kings of the Sun dynasty !

But it is clear that some of the wise, making reference to the
Sun race of the Sun dynasty, have discovered the right interpretation, and state that Pyusawhti reigned in the kingdom
of Arimaddana, being descended through a long line from king
Mahasamata who was of the race of the Sun spirit.   Thus:

All glorious Pyuminsaw the good and great,
Issue of the long line of the Sun spirit,
Sate in the golden kingdom of Rimad, the crown of the earth;
The umbrella, Sandi, fair as lotus-pollen,
Whose stick was coral three spans round,
Nine cubits high stood o'er him, its navel-top of gems . . .

This being so, heed we the familiar proverb of the wise—' Be
it never so old, if bad, reject it ! '   True the phrase ' egg-born bone
of kings ' is not really old, but only seems so; none the less have
we rejected it.

[*A tale of the Ari.*]   And here is an instance how old beliefs
were rejected in the past.   Seeing that the people had been fondly
clinging to the doctrine of the Ari lords for thirty generations
of kings at Pagan, Anawrahtaminsaw, filled with virtue and
wisdom, rejected the rank heresies of the Ari lords and followed
the precepts of Shin Arahan, known as Dhammadassi.   Whereupon those Ari lords, in order that the people might believe their
doctrine, made manuscripts to suit their purpose, and placed them
inside a *thahkut* tree.   And when the *thahkut* tree became covered
with scales and bark they sought and seduced fit interpreters of
dreams, and made them read and publish the manuscripts found in
the *thahkut* tree.   So that the king and all the people misbelieved.

It should be confidently held that only the story in the Old
Pagan Thamaing above recorded is both reasonable in itself and
consistent with documentary evidence.   The above is inserted with
documentary evidence and fitting comment in order to dispel the
doubt about the so-called undetermined oviparous birth of king
Pyusawhti.

[*Death of Thamoddarit,* 152 A.D.]   When Pyusawhti became heir
to the throne he was sixteen years old.   When he had been three
years an heir king Thamoddarit died.   Thirty-two years in the
nether house, forty-five years he flourished; king Thamoddarit

passed at the age of seventy-seven. About the moment of his death a bolide as large as a cartwheel fell in his presence. He was born on a Sunday.

114. *Of king Yathekyaung.*

[*Yathekyaung*, fl. 152–167 A. D.] After the death of king Thamoddarit, Pyusawhti, ere he became king, made his benefactor the hermit turn layman, and made him king. Because the hermit thus turned layman he was afterwards known as Yathekyaung. In the seventy-fourth year Yathekyaung became king. Ninety-one years in the nether house, fifteen years he flourished ; he passed at the age of one hundred and six. About the time of his death the *deinnetthè* coincided with the *thingyan*. He was born on a Monday. It is said in the Nangyaung Chronicle, the Abridged Chronicle, and the Old Chronicle, that Yathekyaung was of the royal race of Tagaung.

115. *Of the reigning of king Pyusawhti after his teacher king Yathekyaung.*

[*Pagan.*] In the eighty-ninth year Pyusawhti became king. He was known as Pyuminhti because he was reared to manhood by the old Pyus. The kingdom was known as Pandupalasa in the time of Kakusandha the Buddha, as Dhammakuti in the time of Konagamana the Buddha, as Dhammadesa in the time of Kassapa the Buddha, as Tampadipa in the time of Gotama the Buddha. Not until the time of Pyuminhti was it known as Arimaddana. (But the Great Chronicle contradicts itself when it says that even in the reign of king Thamoddarit the kingdom was founded under the name of Arimaddana : and again, that in the reign of king Pyusawhti it received the name Arimaddana. The first statement clashes with the second.)

[*The glory of Pyusawhti*, fl. 167–242 A. D.] When Pyuminhti ascended the throne, Brahma on the right and Sakra on the left lifted him by the hand and set him on the throne. He caused spirit drums and harps and trumpets to sound, what time he mounted the throne and was anointed king. His queens were two, Thirisandadevi daughter of king Thamoddarit, and the Naga princess Irandadevi, offered by the Nagas deferring to his glory and might. Moreover, Sakra presented him with royal articles of use and pomp together with five regal emblems. Among the royal articles of use and pomp he presented eight umbrellas with handles of coral, nine and a third cubits long, three spans in circumference, with leaf-canopies of one hundred folds, exceeding delicate and soft, wrought with *kamuttara* lotus-thread, with hangings of the banyan-leaf pattern variegated with the nine priceless gems, wrapped in radiance down to the base, the top-navel studded with jewels and precious stones. Moreover, he gave the *hsaddan* flying elephant with six-rayed tusks, called Girimekhala, sprung from Hsaddan mere, and the horse of noble breed sprung from near the Sindhu river. And the Naga king presented thirty domestic white elephants, together with the *hsaddan* she-elephant called Mahasubhatta, of the race of the *hsaddan* flying elephants; four thousand domestic black elephants unblemished; seven hundred black *katha* elephants; six thousand domestic horses and six thousand state horses unblemished. Moreover, he sent three women to attend on him—a Naga stewardess to mind the royal food, a Naga to offer the royal apparel, and a Naga to offer the royal headdress; together with the royal articles of use and pomp to quell the malice of his foes; also one hundred and eighty Naga youths, mighty to subdue the enemy. These Naga youths whenever the king went forth had alway to wait by the stairs; and for fear of the Garulas they waited with hair tied up in a knot shaped like a bird-snare, holding canes in their hands. And when the king went forth they followed with canes in their hands, keeping on the left hand and on the right while the king strode before. The king had four marshals of war: Rajavaddhana, Devavaddhana, Dhammavaddhana, and Nagavaddhana. He had eight thousand subalterns, sixteen thousand captains, one hundred crores of valiant foot-soldiers, three crores and six million cavalry, six million fighting elephants.

The twelve great festivals held in the reign of this king are these: one for the piercing of the great bird; one for the piercing of the great boar; one for the piercing of the great tiger; one for the piercing of the flying squirrel; one festival in honour of his ascending the throne amidst men, spirits, Nagas, Sakra, Brahma, and the sounding of spirit harps and trumpets; one for the meeting of his royal mother at Shwezigon; one for the climbing of Mt. Poppa to review his innumerable fourfold army, parading his strength; one in honour of his own march with a force of elephants and horse, and his assault and victory when Tarop soldiers, more than one hundred crores in number, reached the town of Kosambhi on the frontier of the kingdom ; three for the three showers of gems that fell during his reign and were gathered by the people—twelve festivals in all.

The handmaids waiting on his two queens were these : two thousand attendants wearing livery crowned with the red ruby, two thousand attendants wearing livery crowned with the dark ruby, two thousand attendants wearing livery crowned with the spotted ruby, two thousand attendants wearing livery crowned with emerald, two thousand attendants wearing livery crowned with pearl, two thousand attendants wearing livery crowned with diamond, two thousand attendants wearing livery crowned with precious stones, two thousand attendants wearing livery crowned with coral—in all, sixteen thousand attendants. Eight thousand surrounded each of the queens.

Irandadevi had no son nor daughter. Queen Sandadevi gave birth to prince Htiminyi. When he came of age he was made heir. He was of noblest birth, on the father's side and on the mother's side.

Pyuminhti was a glorious prince with might of arm and dominion, and Sakra and the Naga king alway succoured him, insomuch that all the kings of Jambudipa Island had to present him with letters of ceremony, gifts and presents, virgin daughters, jewels, elephants, and horses. The king possessed all the seven qualities of good men, including faith, virtue, the sense of shame, and the fear of reproach ; he was master of the ten kingly duties. He upheld aright the Lord's religion. For the good of future kings he conferred with Gavampati, Rishi, and Sakra, and composed the code of law beginning with the verse ' Atthesu dhammasatthesu '. He built a cave-temple with an image of the Lord at the place where the skull of the great bird was buried, and another at the place where the bird was pierced. Many other pagodas, *gu*, monasteries, grottos, and cave-temples did he build. He had compassion on his ministers, headmen of villages and circles, and the people, both laymen and saints, as though they were children of his bosom. Such are the works of merit he piled up. Thirty-five years in the nether house, seventy-five years he flourished ; he passed at the age of one hundred and ten. About the time of his death the Thursday planet passed across the disc of the moon ; all day long it was dark like night. It is said that the king was five cubits in

stature; the circumference of his body three cubits. He was born
on a Tuesday.

116. *Of the six kings from Htiminyi, son of king Pyusawhti, to king
Thihtan.*

[*Htiminyi*, fl. 242–299 A. D.] In the 164th year his son Htiminyi
became king, receiving the ceremony of anointing. Fifty years in
the nether house, fifty-seven years he flourished; he passed at the
age of one hundred and seven. About the time of his death the
deinnetthè coincided with the *thingyan*; the Thursday planet passed
across the disc of the moon. He was born on a Wednesday.

[*Yinminpaik*, fl. 299–324 A. D.] In the 221st year his son Yinminpaik became king. Fifty years in the nether house, twenty-five years
he flourished; he passed at the age of seventy-five. About the time
of his death the Thursday planet alighted on the moon; the earth
quaked for full seven days. The day of his birth was Thursday.

[*The tooth relic brought to Ceylon.*] At this point the Great and
the New Chronicles state that in the forty-fourth year of Htiminyi
princess Hemamala and prince Danta, daughter and son-in-law of
king Kumasiva, brought the sacred tooth from Dantapura in the
kingdom of Kalinga and crossed over to the island of Ceylon.
Poems, both *kabya* and *linka*, have also wrongly been composed
after the Chronicles. They agree not with what comes in the
books nor with the Kalyani inscriptions. This is how they differ:

It is stated in the Dipavamsa that in the 811th year of the
religion Mahasena was king (we include the years in which he had
flourished). He was the sixtieth in descent from king Vijayakumma,
who first ruled Ceylon for thirty-seven years beginning from the
day when the Lord entered *parinirvana*. The Kalyani inscription
agrees with the Dipavamsa, stating, 'When three hundred and
fifty-seven years had passed since the building of the Abhayagiri,
king Mahasena reigned in the island of Ceylon for twenty-seven
years.' The Mahavihara was built in the 236th year of the
religion; the Abhayagiri was built 218 years later; 357 years
thereafter Mahasena became king. The total of these three dates
gives the date of the reign of Mahasena, namely the 811th year of
the religion. By subtracting therefrom 622 *dodorasa*, the year 189
is obtained. By adding 27, the years of Mahasena's reign, we
obtain 216, or the 838th year of the religion, being the year when

his son Kittisirimegha became king. Now the Nalatadhatuvamsa states that in the ninth year of the reign of this king, princess Hemamala and prince Danta brought the lower left tooth-relic from Dantapura in the kingdom of Kalinga: 'On inquiry made after reaching Anuradhapura it proved to be in the ninth year of Kittisirimegha.' 'In the ninth year of Sirikittimegha, lord of men and son of Mahasena' occurs in the Dathadhatuvamsa. 'It was then the ninth year of Kittisirimegha, son of king Mahasena' occurs in the sub-commentary on the Dathadhatu-vamsa. 'In his ninth year he brought from Kavilakalinga the tooth-relic of the great sage, the Brahma' occurs in the Culavamsa. Thus, in accordance with the account given in the various books, by adding the nine years in which he flourished to 838, era of the religion, the year when king Kittisirimeghavanna ascended the throne, we obtain 847—or 225 if we add the nine years in which he flourished to 216, the year of his accession.

Consider now, in reference to what is said in those Chronicles, the statement that in the forty-fourth year of the reign of Htiminyi the sacred tooth arrived in Ceylon. Htiminyi became king in the 786th year of the religion. Add 44 years of his reign, and we obtain the 830th year of the religion. Add 44 years to 164, and we obtain 173.[1] Hence the statement that in the forty-fourth year, when Htiminyi flourished, the sacred tooth reached Ceylon from Jambudipa in the reign of Kittisirimegha, conflicts with the Dipa-vamsa and Kalyani inscriptions, for Kittisirimegha had not even become king; there is a gap of seventeen years.

Hence it was not in the reign of Htiminyi, but in the fourth year after his son king Yinminpaik ascended the golden throne, that a certain warlike king, desirous of the sacred tooth, came to do battle, and king Kumasiva perished in the fight. Hearing the tidings his royal daughter Hemamala and prince Danta, son of the king of Ucceni country, bore the sacred tooth till it reached the island of Ceylon in the ninth year of the reign of Kittisirimeghavanna, in the 447th[2] year of the religion, or 216.[3] The Dathadhatuvamsa records how a welcome was prepared for it and abundant honour and worship. It was placed in the Dhammacakka monastery built by Devanampiyatissa. The monastery was called Dathadhatughara from that day.

[1,2,3] *errors for* 208, 847th, 225 *respectively.*

Thus the story should be accepted simply as it occurs in the books. The above account has been extracted from the books and here inserted in order to make manifest from the root the date when the sacred tooth reached the island of Ceylon.

[*Paitthili,* fl. 324–344 A.D.] In the 246th year his son Paitthili became king. Forty-one years in the nether house, twenty years he flourished; he passed at the age of sixty-one. About the time of his death the sun-comet appeared seven times the height of a palm tree; half the stars in the sky vanished. The day of his birth was Thursday.

[*Thinlikyaung,* fl. 344–387 A.D. *Founding of Thiripyissaya.*] In the 266th year his son Thinlikyaung became king. It was only in his reign that the group of nineteen villages was dissolved, and he founded and built the city of Thiripyissaya at the site of Lokananda where he lived. He named it Thiripyissaya. He was master of the ten kingly duties and had compassion on the people, both laymen and saints. And the ministers and headmen of villages and circles and all the people loved him and made great prayers on his behalf. In his reign there fell three showers of gems. The Mahagiri brother and sister came, and he settled them on Mt. Poppa. Fifty-three years in the nether house, forty-three years he flourished; he passed at the age of ninety-six. About the time of his death there was a thunderstorm for full seven days and many trees were shattered. He was born on a Sunday.

117. *Of the Mahagiri spirits, brother and sister, in the reign of king Thinlikyaung.*

[*The children of the Tagaung blacksmith.*] This is the story of Mahagiri, brother and sister. Nga Tindè, son of Nga Tindaw, blacksmith of Tagaung, was famous for his vast strength. It is said that once he wrenched even the tusk of a grown male elephant. When the Tagaung king heard of it he commanded his ministers saying 'This man will rob me of my prosperity. Seize him and do away with him!' So Nga Tindè, fearing to lose his life, ran away a far journey and lived in the deep jungle. And the king was afraid; so he took the young sister of Nga Tindè and raised her to be queen. Long after, the king said to the queen, 'Thy brother is a mighty man. Send for him straightway, and I will make him governor of a town.' And Nga Tindè came, thinking,

' He hath raised my sister to be queen, and now he sendeth for me,
desiring me to enter his service.' But the king had him seized by
guile and bound to a *saga* tree, and he made a great pile of fuel and
coal, and caused the bellows to be blown. And the queen descended
into the fire saying, ' Because of me, alas, my brother hath died ! '
It is said that the king clutched the queen's topknot and rescued
only her head and face, but her body was burnt.

[*The Mahagiri spirits.*] After their death, brother and sister
became spirit brother and sister and dwelt in the *saga* tree. Any
man, horse, buffalo, or cow who entered so much as the shade of that
saga tree, died. And when this verily befell, they dug up the *saga*
tree from the root and floated it in the river Irrawaddy. Thus it
reached Pagan; and they carved images of the spirit brother and
sister and kept them on Mt. Poppa. And king, ministers, and
people visited them once a year.

[*Kyaungdurit*, fl. 387–412 A.D.] In the 309th year the king's
son Kyaungdurit became king. Fifty-five years in the nether
house, twenty-five years he flourished ; he passed at the age of
eighty. About the time of his death the moon showed a comet
and the Pleiades crossed the disc of the moon. He was born on
a Wednesday.

118. *Of the going of Ashin Buddhaghosa to Ceylon to bring the
sacred Pitakas, and his copying of them.*

Concerning this the Great Chronicle says that the famous elder,
Ashin Buddhaghosa, crossed to the island of Ceylon from the
Thaton kingdom to bring the Pitakas. The New Chronicle says
that he crossed from the Middle Country. This is the story :

[*Buddhaghosa.*] Till after the 900th year of the religion the
line of pupils great and small, from Ashin Yonakamahadhammarak-
khita and Ashin Sona-Uttara the elders, recited the three Pitakas
from memory only. There were no letters in Jambudipa. At that
time a Brahman youth born near the great Wisdom Tree had completed his studies in medical and Vedic treatises and was roaming
about to defeat the doctrines of others in Jambudipa ; and he came
to a monastery. Ashin Revata the elder heard him reciting with a
pure and even tone, and he thought ' This man is learned. He is
worth comparisons.' So he asked ' Who is it making a noise like
a donkey's bray ? ' and he put many questions. Ashin Revata

answered them all. But when the Brahman youth was questioned on the Law he was unable to answer. So he turned monk in order that he might learn the Vedas, and he studied the three Pitakas. Thereafter he became famous as the Lord, and began to be known by the name Ashin Buddhaghosa.

[*He goes to Ceylon.*] Now Ashin Revata knew that Ashin Buddhaghosa desired to write commentaries on the works Tappacchanodaya and Atthasalini, and he said, ' Here in Jambudipa island there is only the Pali; not the commentaries, nor the divers doctrines of the masters. The commentary that is in the island of Ceylon is pure. Ashin Mahinda the elder carried to Ceylon the sacred Pali canon of the Three Councils. Go to Ceylon and hearken to the Ceylonese tongue ; hearken to the Magadha tongue ; and translate into the Magadha tongue the commentaries kept in the Ceylonese tongue, after studying the series of works by noble elders such as Sariputta.' And he sent him away. This agrees with the Culavamsa.

At that time king Dhammapala, twenty-fifth in unbroken descent of son and grandson from king Siharaja the first king of Thaton called Suvannabhummi, was ardent in his zeal for the religion ; and he exalted Ashin Buddhaghosa and gave him a white elephant with four high ministers to attend him. And Ashin Buddhaghosa crossed to the Middle Country from the seaport of Bassein, and had drawings made after the likeness of the great Wisdom Tree and the seven sites, Nerañjara and Pupparama monastery and the others, and he purposed to cross over to the island of Ceylon. This agrees with history.

Then Sakra, king of spirits, thousand-eyed, cleansed the organ of the monk's sight and offered two *chebula* fruits, potent on being eaten to give contentment without hunger; also an iron stile that did one's utmost bidding. So he went down to the seaport Bhangari in the Deccan and crossed and reached Ceylon by ship. This agrees with the Buddhaghosuppatti and Sasanavamsa.

[*His writings.*] Then he hearkened to the Ceylonese commentary and the orthodox doctrines in the presence of the elder Sanghapala at Mahaviharapadhanaghara in the island of Ceylon, and there first he made the treatise Visuddhimagga. Then he translated into the Magadha tongue all the books of commentaries. This agrees with the Culavamsa.

Moreover, after studying with the Ceylon teacher Ashin Buddha-mitta these three treatises—the Great Commentary, the Great Paccarita Commentary, and the Kurundi Commentary, he wrote many books. This agrees with the conclusion of the Commentary on the Vinaya Parivara by Ashin Buddhaghosa.

[*He brings the Pitakas to Thaton.*] Thus, when the great elder Ashin Buddhaghosa had given king Mahanama a white elephant and sought leave to depart, he brought one out of the three copies of the Visuddhimagga which he had made, together with the Three Pitakas and the commentary on the Three Pitakas, and crossed over to Jambudipa. And Sakra came to him and said : ' In Jambudipa, in the Middle Country, there is no standing-place for the religion. The religion should shine. The religion shall stand and shine for five thousand years in such places as the distant jungle settlements in the south-east corner of the Middle Country, nine hundred (*yojana*) in circumference—Tharehkittara, Thiripyissaya, Ramañña-desa. Carry it thither.' So he took it and crossed over and reached the city of Thaton, called Sudhammavati. And when the tidings were known there was a general cry throughout all the kingdom of Ramañña, and king and queen, men and women, monks and laymen, all welcomed the religion with divers festivals, assemblies, celebrations, and almsgivings. As though the Lord Omniscient had appeared in their midst, they reverently raised the Pitakas, and coming to the city-palace they built a tabernacle in a lovely place in front of the golden palace, and there they laid the treasures of the religion.

[*The lineage of Anomadassi.*] At that time the chief elder of the religious order was Ashin Anomadassi. This is his lineage : of the two monks of the Third Council, Sona and Uttara, who came to Suvannabhummi in the cause of religion, Ashin Sona the elder had ten pupils who abode with him, the chief of whom was Ashin Mahasobhita; his pupil was Ashin Mahasomadatta; his pupil, Ashin Sumanatissa; his pupil, Ashin Sobhaga; his pupil, Ashin Somadatta; his pupil, Ashin Anomadassi. When Ashin Anomadassi was in charge of the religion, divers saints and monks who were practising piety in the countries of Burma, Mon, Arakan, Shan, Yun, Linzin, and Sokkate, came one by one and studied and took away the sacred Pali and the commentary, which had only been handed down by word of mouth from teacher to teacher; and so in divers distant places even now the religion spreads and shines. This agrees with the Sasanavamsa and the Thaton Chronicle.

Thus until the 450th year of the religion, the Pitakas, the canonical books of the religion as fixed by the Three Councils, were handed down by noble saints by word of mouth, ever since the elder Ashin Mahamahinda came to the island of Ceylon in the 236th year of the religion and upheld and promoted the religion, with the help of king Devanampiyatissa, sixth in descent from king Vijaya, the first ruler of Ceylon. And in the sixth year of the prosperity of king Vattagamani, twenty-fourth in descent, five hundred noble saints, foreseeing the weak-mindedness of future generations, inscribed on palm leaf the characters of the canonical books at a fourth Council similar to the other Councils. Then in the reign of king Buddhadasa, sixty-third in descent, a certain preacher of religion translated and wrote down in the Ceylonese tongue the Sutta and Abhidhamma Pitakas. But it was not till the reign of king Mahanama, sixty-sixth in descent, who became king in the 946th year of the religion, that the great and noble elder Ashin Buddhaghosa transcribed them in the Magadha tongue, so that they reached Jambudipa Island and the great kingdom of Thaton, called Suvannabhummi.

[*Suvannabhummi.*] The Great Chronicle and others say Suvanna-bhummi is Thaton, or also Zimmè. The Kalyani inscription says 'In Ramaññadesa, called the kingdom of Suvannabhummi.' The Thaton Chronicle mentions the founding of Suvannabhummi, when the Rishi and Sakra helped king Siharaja, and then says the folk moved south only in the reign of king Upadeva, sixth in descent, and founded Thaton, called Sudhammavati. But seeing that the account of the arrival of the missionary elders, Ashin Sona and Uttara, in the reigns of Jotakuma Siridhammasoka, grandson of that king Upadeva, agrees with the statement in the books that the elders Ashin Sona and Uttara were sent on mission to Suvannabhummi, only Thaton should be understood by Suvanna-bhummi.

[*Date of Buddhaghosa's visit to Ceylon.*] Again, the Great Chronicle says that it was in the forty-second year after the accession of king Thinlikyaung that Ashin Buddaghosa crossed over to Ceylon. But in the forty-fourth[1] year of the reign of this

---

[1] *error for* forty-second.

king, being the 930th year of the religion or 308, Mahanama
had not even come to the throne; there is a gap of sixteen years.
So it was not in the reign of king Thinlikyaung, but in the
fifteenth year of the reign of his son king Kyaungdurit that
Mahanama became king, in the 946th year of the religion or
324. This is found in the Dipavamsa and agrees with the
Kalyani inscription and the Sasanavamsa.

The above account has been omitted in the Great and Middle
Chronicles, but is here inserted with extracts according to the
books, in order to make plain the story of the arrival in Burma
of the Pitakas, bedrock of the religion.

[*Thihtan*, fl. 412–439 A.D.] In the year 334, Thihtan, son of
king Kyaungdurit, became king. Thirty-five years in the nether
house, twenty-seven years he flourished; he passed at the age
of sixty-two. About the time of his death lightning fell for full
seven days; the shadow was reversed. He was born on a Saturday.

119. *Of the usurping of the throne by Mokhkaman and Thuyè,
ministers, not of the royal bone.*

[*Mokhkaman and Thuyè*, fl. 439–497 (494?) A.D.] In the year
361, three ministers, not of royal bone, quarrelled, and the minister
called Mokhkaman was victorious and ruled for three months.
Then Thuyè wrested the throne from Mokhkaman and reigned.
When Mokhkaman was about to die, a shower of gravel fell.
King Thuyè was thirty-two years in the nether house and passed
in the fifty-eighth[1] year of his prosperity. About the time of his
death the bank of Nyaung-u steadily subsided. He was born on
a Thursday.

[*Tharamunhpya*, fl. 494–516 A.D.] In the year 416, the
ministers found king Thihtan's grandson in hiding and set him
on the throne. He received the name Tharamunhpya, and reigned.
Fifty-five years in the nether house, twenty-two years he flourished;
he passed at the age of seventy-seven. About the time of his death
stars fought each other. He was born on a Friday.

120. *Of the eight kings from king Thaittaing, son of king Thihtan,
to king Htunchit.*

[*Thaittaing*, fl. 516–523 A.D. *Founding of Tampavati.*] In the
year 438, Thaittaing, son of that king, came to the throne. He

[1] fifty-fifth ?

was a man of great stature. He forsook the city of Thiripyissaya, and founded a city at Thamahti, and he called it Tampavati and dwelt there. Forty-five years in the nether house, seven years he flourished; he passed at the age of fifty-two. About the time of his death a constellation passed across the disc of the moon; lightning fell for full seven days. He was born on a Saturday.

[*Thinlikyaungngè*, fl. 523–532 A.D.] In the year 445 his son Thinlikyaungngè became king. Thirty-five years in the nether house, nine years he flourished; he died at the age of forty-four. About the time of his death the water of the river flowed up country; a heavy rain fell. He was born on a Monday.

[*Thinlipaik*, fl. 532–547 A.D.] In the year 454 his younger brother Thinlipaik became king. Twenty years in the nether house, fifteen years he flourished; he passed at the age of thirty-five. About the time of his death smoke issued from the royal house. He was born on a Saturday.

[*Hkanlaung*, fl. 547–557 A.D.] In the year 469 his younger brother Hkanlaung became king. Thirty-two years in the nether house, ten years he flourished; he passed at the age of forty-two. About the time of his death waves boiled up furiously in the river, and there was no wind. He was born on a Friday.

[*Hkanlat*, fl. 557–569 A.D.] In the year 479 his younger brother Hkanlat became king. Thirty-nine years in the nether house, twelve years he flourished; he passed at the age of fifty-one. About the time of his death an ogre wandered laughing over the whole country for full seven days; and the people who heard the ogre's laugh durst not sleep. He was born on a Wednesday.

[*Htuntaik*, fl. 569–582 A.D.] In the year 491 his son Htuntaik became king. After the custom of kings he went forth with golden buffaloes, golden oxen, and a golden plough, to observe the solemn ceremony of ploughing. And as he ploughed the oxen took affright at the cotton sleeve of the king's golden cloak being blown to and fro by the wind, and they bolted, and the king fell within the arc of the ploughshare and he died. Thirty-five years in the nether house, thirteen years he flourished; he passed at the age of forty-eight. About the time of his death a star crossed the disc of the moon; many stars came out in the daytime. He was born on a Monday.

[*Htunpyit*, fl. 582–598 A.D.] In the year 504 his son Htunpyit became king. Thirty years in the nether house, sixteen years he flourished; he passed at the age of forty-six. About the time of his death two suns appeared; there was no shadow cast; the Thursday and Friday stars fought. He was born on a Thursday.

[*Htunchit*, fl. 598–613 A.D.] In the year 520 his son Htunchit became king. Twenty-two years in the nether house, fifteen years he flourished; he passed at the age of thirty-seven. About the time of his death the Thursday star went trampling on the Pleiades; moreover the moon showed a comet. He was born on a Wednesday.

121. *Of king Sangharaja, not of royal bone, teacher of the queen of king Htunchit.*

[*Poppa Sawrahan*, fl. 613–640 A.D.] In the year 535, Sangharaja, chaplain of the queen, became king. He is known as Papasotthamintaya, also as Poppa Sawrahan. He was deeply learned in the Pitakas and Vedas, and of a very beautiful complexion, and endowed with faith and virtue. When king Htunchit was not, he was made king, so pleasing was he to the king and queen. And Shweonthi, son of king Htunchit, fled in fear and feigned madness, and lived as a beggar at Palin. But Poppa Sawrahan observed the ten kingly duties and loved the people, laymen and saints, as though they were his own womb-children.

But the Mahagiri spirit would not appear nor speak a word, for the king was not of royal bone of the Sun dynasty. And when the king consulted his wise men thereon, they said that because the king was not of royal bone of the Sun dynasty, the spirit would not appear nor speak a word. So the king, exclaiming, 'Ever blessed be the Sun dynasty!', called forth prince Shweonthi from seclusion, and gave him in marriage to his daughter, and made him heir.

[*A new era established.*] With the twenty-seventh year after he ascended the throne, the *khachapañca* number was fulfilled and 560 years were dropped, and the *pashuchiddaramuni* era was kept up for shortness. Thus the year 2 was established. In starting a new era, these four elements must agree in order to calculate the land's presiding asterism : First make the calculation according to the (two) rules of Sujidhat; then calculate the *dhat*, and also the *adhipadi*. To establish a conformity between the two eras,

these four elements must be satisfied. Collect materials to calculate
Thamathaw (in two formulae), choose a time when the months
to be intercalated reach their maximum, and set the solar new
year day at zero. When it was the year 562, Poppa Sawrahan
dropped 560, and called the remainder 2, short era. Taking into
count the era abolished by the king, he was thirty-seven years
in the nether house, twenty-seven years he flourished; and he
passed at the age of sixty-four. About the time of his death seven
vultures alighted on the palace; light streamed from the earth.
He was born on a Sunday.

122. *Of the three kings from king Shweonthi, son of king Htunchit, to
Minhkwe.*

[*Shweonthi*, fl. 640–652 A.D.] In the year 2, short era, his
son-in-law Shweonthi became king. Thirty-five years in the
nether house, twelve years he flourished; he passed at the age of
for even. About the time of his death a tiger entered the
palace. He was born on a Friday.

[*Peitthon*, fl. 652–660 A.D.] In the year 14 his younger brother
Peitthon became king. Forty-one years in the nether house, eight
years he flourished; he passed at the age of forty-nine. About
the time of his death the Pleiades crossed the disc of the moon;
many vultures hovered about the palace and made as though to
swoop. He was born on a Friday.

[*Peittaung*, fl. 660–710 A.D.] In the year 22 his son Peittaung
became king. Peittaung and Ngahkwe were brothers. Twenty-
two years in the nether house, fifty years he flourished; he passed
at the age of seventy-two. About the time of his death the
deinnetthè coincided with the *thingyan*. He was born on a Saturday.

[*Ngahkwe*, fl. 710–716 A.D.] In the year 72 his younger brother
Ngahkwe became king. Fifty-five years in the nether house, six
years he flourished; he passed at the age of sixty-one. About the
time of his death the Thursday star showed a comet for fifteen
days; the shadow was reversed. He was born on a Monday.

123. *Of king Myinkywe.*

[*Myinkywe*, fl. 716–726 A.D.] In the year 78 Myinkywe became
king. He was not of royal bone, but a Kokko Taungpa villager,
servant of a rich man. His mother had been left in charge of

a plantation, and she had intercourse with an ogre and gave birth to the king. Once the rich woman, his mistress, made him look after a horse, and the horse was lost. So in fear of his mistress he entered the king's service. And the king kept him in close attendance, and because he was a man of power and strength he became chief groom of the stables. Now the king loved his horses, and he was wont to go to the stable in the daytime when men were at peace, and to stay there, a queen attending him. Thus came they many times; and the chief groom and the queen had speech together. And one day when the king went forth to sport in the forest, he became separated from his ministers and followers, and the groom killed him. Then he put on the royal robes, mounted the horse, and returned to the city. And when he reached the palace one of the queens disobeyed him, and he slew her, and the others did as he commanded them. Moreover the ministers, fearing lest the country and villagers should fall into disorder, did as he bade them. Twenty-one years in the nether house, ten years he flourished; he passed at the age of thirty-one. About the time of his death the Thursday star crossed the disc of the moon. He was born on a Saturday.

124. *Of the ten kings from king Theinhka to king Tannek.*

[*Theinhka*, fl. 726–734 A.D.] In the year 88 Theinhka became king; he was of royal bone. For Myinkywe not having a son, the ministers made search for one of royal bone and made him king. Forty-three years in the nether house, eight years he flourished; he passed at the age of sixty-one. About the time of his death the sky seemed like dots of blood for full seven days. He was born on a Wednesday.

[*Theinsun*, fl. 734–744 A.D.] In the year 96 his son Theinsun became king. Fifty-five years in the nether house, ten years he flourished; he passed at the age of sixty-five. About the time of his death three tigers entered the palace, and one climbed even to the throne. He was born on a Tuesday.

[*Shwelaung*, fl. 744–753 A.D.] In the year 106 his son Shwelaung became king. Thirty-five years in the nether house, nine years he flourished; he passed at the age of forty-four. About the time of his death bees swarmed about the palace; a bitch littered on the throne. He was born on a Wednesday.

[*Htunhtwin*, fl. 753–762 A.D.] In the year 115 his son Htunhtwin became king. While at sport in the forest, the king fell from his horse and was pierced by a cutch thorn and died. Twenty-six years in the nether house, nine years he flourished; he passed at the age of thirty-five. About the time of his death the *deinnetthè* coincided with the *thingyan*. He was born on a Saturday.

[*Shwehmauk*, fl. 762–785 A.D.] In the year 124 his son Shwehmauk became king. He was full of vigour and energy, able both to devise a thing and to perform it. Twenty years in the nether house, twenty-three years he flourished; he passed at the age of forty-three. He was born on a Thursday.

[*Munlat*, fl. 785–802 A.D.] In the year 147 his younger brother Munlat became king. Thirty-nine years in the nether house, seventeen years he flourished; he passed at the age of fifty-six. About the time of his death eight planets were in conjunction in one sign of the zodiac; the Saturday star showed a comet. He was born on a Wednesday.

[*Sawhkinhnit*, fl. 802–829 A.D.] In the year 164 his son Sawhkinhnit became king. Thirty-six years in the nether house, twenty-seven years he flourished; he passed at the age of sixty-three. About the time of his death the Saturday and Friday stars entered the moon. He was born on a Thursday.

[*Hkèlu*, fl. 829–846 A.D.] In the year 191 his son Hkèlu became king. Thirty-five years in the nether house, seventeen years he flourished; he passed at the age of fifty-two. About the time of his death the Thursday star crossed the disc of the moon; the Friday star showed a comet; the *deinnetthè* coincided with the *thingyan*. He was born on a Sunday.

[*Pyinbya*, fl. 846–878 A.D. *Building of Pagan*, 849 A.D.] In the year 208 his younger brother Pyinbya became king. He was so called because as a young prince he *ate* the village of Pyinbya. Forty-five years in the nether house, thirty-two years he flourished; he passed at the age of seventy-seven. In the third year after the accession of king Pyinbya the city of Pagan was built; the year of the building was 211. In 219 he founded the city of Taungdwin and gave it the name Rammavati. About the time of his death the Friday star showed a comet; the *deinnetthè* coincided with the *thingyan*. He was born on a Monday.

[*Tannek*, fl. 878–906 A.D.] In the year 240 his son Tannek

became king. He loved horses and was a master of horsemanship. It was his wont to go to the stable at night to look at them. While he was looking at them Sale Ngahkwe killed him. Twenty-eight years in the nether house, twenty-eight years he flourished; he passed at the age of fifty-six. About the time of his death the Friday star showed a comet; the *deinnetthè* coincided with the *thingyan*. He was born on a Friday.

125. *Of Sale Ngahkwe.*

In the year 268 Sale Ngahkwe became king. This is the tale of Ngahkwe :—

[*The Story of Sale Ngahkwe*, fl. 906–915 A. D.] When Theinhkun the aforesaid fought his brother, the elder won and the younger fled and lived in hiding at Sale. He had a grandson Ngahkwe, whose parents took and sold him into the house of a certain wealthy man. Now Ngahkwe loved betel-flower, wax, unguents, and scented powders; he loved good clothes and good victuals. It is said that he failed not to comb his hair three times a day.

One day the rich man, his master, sent him on board a boat to pole it along. That night before reaching Pagan, he dreamed a dream, and lo! his bowels issued from his navel and encircled the city of Pagan. Early in the morning he came poling the boat upstream, and as he poled he hit a jewelled salver so that it came up cleaving to his pole. And when Ngahkwe saw it he said 'My dream surely is hard to come to pass. Must I be content with a jewelled salver?' And he thrust it back into the river.

So he came to Pagan and went to the house of the counsellor, chaplain of the king. Now the brahman was out, so he told the tale to his wife, the brahmani. And she did but say 'Thou shalt be great in glory, long in life.' So Ngahkwe seeing that she took no pains to interpret, descended and went away. At that moment the brahman came and asked his wife 'Who came after I left?' And she replied: 'A youth came to tell a dream and I interpreted it so.' Her husband the brahman when he heard the dream, cut off his wife's topknot and threw it down; at the same moment that he threw it, lightning struck the topknot of hair. And the brahman straightway followed him up who had told the dream, and called after him, and when he overtook him he said: 'Where livest thou, young sir? Of what race art thou? The dream that thou hast seen, young sir, is surely hard to come to pass. Practise piety! Ere long thou shalt be ruler of the kingdom of Pagan. And when thou becomest king, young sir, do not forget me!'

When Ngahkwe had done his selling and buying he went down home to Sale. And the rich man his master was harsh to Ngahkwe and used him hotly. And Ngahkwe could endure it no longer, but entered the service of king Tannek. When the king saw the youth's appearance he took pity on him and appointed him groom of the stables. Now the king came daily with a young concubine to the stable. And the king called the groom and said 'Groom, put the horse-dung in a pit afar off, and set fire to it where it is dry. And so what dung thou puttest in later, will dry in the heat of the fire and be consumed.' And he did as the king said. One day the groom and the young concubine had speech together, and he pushed the king into the dung-pit. And he threatened the queen and concubines insomuch that they did as he bade them, and he became king.

Ngahkwe, as ogre-guardian of a mountain who once shielded the Lord from the sun by three *in* leaves, had received a prophecy that he would become king thrice in this country. So he was great in glory and might. Being reborn from the state of an ogre, he was exceeding wrathful and haughty; he was gross and gluttonous in eating. The ministers and followers were sore afraid and waited upon him. He nursed anger against his master at Sale for treating him harshly, and when he became king he slew him. It is said that whenever he laid hands on men who resembled his former master, he had them thrown into a pond and pierced them with his lance from the back of an elephant, calling them pigs. But when he had done this often, the ministers and followers gave a vast bribe to the master of the elephants, and he, while the king was sporting in the water of the pond, cut the cord underneath so that the howdah slipped, and the king and the howdah fell into the water. And the ministers and followers threw each a handful of mud, and he died. The pond is known as Nyuntalephpek to this day.

Fifty years in the nether house, nine years he flourished; he passed at the age of fifty-nine. About the time of his death an ogre came with body as tall as a palm tree and stood upon the king's breast. He was born on a Saturday.

126. *Of king Theinhko, son of Sale Ngahkwe.*

[*Theinhko*, fl. 915–931 A. D.] In the year 277 his son Theinhko became king. Twenty-five years in the nether house, sixteen years he flourished; he passed at the age of forty-one. This was the manner of his death. He rode abroad for sport in the forest, and being hungry he plucked and ate a cucumber in a farmer's plantation. And because he plucked it without telling him, the farmer struck him with the handle of a spade that he died. About the time of his death the Friday star showed a comet; the Thursday and Friday stars fought. He was born on a Saturday.

127. *Of Nyaung-u Sawrahan.*

In the year 293 Nyaung-u Sawrahan became king. It was on this wise :—

[*The farmer king, Nyaung-u Sawrahan,* fl. 931–964 A. D.] Theinhko's groom came up and said 'Ho! farmer, why strikest thou our master?' He answered 'Thy king hath plucked and eaten my cucumber. Did I not well to strike him?' And the groom spake winding words and said, 'O farmer, he who slayeth a king, becometh a king.' But the farmer said, 'I will not be king. Hath not my cucumber grown in my garden like pups sucking milk?' Then said the other, with winding words persuading him, 'Farmer! not only shalt thou have thy cucumber, thou shalt also flourish as a king. To be a king is exceeding glorious. Verily he hath good clothes, good victuals in abundance, gold, silver, elephants and horses, buffaloes, oxen, goats, pigs, paddy and rice!'

So at last the farmer consented and followed him. And the groom, letting no one know it, brought the farmer within the palace and told the whole story to the queen, who praised him for his wisdom. And the queen fearing that the country and villages would be cast into turmoil, let none come in nor go out, saying 'The king's body is not safe.' And she directed the farmer and made him bathe in warm water and cold, and rub himself with bath powders to remove all dirt and disease. And when a young concubine flouted him the queen said 'Who shall drub this slave-woman?' Whereupon a stone statue at the door came running and drubbed her with its elbows that she died. And the whole palace saw it and feared as though it would eat their flesh.

On the day before the seventh day the queen sent and caused to

sound a metal gong throughout the kingdom saying 'The king
goeth abroad to-morrow. Enter, all ministers, both high and low ;
let none be absent !' So at dawn all the ministers and followers
ascended the king's palace. When they were met, the door of the
throne was suddenly opened, and the ministers and the followers
raised hands and did obeisance. But one minister uttered words
of disdain saying, ' Verily this is not our lord. And the queen hath
not consulted us.' Thereupon the stone statue at the door ran yet
again and drubbed him with its elbows that he died. And the
ministers both high and low and the whole country saw it, and
feared as though it would eat their flesh.

The groom was astute in statecraft. With winding words he
persuaded the farmer to go with him, knowing 'The king hath
been struck to death by a stick. If I take the horse with the royal
robes and gear and return without him who struck the blow, the
whole people, the queen and the ministers will say, "The groom
hath killed the king ! " The farmer who struck the blow must bear
witness.' And because he was a man of subtle wit, it seemed good
to him to prove to the queen first that this man struck and killed
the king, without letting any know of it on his coming to the
palace. So the wise have said.

[*The power of the Ari.*] Now the farmer became king and was
great in glory and power. At his cucumber plantation he made
a large and pleasant garden, and he wrought and kept a great
image of Naga. He thought it good thus to make and worship
the image of Naga, because Naga was nobler than men and his power
greater. Moreover he consulted the heretical Ari monks regard-
ing the *zigon* pagodas in the kingdoms of Yathepyi and Thaton,
and he built five pagodas—Pahtogyi, Pahtongè, Pahtothamya,
Thinlinpahto, Seittipahto. In them he set up what were neither
spirit-images nor images of the Lord, and worshipped them with
offerings of rice, curry, and fermented drinks, night and morning.
He was also known as Nattaw-kyaungtaga-minchantha. However,
since the root beginning made by Ashin Punna the elder in the
lifetime of the Lord Omniscient, throughout the reigns of the
dynasties of the Burmese kingdoms of Tagaung, Tharehkittara,
Arimaddana, and Thiripyissaya, there flourished the *paramattha*
order, the *samuti* order, the sacred writings, their study and intuition. But afterwards the religion gradually grew weak from the

reign of king Thaittaing, founder of the city of Tampavati, and because there was no Pitaka or sacred writ, only the doctrines of the Ari lords at Thamahti were generally adopted, and in the reign of king Sawrahan the king and the whole country held these doctrines.

Although in verity king Sawrahan should have utterly perished, having killed a king while he was yet a farmer, he attained even to kingship simply by strong *karma* of his good acts done in the past.   In the Law of the Lord it is written, ' What is not thought of, happens ; what is thought of, fails '.   And the meaning is this. Those who have the strong *karma* of good acts done in the past prosper without much ado.   Those who have not the strong *karma* of good acts done in the past may fail, though they try hard and struggle and expect success.   Therefore though all creatures may strive hard to become wealthy and great, they shall not speed if there is not the *karma* of their previous acts.   And there are many proofs to show how often men who have strong *karma* of the past, prosper without much ado.   When Nyaung-u Sawrahan, at the time of Sakra's coming and exalting king Kyaungbyu, stood in the front of the palace and cried, ' Who shall be king while I live ?', the *karma* of his past good acts was exhausted insomuch that the stone statue at the door pushed him down and he fell head foremost from the palace-front and died.

Forty-five years in the nether house, thirty-three years he flourished ; he passed at the age of seventy-eight.   About the time of his death eight planets were in conjunction in one sign of the zodiac ; an ogre was seen in the palace.   He was born on a Wednesday.

128. *Of Kunhsaw Kyaungbyu.*

In the year 326 Kunhsaw Kyaungbyu became king.   His story is on this wise :

[*Kunhsaw Kyaungbyu becomes king*, fl. 964–986 A.D.]   One of the queens of king Tannek, what time Sale Ngahkwe killed the king and came to the throne, ran down from the palace with a child in her womb, for she would not brook becoming queen to Ngahkwe.   She dwelt in Kyaungbyu, which is known as Naga-kyaung, for by that way Suvannasota went to the Naga country ; it is also called Shwegyaung.   There Kyaungbyumin was born. While he was a boy he played with other children and they mocked

him, saying ' Aha ! Son without a father ! ' And he said, ' Mother,
these village children mock me saying I am a son without a
father.' And his mother said, ' Noble son, thy father was no
common man ; he was the king of this country. But one killed
thy father and robbed him of his royal estate. And I feared he
would make me his wife, and while thou wast still a babe in my
womb, I gat me away and hid, and so gave birth to thee.' And
when Kyaungbyumin heard it, he made a solemn vow and said,
' May I be as my father was.' So he went and served the king.

Now the king made the place Let-htot purveyor of the king's
betel. Some chronicles say he purveyed betel at Myaunghla in the
south. And Kyaungbyumin was a gentle son and supported his
mother by his toil. Every day she dressed his food neatly and did
it up in a bundle. And her son was wont each day to untie the
food wrapped up by his mother and eat it under a big *Saunggyan*
tree. And before he ate, he first made offering to the *Saunggyan* tree. Now the tree-spirit thought ' He hath alway given me
the firstlings whenever he eateth his food. What shall befall the
youth ? ', and he saw that ere long he would be king. So he showed
himself and said, ' Thou hast given me the firstlings of thy food
daily. If thou desirest glory, maintain thy refuge in the Five
Precepts. Speak the truth and err not. Repeat thou the ten
memorable things till thou canst say two thousand of them daily.'
After the spirit spake to him on this wise the prince was ever care-
ful so to do. (In view of this story it should be evident that in
the Pagan kingdom the religion did not wholly disappear.)

Now Sakra and other spirit-guardians of the religion helped
Kunhsawmin till it was noised abroad that a future king should
appear in the country of Pagan. And the people went in tumult
to Mt. Tuywin saying, ' This day the future king will come. We
shall see him and adore him.' And Kunhsawmin thought likewise. ' I will purvey betel early and go and see the coming king.'
So he asked his mother to wrap up his food betimes, and she did so,
and her royal son took the bundle of food and set out while it was
yet night. When he reached Let-htot he made haste and purveyed
the betel and hurried away to see the coming king. Now Sakra,
disguising himself as an old man riding a horse, spake thus from
horseback to Kunhsaw : ' Young man, be pleased to take this horse
I am riding to Pagan. I must tarry here.' And Kunhsaw said,

'Grandfather, I must be in time to see the coming king. I cannot take thy horse.' But the old man whose horse it was replied, 'Young man, is it not faster going on horseback than on foot? Ride me then this horse. Wear also this ruby hairpin, this ruby ring. Grasp also this lance and sword. If I tarry long, ride this horse and go till thou art in the bosom presence of the king.'

So Kunhsaw wore the ring, fixed the hairpin, grasped the Thilawuntha sword and the Areindama lance that Sakra gave him, and urged on the horse amain that he might see the coming king. And all the ministers, both great and small, and the people seeing Kunhsaw coming on horseback, did obeisance, for he shone radiant with the ornaments of Sakra like the sun-child new risen. And Kunhsaw entered and rode into the palace, and he remembered and said, 'Verily it must be I myself. Of old, too, the *saunggyan* spirit spake of it.' But king Sawrahan was standing in the front of the palace, and he cried, 'Who durst enter while I live?' Thereupon the stone statue at the door pushed him down, and he fell headlong from the palace-front and died.

[*Birth of Kyizo, Sokkate, and Anawrahta.*] King Nyaung-u Sawrahan had raised three princesses to be his queens, and called the eldest sister Taungpyinthi, the middle sister Alèpyinthi, the youngest Myauppyinthi. When the king died the eldest of the three, Taungpyinthi, had conceived Kyizo nine months, and Alèpyinthi had conceived Sokkate six months in the womb. When Kunhsaw became king he raised them to be his queens, and queen Myauppyinthi gave birth to Anawrahtaminsaw.

[*Dethronement of Kunhsaw, 986 A.D.*] When Kyizo and Sokkate came of age they built a pleasant monastery and said to king Kunhsaw, 'Come and call thy blessing on the monastery'. And the king took no heed nor scrutiny but hearkened to them. And Kyizo and Sokkate seized the king and threatened him and made him become a monk. And they spread the rumour far and wide that the king in his zeal for bliss hereafter had become a monk.

King Kunhsaw Kyaungbyu was fifty-eight years in the nether house; twenty-two years he flourished; he fell from the throne at eighty. He was born on a Sunday. About the time of his fall a miracle was seen in the Pahto pagoda; the Friday star trampled on the moon; the moon was a full circle on the second day of waxing; the earth quaked seven days; the water stood still in the river.

129. *Of king Kyizo and king Sokkate.*

[*Kyizo*, fl. 986–992 A.D.] In the year 348 Kyizo became king. He built a royal box in the marshes of the Chindwin and visited the ten villages of Bangyi, hunting *thamin*. One day a hunter lay waiting for *thamin* at the place where they drank water. The king likewise came to the spot to wait for *thamin*, and the *thamin* seeing the king took fright and ran. And the hunter knew not that it was the king, but shot with the bow and hit him that he died. Twenty-two years in the nether house, six years he flourished as king; he passed at the age of twenty-eight. About the time of his death an ogre laughed for a full half-month and threw stones at the palace. He was born on a Tuesday.

[*Sokkate*, fl. 992–1017.] In the year 354 his younger brother Sokkate became king. Anawrahtasaw attended on him.

[*His fight with Anawrahta.*] Anawrahtasaw's mother lived with king Kyaungbyu, ministering to him, and Anawrahtasaw lived with his royal father and mother. One day while he was in attendance, his elder brother Sokkate addressed him, ' Nyitha-naungmè.' Anawrahtasaw told that word to his father king Kyaungbyu. And his father said, ' Because he wisheth to take thy mother, thus he speaketh.' And Anawrahtasaw was exceeding wroth, and he begged for the horse and weapons and gear that Sakra gave his father. And his father gave him the Areindama lance, the Thilawuntha sword, the ruby ring, and the ruby hairpin. ' But for the horse ', quoth he, ' it hath been at large since I fell from the throne. Show this ring I am wearing, and it will suffer itself to be caught. And when thou hast caught it, take it and gather thy followers, as many as thou canst, to Poppa. But till thou art strong, fight not against thy brother.' Some say that Anawrahtasaw caught the horse of king Kyaungbyu from the hands of king Sokkate. And when he had shown the ring and caught his father's horse, he went to Poppa and mustered his forces. King Sokkate took his mother and raised her to be queen ; but in some chronicles it appears that Anawrahtasaw carried away his mother.

Now when he had mustered his forces he marched on Pagan, and sent a message to his brother saying, ' Wilt thou give up the throne, or wilt thou do battle? ' And when Sokkate heard the words of his younger brother he was exceeding wroth, and answered :

' His mother's milk is yet wet upon his lips ; and saith he, he will fight me. Let all my ministers look on. I will fight him, man to man, on horseback.' When Anawrahtasaw heard his brother's words he was glad ; and when the appointed day was come, he took the lance and sword his father had given him, and mounted the demon horse and came to the stream of Thamahti. And Sokkate his brother saw him coming and went forth to meet him. Then said Anawrahtasaw : ' Brother, thou art the elder, strike thou first.' And Sokkate thrust at him with his lance. But Anawrahtasaw parried it with the Areindama lance, Sakra's weapon, and it reached not his body, but pierced the pommel of his saddle. And when Sokkate saw it, he was sore afraid and trembled. Then said Anawrahtasaw : ' Brother, thy turn is over. Now it is mine. Meet it as best thou canst.' And he smote him and pierced him with the Areindama lance, so that it went in at the front and came out behind. And Sokkate's horse ran away with him to the river, and there he died. The place is known as Myinkaba to this day.

Now the mother of Anawrahtasaw heard that Sokkate was dead, pierced by her son's lance ; and she let her breast-cloth fall and wailed and cried aloud, ' Pottalin, Pottalin.' And they built a pagoda at that place and called it Pottalin. Moreover, they built a pagoda at the place where the mother's breast-cloth fell, and called it Wut-yin-kyut.

Sokkate was twenty-eight years in the nether house, and twenty-five years he flourished ; he passed at the age of fifty-three. About the time of his death two bolides as large as panniers fell in solid lumps near the palace. He was born on a Saturday.

130. *Of Anawrahtaminsaw.*

[*Anawrahta*, fl. 1017–1059.] When Anawrahtasaw had smitten his elder brother, he went to his father's monastery and begged him to be king. But his father said : ' I am old to look upon, old in years. Be thou king thyself.' In the year 379 Anawrahtasaw ascended the throne and was anointed king. He arrayed his father in all the articles of royal pomp and use and the five symbols of royalty, and made the monk king, who, surrounded by his women who ministered to him, received monk-kingship in the monastery. Although it is not said in the chronicles that Nawrahtasaw ascended the throne in the year 379, yet it may be known from a sentence

of the inscription in the pagoda built by Myauppyinthi, his queen :
' Anawrahtaminsaw became king on Monday, the eighth day after
the full moon of Pyatho, in the year *tharawun* 379, and he reigned
and governed righteously the people of the kingdom, with the
prince, queen, and ministers, both great and small.'

Now Anawrahtaminsaw could not sleep for full six months,
because he had slain his elder brother. Then Sakra visited him
with a dream, saying, ' O king, if thou wouldst mitigate thine evil
deed in sinning against thine elder brother, build many pagodas, *gu*,
monasteries, and resthouses, and share the merit with thine elder
brother. Devise thou many wells, ponds, dams and ditches, fields
and canals, and share the merit with thine elder brother.'

[*Princess Pancakalyani.*] When the king ascended the throne,
he sent a royal envoy with store of gifts and presents, saying,
' Search me the face of Jambudipa and find a princess worthy
of me, beside Sawlu's mother.' So the royal envoy went seeking
high and low a lady worthy of the king.

Now princess Sanghamitta, eldest of the seven daughters of the
king reigning in Vesali in the Middle Country, was practising
piety in a certain garden with some saintly nuns. At that time
a bael tree planted by the nun Sanghamitta bore a bael fruit as
large as a jar. And when it became ripe it fell, and lo ! there
came out of it a young daughter, beautiful exceedingly, with all
the signs of royalty, great and small. And the saintly nuns offered
her to the king of Vesali, who named her Ruciyapabhavati and
gave her in marriage to his son and heir. Not long afterwards
the king his father passed away to enjoy a home among the spirits,
and the son, his heir, reigned in his stead, and was anointed king.
He raised Ruciyapabhavati to be his chief queen, and she gave
birth to a daughter called Pancakalyani. She was exceeding fair
to look upon, with all the signs of royalty, and she was kept in
a *pyatthad* with a single post.

When the envoy heard thereof, he went to the kingdom of
Vesali and offered store of gifts and presents, and said, ' I am come
to ask for the princess Pancakalyani, because Anawrahtaminsaw,
ruler of the great kingdom of Paukkarama, hath no queen.' And
the king of Vesali set her in a palanquin and gave her away with
a troop of eighty handmaidens, saying, ' I cannot but grant what
king Anawrahta hath asked.' And the royal envoy took the

princess and departed. She had all the five virtues of beauty and
none of the six blemishes. She was delicate and gentle, and of the
colour of new-burnished gold. And when the royal envoy saw how
fair she was, he could not refrain himself, but one day they came
together. And the envoy thought: 'If we come to Paukkarama
with all this troop of attendants and they tell the king and he give
ear, I shall be utterly destroyed.' So of all the attendants that
came with the princess he left one behind in turn at each town and
village; and so they came to Dhaññavati.

Now when king Anawrahtaminsaw was informed of their coming,
he went forth to meet them with his fourfold army, and having
received that which was offered him, he returned home with his
army. The place is well known as Minpyantaung unto this day.
And when he reached Arimaddana his royal home, he was about to
usher into the golden palace the princess offered him from Vesali,
whom he had welcomed and brought home with him, when he who
had at the first been sent as royal envoy and had brought her,
said: 'Vesali is not a kingdom with a name only. It is a great
kingdom, a great country, where dwelt kings of yore, virtuous and
noble kings. If she were the own and true daughter of the lord of
a great kingdom and a great country, he would not have presented
her with so small a state. Even though he hath offered her, not
daring to offend the majesty of thy golden glory, he still might
decently have done so under the charge of high ministers and
officials, and added (as is ever the custom due in palaces) a married
lady, a nurse and a guardian, servants and followers, sons and
daughters of good family, and people skilled in housework and
victualling, in topknots and tails of hair, in needlework, stencilling
and embroidery; and persons deft in frying and frizzling, roasting,
baking, dressing and boiling, with their bags and baggage. But
she hath with her no high minister, nor official, no married lady,
no sons and daughters of good family, no retinue nor attendants,
nurse nor carrier; no people skilled in topknot and hairtail, in
needlework, stencilling and embroidery, in frying and frizzling,
roasting, baking, dressing, and boiling. The princess now presented
thee is not the own daughter of the king of Vesali!'

And when he heard the speech of the royal envoy, he took no
heed nor counsel, but believed him and waxed wroth, and cried:
'He giveth not his own daughter, but a foster-daughter to such

a king as I !' So he lodged the princess in the West Chamber and
gave her in charge to his minister at Pareimma.

[*The birth and perils of Kyanzittha.*] Now when she reached
Pareimma and Nawrahtaminsaw's child in her womb was ready to
be born, there was a great earthquake. And Nawrahtaminsaw
questioned his masters of white magic and black, saying, 'Why
quaketh the earth?' And they spake into his ear: 'O king, one
who shall be king hath been conceived in the north quarter.' And
Nawrahtaminsaw, it is said, made search for all women with child
in the north quarter and put to death over seven thousand. But
the mother of Kyanzittha was hidden by a Naga youth and died
not, but escaped. And the king questioned his masters of white
magic and black, saying, 'Is he dead?' And they spake into his
ear: 'Not dead, but born from his mother's womb!' And he
made search, it is said, for all suckling babes in the cradle, and again
killed over six thousand. But Kyanzittha was hidden by the Naga
youth and died not, but escaped. And the king asked: 'Is he dead?'
And they answered: 'Not dead yet, but the size of a cowboy!' And
he made search, it is said, for children of the age of cowboys, and
again killed over five thousand. But Kyanzittha was hidden by the
Naga youth, and was left over and was not counted among the slain.

Because he was *left over* and was not counted among the slain,
some chronicles write Kyanyittha. Moreover, because of all the
marks and *signs of beauty* he possessed, some chronicles write Kyanzittha; they also write Pareimmazittha, because he was born at
Pareimma. Because of his wheel-mark of royalty, and because the
waterpot fell back when they gave him to drink, he is also written
Kayalanzittha. The Zigon Thamaing says that king Nawrahta
himself gave him the name Kyanzittha, because he was *left over*
each time the king *made search*. Furthermore, because he was the
lord of the Ngahtihlaing village-headman, he is also called Htihlaingshin. (This note we add in its appropriate place.)

Whereas some chronicles state that the king, even at Dhaññavati town, believed the words of the royal envoy and sent and kept
the princess Pancakalyani at Pareimma, and moreover that Kyan-
zittha was the son of a Naga: it should rather be held that the
princess Pancakalyani was sent to Pareimma only after she reached
the royal abode, in view of the plain fact of the Pahsittop pagoda.
This was built and honoured by Kyanzittha when he became king,

saying 'Here my mother sank upon her knees!'; for here she knelt and worshipped the golden palace when the king, who had brought her from Dhaññavati, was about to set her on the golden throne, and then, hearkening to the words of the royal envoy, he sped her rather to Pareimma.

As for the theory that Kyanzittha was the son of a Naga:—In the inscription of the Hlèdauk pagoda, built at Kyawzitait Taungbyongyi in the year 470 by his grandson Alaungsithu when he marched to battle with the Talops of Gandhala, it is written: 'Happy and full of years is the old king, builder of the Shwegu, the beloved grandson of Htihlaing-ashin Kayalanzittha, who was the beloved son of king Nawrahta.' This inscription, made in the reign of king Alaungsithu to make plain in times to come that Kyanzittha was the beloved son of Anawrahtaminsaw and descended from an unbroken line of kings, has been forgotten. It appears that, even as it is wrongly said that Pyusawhti the former king of Pagan was son of a Naga, so too it has been wrongly believed and stated that Kyanzittha was son of the Naga and that the Naga came to shelter him because he was his father; whereas the Naga youth was constrained to shelter and protect him simply because he was a man of great glory and power. In fact, it can only be assumed that the Naga, as it is said, protected Htihlaingshin Kyanzittha because he was the coming king unborn who would uphold the great religion by his glory, power, and authority; for even so it is said of others—of prince Susunaga, ruler of Pataliputta in the Middle Country, that while he was still young a Naga protected him; and again of Hpwasaw, queen of king Uzana of Pagan, that while she was young her father put her to sleep in the forest and a great hamadryad came and watched over her.

[*Anawrahta discovers him.*] Now Kyanzittha's mother entrusted her son to the king's chaplain and he became a monk. And the masters of white magic and black spake yet again, saying, 'He hath become a monk!' And the king asked them: 'How may this be known?' And they answered: 'Invite thou them to a meal, and when it is ended offer them water in a water-pot; and lo! from the mouth of him who shall be king the wheel-mark will stand out radiant.' So the king invited all the monks in order; each day he served and gave them to eat. One day he invited Kyanzittha and served and gave him to eat. When the meal was over, in due time

he offered him drinking-water in a waterpot. And lo! from Kyanzittha's mouth the wheel-mark stood out radiant; and the king saw
it and was aghast, and the pot fell back. And the king cried,
entreating him: 'Wilt thou rob me of my throne?' And the
masters of white magic and black spake into his ear, saying, 'He
shall be king in the second generation after thee.' And the king
said: 'Ye tell me this but now. Alas! I have killed many, thinking he would rob me of my throne!' And he made Kyanzittha
become a layman, that he might attend in his presence. He took
pity on him being his own son, and named and called him Kyanzittha.

[*Exploits of Kyanzittha and his men.*]   Now in Myinmu there
was one called Nga Htweyu; it was said that he could go up and
down a thousand palm trees in a given time, cutting their fruit.
When Anawrahtaminsaw heard of it he sent for him and made him
dwell continually with Kyanzittha. Moreover, in the parts of
Poppa there was one called Nga Lonlephpè who, it is said, could
harness threescore yoke of oxen and drive the plough up and down
over a whole field, keeping a straight furrow and the harness
square. When the king heard of it, he sent for him and made
him dwell continually with Kyanzittha and Nga Htweyu. And in
Nyaung-u there was one called Nyaung-u Hpi, who could, men
said, run down from the top of the cliff at Nyaung-u, swim across
the river, and reaching the further bank at Aungtha swim back
without touching the shore with his feet, and reaching Nyaung-u
run back up the cliff. When the king heard of it, he sent for him
and made him dwell continually with Kyanzittha and his men.

Once it was told the king that at Let-htot there were four horses
without an owner, richly caparisoned, and they could not be caught.
So the king sent the four heroes to catch them—Kyanzittha, Nga
Htweyu, Nga Lonlephpè, and Nyaung-u Hpi. And they made
a fenced pathway into a yard, and they filled the yard with water;
and the four horses fell into the water and swam, and as they
swam the heroes mounted and rode them. And they took them
and presented them to the king; and the king gave them the
horses, saying, 'Ye are four. Rear these four horses, and bear my
yoke.' Now the four horses were demon horses, of immeasurable
worth. The horse ridden by Anawrahtasaw was called Kandi-
kalek-hla; the horse ridden by Kyanzittha was called Hnalonhkun-
gaung; the horse ridden by Nga Lonlephpè was called Lemoyi-

hkaung; the horse ridden by Nga Htweyu was called Hnalonlyin-
taing; the horse ridden by Nyaung-u Hpi was called Hnalon-
atumashi.   These are the names of the five demon horses.

[*Death of king Kyaungbyu,* 1021.] In the fourth year after
Anawrahtasaw became king, his father king Kyaungbyu passed
away.   Fifty-eight years in the nether house, twenty-two years he
flourished; thirty-one years dethroned or a monk-king, he passed
at the age of one hundred and fifteen, in the year 383.

The Great Chronicle says that Anawrahtaminsaw became king
in the year 364, and in his fourth year king Kyaungbyu passed
away.   The inscription of the Mahti monastery, built and dedicated
to his father by Anawrahtaminsaw, shows that it was built in the
year 382.   If we compare the inscription of the Mahti monastery
with the date given in the Great Chronicle, it is as though king
Kyaungbyu passed away full fourteen years before the monastery
was built.   Hence the statements that in the year 329 Anawrahtasaw
became king, that three years after becoming king he built the
monastery, and that one year after the monastery was built king
Kyaungbyu passed away, tally with the inscriptions in various
places and with the New Chronicle.

[*Epilogue.*] Here endeth the third part of the Great Royal
Chronicle, sifted and prepared in accordance with all credible
records in the books after consulting learned monks, learned brahmans, and learned ministers: written in the sacred chamber in
front of the royal Palace of Glass and divers-coloured jewels,
beginning from the first waxing of Nayon in 1191, in the reign of
His Majesty, sovereign of umbrella-holding kings of divers great
kingdoms and countries, master of mines of gold and silver, ruby,
amber, and all other gems, builder of the fourth city of Ratanapura
and the palace, lord of the *hsaddan* king of elephants, lord and master
of white elephants, lord of the universe, and great captain of the law.

The third part of the Great Royal Chronicle is ended.

PART IV

Honour be to Him, the Blessed One, the Saint, the Lord Buddha !

[*The Ari.*] In the reign of Anawrahtaminsaw the kingdom was
known as Pugarama.   Now the kings in that country for many
generations had been confirmed in false opinions following the

doctrines of the thirty Ari lords and their sixty thousand disciples who practised piety in Thamahti. It was the fashion of these Ari monks to reject the law preached by the Lord and to form each severally their own opinions. They wrote books after their own heart and beguiled others into the snare. According to the law they preached, a man might take the life of another and evade the course of *karma* if he recited the formula of deprecation ; nay, he might even kill his mother and his father and evade the course of *karma* if he recited the formula of deprecation. Such false and lawless doctrine they preached as the true doctrine. Moreover, kings and ministers, great and small, rich men and common people, whenever they celebrated the marriage of their children, were constrained to send them to these teachers at nightfall, sending, as it was called, the flower of their virginity. Nor could they be married till they were set free early in the morning. If they were married without sending to the teacher the flower of their virginity, it is said that they were heavily punished by the king for breaking the custom.

This sending of the flower of virginity means an act of worship. Hence scholars connect in meaning this 'sending to the monastery to worship' with the word *viharamaho*. And scholars in their stone inscriptions use this phrase, 'the time of the first sending to the monastery'. And in the Bayinhnamadaw Egyin Nawade has written : 'the time of sending to the glorious gem, the Vijaya shrine'.

But Anawrahtaminsaw was a king of ripe perfections, and when he heard and saw these wrong and lawless doings he was displeased, knowing them for false doctrine. And he yearned vehemently to discover the true Law.

131. *Of the coming of Shin Arahan from the kingdom of Thaton to the kingdom of Pagan.*

[*The coming of Shin Arahan.*] At that time, from the kingdom of Thaton, called Sudhammavati, there came to Pagan Shin Arahan, or Dhammadassi. This is the story of Shin Arahan.

Certain noble saints, perceiving that the religion had not yet shone in the kingdoms of the Western Country and Tampadipa, approached Sakra, saying, 'Help us to entreat one who can build the religion !' And Sakra entreated a spirit in Tavatimsa, country

of the spirits, insomuch that he suffered himself to be conceived
in the womb of a Brahmani. When the days and months were
fulfilled, and the child was born, it was the noble saint called
Silabuddhi. When he grew up he became a monk, and learning
the books of the Pitakas attained saintship; he was famous and
well known as Arahan over the whole face of Jambudipa. And
the saint said: 'The religion standeth not yet in the kingdoms
of the Western Country and Tampadipa.' So he came to Pugarama
and dwelt in a forest not near nor far from the capital. And
Sakra prevailed upon a certain hunter to see Shin Arahan. And
when the hunter saw him, he said, 'Here is a reverend man
and an amiable. He must be eminent and noble. I will take him
to the capital and present him before the king.' So he took
him, and Shin Arahan followed with the eight things needful.

[*He preaches before Anawrahta.*] So they came before the king;
and the hunter said, 'I found this man in the forest, and I have
brought him hither.' When the king beheld the great and glorious
Shin Arahan, he was glad like the young bud of a lotus that hath
found sunshine, and he thought, 'Verily this man is not of low
degree, but noble. The noble Law should be within him.' And
he thought, 'If he be of high degree, he will take a high seat,
if he be of low degree, he will take a low seat.' So he said: 'Sit
where it is meet for thee to sit!' And Shin Arahan, wishing
to show how truly great he was, ascended the high royal throne
and sate there.

And the king saw it and thought: 'Verily his room is large.
Let me ask after his race.' And he said, 'Master, of what race
art thou? Whence comest thou? Whose doctrine dost thou
follow?' And Shin Arahan made answer: 'My race is that of
the Lord Buddha, possessor of the nine qualities beginning with
sanctity, the six glories beginning with lordship, and the four
incomprehensibles beginning with intuition. Thou sayest, whose
doctrine do I follow? I follow the doctrine of the sermon
of authority, most fine, subtle, difficult and profound, preached
by the Lord—the Lord Buddha.' And the king was full of joy
and rapture, and spake again, entreating him, 'My Lord, preach
me somewhat—yea, but a little—of the Law preached by the Lord,
the Master!' And Shin Arahan preached the Law, beginning
with the things not to be neglected, the sermon preached by the

novice Nigrodha to king Siridhammasoka. Then the king's heart was full of faith, steadfast and immoveable ; faith sank into him as oil filtered an hundred times soaks into cotton an hundred times teased.

When he had made an end of preaching, the king spake again : ' Where is my master, the Lord—the Lord Buddha? How much is the sum of the Law preached by the Lord? Liveth there any disciple and son of the Lord save thee, my master ?' Ashin Arahan made answer : ' The Lord Omniscient, adorned with the six rays, and the thirty-two greater and eighty lesser signs, clothed in glory of great and matchless grace, possessor of the ten powers of knowledge—attained mastery near the great Wisdom Tree. Thereafter for forty-five whole rain-seasons he exhorted all men, spirits, brahmas, and other beings in his great pity and compassion, and gave them to drink the rich ambrosia of the Law. Thereafter he entered *parinirvana,* causing all the world-elements to quake, in the *ingyin* garden, the pleasance of the Malla princes, in the kingdom of Kusinara. Eleven kings, founders of kingdoms, took the eight holy relics of his body and severally worshipped them. Seven of these relics, the noble scholars who attended the Third Council brought and showed to king Siridhammasoka, who built fourscore and four thousand pagodas. One portion of the relics Naga took away and hid in his stomach, but the novice Sumana found it and offered it to Abhayadutthagamani, ruler of Ceylon island, who built a great *zedi.* The upper right tooth Sakra took up to Tavatimsa and worshipped it. The lower right tooth Nagas took away and worshipped in the Naga country. The lower left tooth was brought from Kalinga kingdom to the island of Ceylon, and was ever worshipped by the kings. The upper left tooth was ever worshipped by the kings of the Tarop kingdom, called Gandhala.'

On this point the Great Chronicle writes that the upper left tooth was in the island of Ceylon. This does not agree with the Dathadhatuvamsa.

' The Law preached by the Lord is reckoned thus :—Dhamma and Vinaya, two ; Pitaka, three ; Nikaya, five ; Anga, nine ; Dhammakhandha, fourscore and four thousand. The religious sermons thus reckoned were written by certain of the Order, presented thrice before the Councils in the Middle Country, inscribed

on palm-leaf in the island of Ceylon, and offered to the king of
Thaton. Thus there were in Thaton thirty sets of Pitakas.

' And thou hast asked—Is there any monk of the Order, save
myself, a disciple of the Lord ? Yea, verily; besides myself there
are the *paramattha* Order and the *samuti* Order.'

[*Gratitude of Anawrahta.*] Thus he spake. And when Anawrahtaminsaw heard the words of Ashin Arahan, he was seized with an
ecstasy of faith unbounded, and he said, ' Master, we have no other
refuge than thee! From this day forth, my master, we dedicate
our body and our life to thee ! And, master, from thee I take my
doctrine ! ' And he built and offered him a monastery in the
forest, adorned with nought but gems, exceeding pleasant. Moreover he rejected the doctrines of the Ari heretics.

[*Lineage of Shin Arahan.*] It appears in the Thaton Chronicle
that when there were dearth and famine throughout the kingdom
of Thaton, the three perils having come to pass in the reign of
king Manuha, a hunter found a novice roaming in the forest and
presented him to Pagan Anawrahtasaw. He was Shin Arahan,
but his original name was Shin Dhammadassi; he was known as
Ashin Arahan only after he came to Pagan. This is his lineage.
Ashin Upali, pupil in the presence of the Lord Omniscient, lived
yet in the 30th year of the religion after the Lord entered *parinir-*
vana, and himself made *parinirvana* at the age of seventy-five.
His pupil was Ashin Dasa; his pupil Ashin Sona; his two pupils
Ashin Siggava and Ashin Candavajji. When Ashin Moggaliputta
Tissa presiding over one thousand saints held the Third Council,
Ashin Sona the elder was sent to Suvannabhummi to build the
religion. His pupil was Ashin Sobhita; his pupil Ashin Soma-
datta; his pupil Sumanatissa; his pupil Ashin Sobhaga, his pupil
Ashin Somadatta; his pupil Ashin Anomadassi; his pupil Ashin
Adhisila ; his pupil Byanadassi. Ashin Byanadassi went daily
from Thaton to worship at the great Wisdom Tree in the Middle
Country. His two pupils were Ashin Mahakala and Ashin
Silabuddhi.

[*The Ari disgraced.*] The noble saint Ashin Dhammadassi having
come to Pagan ministered to the religion. When the king and all
the people forsook their own opinions and were established in the
good Law, the Ari lords lost their gain and honour and bore great
hatred against Shin Arahan. And the king fearing that the Ari

would practise ill against him, took good heed and appointed guards enough to defeat the thirty Ari lords and their sixty thousand disciples. At that time there came many saints and novices from Thaton, and Shin Arahan made saints and ghostly counsellors of those who were faithful in the religion. And the king unfrocked the thirty Ari lords and their sixty thousand followers and enrolled them among his spearmen and lancers and elephant dung-sweepers. And the king said : ' Our royal grandsires and great-grandsires who ruled this kingdom in unbroken line, followed the doctrines of the Ari monks. If it were good to follow them again, I would fain follow them ! ' So fain was he, it is said.

132. *Of the mighty men of valour, the Kala brothers.*

[*The dead fakir.*] At that time two Kala brothers were ship-wrecked near Thaton, and they rode a plank and reached Thaton. And they went into the presence of the chaplain of the Thaton king and attached themselves to him. And the monk loved and regarded them and kept them continually near him. One day he called the young Kala brothers and went to dig herbs for medicine in the forest. When he entered the forest he found a fakir, possessed of mystic wisdom, dead with the marks of violence upon him. Now the monk, chaplain of the Thaton king, was a perfect scholar of the Pitakas, Vedas, medicine, and charms, and seeing the dead body of the fakir he said : ' If a man were to roast, fry, stew, or seethe the dead body of this fakir and eat it, he would lose all manner of diseases, and his life and all its elements would last for ever. A ten days' journey he could go in a day. He could bear the weight of a thousand (viss). He could even seize a full-grown male elephant by the tusk and fell him. Or again, if we acted not on this wise, but if we steeped this dead body of the fakir in medicine, our life would last long, and ye and I, leaning on the virtues of the fakir, would get many benefits. Therefore, ye twain, shoulder me the dead body. When we reach the monastery I will collect medicine and see to it.'

So the Kala brothers shouldered the dead body of the fakir and carried it. Now this is the nature of fakirs' dead bodies. Lifeless, they are said to be about the size of a natural seven months' babe. And because they eat only Abbhantara mangoes and rose-apple fruits, their fragrance is great, like that of *nanthabu* plantains.

When they reached the monastery they stored up the body with care. One day when the chaplain of the Thaton king had gone to the palace, the young Kala brothers roasted, fried, and ate the fakir's dead body. When they had eaten it they said, ' Let us test whether what our teacher told us be true or no!' So they made assay, and lo! they could lift a stone slab ten cubits in length, eight cubits in breadth; and they put it at the foot of the stairs of the monastery. And when the chaplain of the Thaton king returned from the palace and saw the stone slab, he questioned them, for he divined that they must needs have roasted, fried, and eaten the dead body of the fakir, and so lifted the stone slab and placed it there. And the Kala brothers confessed that they had verily eaten it. And the chaplain of the Thaton king abode in silence.

[*One Kala murdered.*] From that day forward the young Kala brothers had the strength of a full-grown male elephant. After a long while the Thaton king grew sore afraid of them and sought to lay hands on them. He seized and killed the elder brother while he was asleep in his wife's house. But the younger brother fled from the kingdom of Thaton, and coming to Pugarama attended on Anawrahtaminsaw. And Anawrahtaminsaw seeing the looks and bearing of the Kala, took pity on him and kept him continually near him.

When the Kala was killed, the king of Thaton asked the chaplain what should be done with him. And he said : ' Cut up the body of the young Kala and bury the right hand in such a place. Bury likewise the left hand, the right thigh, and the left thigh, the head, the intestines, and the liver, in such and such places. If this be ordered with divers charms and ceremonies, this city of Thaton, though it be assaulted by all manner of foes, cannot be conquered.' So the king of Thaton did so, and buried them with manifold and divers charms and rites and ceremonies. From that day forward no enemy could daunt nor frighten the kingdom of Thaton.

[*The other Kala at Pagan.*] Now Anawrahtaminsaw sent the young Kala who had come to him, ten times a day to Poppa to fetch *saga* flowers. Such power had he, it is said. One day an ogress at Poppa, seeing the young Kala, lusted after him, for they were brought together by *karma* done in their past lives. She took upon her the form of a woman and lay with the young Kala, and two sons were born. When they grew up she presented them to Anawrahtaminsaw, and he seeing their looks and bearing, kept them near him and called them Shwehpyigyi and Shwehpyingè.

133. *Of the journey of king Anawrahta to Thaton and his bringing of the Pitakas.*

[*Anawrahta's mission to Thaton.*] Now Shin Arahan spake to Anawrahtaminsaw : ' There are three elements of the Lord's religion : without the scriptures there can be no study, without study there can be no intuition. The scriptures, the Three Pitakas, thou hast not yet. Only when thou hast obtained them, sending gifts and presents and entreating them of divers countries which have relics of the Lord's body and the books of the Pitakas, may the religion last long.' Anawrahtaminsaw answered and said : ' In what country must I seek and find them ? ' Said Shin Arahan, ' In the country of Thaton are thirty sets, the Three Pitakas in each set. There are also many sacred relics.'

So the king made ready store of gifts and presents and sent a wise minister to Thaton to ask for them with seemly words. But the heart of the Thaton king was rancorous and evilly disposed, and he answered ill. Thereat Anawrahtaminsaw waxed exceeding wroth, and he gathered all his mighty men of valour and marched by land and water. By water he sent eight hundred thousand boats and four score million fighting men. By land he made his four generals march in the van — Kyanzittha, Nga Htweyu, Nga Lonlephpè, and Nyaung-u Hpi—while he marched forth with the main army in the rear. His land force, it is said, contained eight hundred thousand elephants, eight million horses, and eighteen million fighting men. It is said that when the vanguard of the naval force reached Pegu, the whole armament of boats had yet not quitted Pugarama ; and on land also, when the vanguard of the army reached the frontier of Thaton territory, the rear guard had yet not quitted Pugarama.

[*The exhuming of the Kala.*] When Manuha king of Thaton heard that Anawrahtaminsaw had marched forth with an innumerable host, with his four generals on demon horses, he was sore afraid, and shut the city gates and prepared to meet him by fortifying the city. So when the king's army arrived by water and land, the four generals went foremost up to the city walls,

but they could not enter. Though they made many assaults they
were not victorious, because of the charms which had been devised.
Anawrahtaminsaw questioned his masters of white magic and black,
saying, 'What meaneth this?' and they answered, ' He winneth
the victory because he hath devised many charms at Thaton.'
Then spake the Kala footrunner: 'Mine elder brother was put
to death long ago and buried with divers rites and charms. Thou
canst not well win victory until thou hast taken and destroyed
his head and hands and thighs.' So Anawrahtaminsaw sent and
commanded him, saying, ' Bring them from their place of burial!'
And the Kala footrunner entered the city by night and questioned
his brother's wife till he knew the spot where his brother's thighs
and hands were buried, and when he knew it, he brought them from
their place of burial and offered them to the king. And Anawrahtaminsaw questioned yet again his masters of white magic and black,
saying, 'What must I do with them?' And they answered, 'It
were best only to drop the head and hands and thighs of the young
Kala into the sea.' Even as they had spoken, he put the bones
upon a royal barge and dropped them into the sea. It is said that
when they fell a column of water sprang up to the height of a young
palm tree.

[*Capture of Thaton.*]   Not until all these preparations were made
could the royal host of fighting men enter Thaton. And they
captured king Manuha with his family and ministers, and presented
them to Anawrahtaminsaw. He brought away the sacred relics
which were kept in a jewelled casket and worshipped by a line
of kings in Thaton; and he placed the thirty sets of the Pitakas
on the king's thirty-two white elephants and brought them away.
Moreover, he sent off in turn the mighty men of valour and all the
host of elephants and horses. Thereafter he sent away separately,
without mixing, such men as were skilled in carving, turning, and
painting; masons, moulders of plaster and flower-patterns; black-
smiths, silversmiths, braziers, founders of gongs and cymbals,
filagree flower-workers; doctors and trainers of elephants and
horses; makers of shields, round and embossed, of divers kinds
of shields, of shields both oblong and convex; forgers of cannon,
muskets, and bows; men skilled in frying, parching, baking and
frizzling; *yakin* hairdressers, and men cunning in perfumes, odours,
flowers and the juices of flowers. Moreover, to the noble Order

acquainted with the books of the Pitakas he made fair appeal and brought them away. He also took king Manuha and his family and returned home to Pugarama.

[*History of Thaton.*] The first ruler of the kingdom of Thaton was king Siharaja in the lifetime of the Lord. Forty-eight kings in succession, beginning from that king and ending in Manuha, kings of glory, dominion, and power, alway upheld the Lord's religion. All the people abounded in virtue, charity, and other qualities, insomuch that the kingdom was fertile and pleasant as the land of spirits. Siritribhavanadityapavaradhammaraja Manuha, the king who ruled this great kingdom of Thaton, thus established in prosperity and abundance, lord of the thirty-two white elephants, was ruined and the whole country ruined because he had spoken ill to the envoys sent by king Anawrahta.

The Great Chronicle says that in the lifetime of the Lord king Asokadhammaraja ruled in Thaton. But it is told at length in the Thaton Chronicle that during the reign of Siharaja, who had been brother of the saint Ashin Gavampati, the Lord invited by the saint Ashin Gavampati came over to Thaton, called Suvanna-bhummi; that after the Lord entered the bliss of *parinirvana*, the saint Ashin Gavampati brought the thirty-two tooth-relics and offered them for king Siharaja to worship; and so forth. King Siharaja had flourished sixty years, when the Lord entered the bliss of *parinirvana*. Ten years later he entered the world of spirits, and his son Sirimasoka became king. Thus it is seen that in two places the Chronicle agrees not with the Thaton Chronicle.

[*Manuha.*] Anawrahtaminsaw, when he reached Pugarama, made separate quarters for the mighty men of valour to dwell in, and the host of learned men whom he had brought. All the relics of the sacred body he enshrined in a ruby casket richly fraught with gems, and he had them alway near his bed at the place where his head lay, and he worshipped them. Moreover he kept the thirty sets of Pitakas in a *pyatthad* richly fraught with gems, and caused the noble Order to give instruction therein. King Manuha with his attendants lived at Myinkaba. Now the glory of king Manuha, it is said, was this, that whenever he spake a wheel issued radiant from his mouth. So when Manuha visited and bowed his head before Anawrahtaminsaw, that king was aghast, and his hair stood on end. Thereafter, in order to demean

Manuha's glory, dominion, and power, he caused his food to be alway prepared upon a jewelled salver and first dedicated to a pagoda and then set before the king. And king Manuha took no heed nor scrutiny, but ate of it. Thus after a while the radiant wheel that issued from his mouth vanished. Then only, when it vanished, it is said he set his heart at rest, saying, 'Plot I never so shrewdly, it may not be!' Then stricken with remorse, he built a colossal Buddha seated with legs crossed, and a dying Buddha as it were making *parinirvana*; and he prayed saying, 'Whithersoever I migrate in *samsara*, may I never be conquered by another!' The temple is called Manuha to this day.

134. *Of the journey to the Tarop country in the kingdom of Gandhala, and the asking of the sacred tooth.*

[*Anawrahta's mission to Gandhala.*] Anawrahtaminsaw was full of faith in the religion, and he thought : 'In the Tarop country of the kingdom of Gandhala there is an holy tooth. If I ask that holy tooth from the Tarop Utibwa and make it an object of worship to all beings, the religion will shine exceedingly and all creatures be profited throughout the five thousand years of the religion.' So he gathered his elephants, horses, and fighting men throughout the kingdom, and marched to the Tarop country with thirty-six millions by water and thirty-six millions by land, summoning thereto the four riders on demon horses and the Shwehpyi brothers.

[*Anawrahta and the hermit.*] Now when he came, the Tarop Utibwa shut the city gate and stubbornly awaited him. And Anawrahtaminsaw knowing that he was stubborn was fain to look into the matter; and he called Kyanzittha, Nga Htweyu, Nga Lonlephpè, Nyaung-u Hpi, and the Shwehpyi brothers, and he mounted the demon horse and rode to the monastery of the hermit, chaplain of the Utibwa, and found him amidst one hundred thousand attendants in the monastery. Now the hermit knew not of a surety 'This is the sovereign king; this is the minister,' for king Anawrahta and the four riders on demon horses and the Shwehpyi brothers wore gorgeous apparel of inestimable worth. That he might be assured thereof, he spread seven seats of dignity and softness. And Anawrahtaminsaw struck the seven seats with his Areindama cane, and they became one seat, whereon he sate. The four generals, Kyanzittha and the others, with the Shwehpyi

brothers, abode humbly paying homage to the king. When the
hermit, teacher of the Utibwa, saw this thing, he knew that it
was a great king and glorious; therefore he asked, 'Whence comest
thou, and why, into our country?' And when the king knew his
question he made answer: 'I am Anawrahtaminsaw, ruler of the
great kingdom of Pugarama, called Arimaddana. The reason of
my coming is to ask the holy tooth of the Lord Omniscient, that
I may worship it.' When the hermit heard the words of Anawrahtaminsaw he made the matter known to the Utibwa. But he
discerned not between the base and the noble, and regarded him not.

Then spake king Anawrahtaminsaw to the hermit, 'What doth
the Utibwa, ruler of this country, worship, looking to the future
and the present?' And the hermit said, 'Looking to the future the
Utibwa, king of the Law, worshippeth the Lord's holy tooth; looking to the present he worshippeth the Sandi spirit which abideth in
a *tazaungpyatthad* in front of his golden palace.'

[*The taming of the Utibwa.*] But the Utibwa thought the army
which Anawrahtaminsaw had brought with him—it was about
seventy-two million fighting men—to be a little thing, and he
regarded it not. One day, it is said, the reapers of horse fodder
came round to look, bearing bamboos on their shoulders and resting
their chins on their hands; and behold! even they surrounded in
three ranks the king's army of seventy-two million fighting men.
But Anawrahtaminsaw said: 'The Utibwa regardeth me not. He
cometh not forth to offer gifts when such a king as I hath come!
Must it be ever so?' And he called the Shwehpyi brothers and
commanded them, saying, 'Enter this night the Utibwa's palace.
He sleepeth guarded by a wheel, an engine worked by water. Suck
out all the water with a tube, and mark three lines with lime upon
the Utibwa's body. And why? He regardeth me not, neither
cometh he forth to offer gifts when such a king as I hath come!
Must it be ever so? If it is so any longer, I will cut him asunder
even along the lines marked by the lime. Leave ye this message
in writing upon the wall.' And the Shwehpyi brothers hearkened
to his word, and entered by night and sucked up the water and
marked three lines with lime upon the Utibwa's body and left
a writing upon the wall.

At dawn Anawrahtaminsaw called Kyanzittha and commanded
him again, saying, 'When such a king as I hath come, the Utibwa

regardeth me not! Tie a rope around the copper Sandi spirit and strike it with the Areindama cane.' And Kyanzittha hearkened to his word and feared not, but tied a rope around the image of the Sandi spirit; now it was cast in copper and so large that four men with joined hands might embrace it, and it was worshipped by the Utibwa and the whole country ; and he struck it with the Areindama cane. And the spirit lifted up his voice and cried, 'The future Buddha, the king who reigns in Pugarama Arimaddana, is come desiring only to behold the sacred tooth ; and lo ! the Utibwa, the ministers, and all the people regard him not, neither go they forth with gifts to meet him. Me, therefore, he punisheth, and sorely !' And the Utibwa and all the people of Gandhala heard that cry as if it had been shouted in their ears. Moreover the Utibwa saw the three marks of lime made by the Shwehpyi brothers and the writing on the wall, and he feared exceedingly. And hearing the cry of the copper Sandi, he and all the people were sore afraid and humbled themselves, as though he would eat their flesh.

So the Utibwa offered store of gifts and presents, and accompanied by an host of ministers he came to see the king. And he said, 'I knew not that my royal kinsman Anawrahtaminsaw had visited our country. Not until the copper Sandi spirit cried aloud, did I know.' And Anawrahtaminsaw said, 'The reason of my coming to the country of my royal kinsman is not a desire for worldly prosperity. I have come to ask for the sacred tooth, desiring to worship it and so attain transcendent happiness.' And the Utibwa said, 'If the sacred tooth is fain to rest upon thee, take it !' Thus did the two founders of empire at last forgather and speak words of love and fairness. From that day onward for full three months the Utibwa dressed food in gold and silver baking-pans, rice-pots, curry-pots and basons, and daily offered it.

[*Anawrahta fails to get the tooth.*] And Anawrahtaminsaw paid honour and worship and entreated the holy tooth at the palace where it lay. And the tooth, adorned with thirty-two greater and eighty lesser signs and the six rays of noble men, ascended the sky with grace unspeakable and remained passing to and fro. And Anawrahtaminsaw raised the jewelled casket and set it on his head, and did obeisance many times and pleaded. But the tooth abode in the sky and descended not. And when he saw it he was dim, sorrowful, and heartbroken. Then Sakra, knowing that he was heartbroken, and that he would prove a firm upholder of the religion, brought an emerald image and caused it to pass to and fro with the sacred tooth and descend from the sky, and rest within the jewelled casket on the king's head. And Sakra revealed himself and spake : ' There is no prophecy of the Lord that this tooth be worshipped by the king ; there is the prophecy that the religion shall be established for five thousand years in the kingdom of Gandhala. But there is a prophecy that the king shall worship the Lord's frontlet-relic. Now this frontlet-relic king Dwattabaung, ruler of Tharehkittara, brought from the Kanyan country, and built a great *zedi* in Tharehkittara and worshipped it. Take thee the frontlet-relic and worship it ! ' So king Anawrahta was comforted, and he cooked food in the gold and silver baking-pans, rice-pots, curry-pots and basons which the Utibwa offered, and gave it to the hermit, that he might daily offer it to the sacred tooth. So the two kings spake words of joy and gladness, and he went his way taking the emerald image given by Sakra.

[*His visit to Maw.*] When he came to Maw, the Sawbwa, ruler of the nine provinces of Maw, spread out reverently five golden mats. And Anawrahta caused them to be stricken with the Areindama cane, insomuch that the five golden mats piled themselves one upon another in token of the king's power and glory ; and the king took his ease upon the mat. When the Sawbwa beheld it, he offered Sawmunhla his daughter, endued with the five virtues. The king accepted her, and returned by water and land.

[*Death of the Shwehpyi brothers.*] Now when he came to Kyawzi, he put to death at Wayindot the Shwehpyi brothers, for he trusted them not. The spot where they were killed is still known as Kupya banyan tree. And Anawrahtaminsaw built a *gu* at Taungbyon that the religion might last five thousand years for the benefit of all beings, and he called it Hsutaungpyi. Thence he returned on board the royal raft. Now the Shwehpyi brothers had become evil spirits, and as the royal raft floated down they kept catching the rudder so that it could not move. Therefore he questioned his masters of white magic and black, and they spake into his ear, saying, ' Thy servants, the Nga Hpyi brothers, did thee faithful service, O king, but it booted them not ; and now they haunt thee, catching hold of the rudder ! ' So Anawrahtaminsaw ordered the

building of the spirit-palace at the Hsutaungpyi pagoda, his work
of merit at the village of Taungbyon, and that it be worshipped
by the people living throughout the length of Kyawzi. And his
ministers did as the king commanded them. Moreover he left one
pagoda on the summit of Mandalay hill, two also at the Kyek-yek
hills. And when the king came down to the homeland, he kept
the emerald image in the golden palace and worshipped it.

135. *Of Sawmunhla, daughter of the Sawbwa, ruler of the nine provinces of Maw.*

[*Dismissal of Sawmunhla.*]   Now the king kept Sawmunhla,
daughter of the Sawbwa, ruler of the nine provinces of Maw,
continually near him. And an holy relic slept in her earring ; and
when the queen and concubines saw that colours shone therefrom,
they said to the king, ' She is a *yogani*, a witch ! ' And the king
looked, and lo ! the earring shone radiant with colours ; and he
believed that she was verily a *yogani*, a witch, as the queen and
concubines had said ; and he gave order that Sawmunhla was not
worthy of his golden palace, and that she must return to the city-
village of her home. So Sawmunhla humbled herself and did
obeisance to the king and the guardian spirit of the kingdom and
the palace, and went her way with her slaves and attendants.

[*Shwezayan pagoda.*]   Day by day as she went, she tarried at these
halting-places : Nyaung-u village, Nyin village, Palin, Let-htot
village, Kaungzi village, Mt. Tuywin, Wunpate, Myothit the main
halting-place, and Kyunba village.   And when she came near the
site of Shwezayan pagoda, her earring became loose and fell ; and
though it was seen shining in the water, and they dived and
searched and fumbled after it, they could not find nor grasp it. At
last Sawmunhla looked up, and lo ! the sacred relic with the earring
was in the sky, revealing a miracle, for young sparrows gathered
round it twittering.   And she did obeisance and worshipped, and
the holy relic of the earring descended and dwelt once more in her
left ear.   And she was minded to build a pagoda over the holy
relic ; and Sakra, seeing that it would be worshipped by all people
throughout the five thousand years of the religion, disclosed a heap
of piled bricks, and she discovered it.   Therein she enshrined the
holy relic and built a cave-temple with an image five cubits in
height.

Now when Anawrahtaminsaw heard that Sawmunhla had built
a pagoda, and given charity to men and monks in that place with
the gold and silver she had brought from Maw, he caused royal
messengers to go and see; and if she had the portal of the cave-
temple facing east towards the Shan country of Maw, they were to
put her to death; but if the mouth of the central arch faced
the royal home of Pugarama, she should not die. The royal
messengers arrived at dusk, and said, ' We will read and proclaim
the king's command!' But Sawmunhla gave them store of gifts
and bribes, to the end that she might not hear their sentence
till early next morning. And she fed them with good victuals
in abundance, and talked to them graciously, and asked them of
this and of that, feelingly, that she might know the purport
of the king's letter. And the messengers answered in such wise
that Sawmunhla knew all the truth. Then she did obeisance and
worshipped, and made a solemn vow before Sakra, the four regents
of the world, and the Samadeva spirits; and she fastened the
golden shawl she wore, studded with emeralds, and swung it
round: and lo! the Shwezayan pagoda, which was built facing
the east, had its entrance on the west. Early next morning the
royal messengers saw it, and they returned to Pugarama. And
when they arrived and told Anawrahtaminsaw, he offered one
thousand *ta* of land adjoining the pagoda built by queen Sawmunhla, on the tenth waxing of Tazaungmon, in the year 416.

Afterwards in the year 485, king Alaungsithu, lord of the magic
boat, made oblation to the pagoda of the land and villages between
the following limits: on the east Thambaya stream, on the south
the winding Myitngè, on the west Yinmabin on one side of the
Pan stream, on the north Nakè stream and Mt. Nakè. Moreover,
he dedicated fifty families of pagoda-slaves as caretakers to cook
food-offerings and to sweep with brooms. Thereafter in the reign
of king Mohnyin it was again repaired, and the image raised
to an height of more than thirty standard cubits. Thereafter
in the reign of the donor of the five-storied royal monastery,
Mahamingalashwebon, his mother, the chief queen, again repaired
it, and set up a golden umbrella, and covered it with gold down to
the ground. The Great Chronicle and the Middle Chronicle say
nothing of this history of the Shwezigon pagoda, one of the four
famous pagodas; but in this Great Royal Chronicle we take the

opportunity of giving it, in accordance with the Thamaings of Pagan Shwezigon and of Shwezayan.

135 a. *Of the bringing of the relics of the sacred frontlet and the tooth, and the enshrining of them in Shwezigon pagoda.*

[*Anawrahta destroys Tharehkittara.*] Then he marched to Tharehkittara by land and water with a great company of elephants and horses, and destroyed the *zedi* built by king Dwattabaung. And he took the frontlet-relic, set it on a white elephant with a *pyatthad* richly fraught with gems, and brought it away.

The New Chronicle says that the wise like not the saying that king Dwattabaung obtained the frontlet-relic from the Kanyan country. There is this evidence to support them: It is said in the Nalatadhatuvamsa that at the time of the Lord's *parinirvana* the Malla kings received as their share the frontlet-relic; that Ashin Mahakassapa begged it of them and gave it to Shin Mahanan; that six elders—Mahanama, Candaratta, Bhaddasena, Jayasena, Sangharakkhita, and Revata—worshipped it, handing it down from teacher to teacher; that from the time of Shin Revata it passed into the hands of king Mahanaga at the village of Mahagama in Ceylon island, and was worshipped by four kings in succession—Mahanaga, Ghatatanalayaka, Gotabhaya, and Kakavanna; and that it was not till the 360th year of the religion that king Kakavanna enshrined it in the Mahirangana pagoda. But the Arakan Chronicle and the Mahamuni Thamaing state that in the reign of king Candagotta, nephew of king Dhulacandara, Nawrahtaminsaw marched to Arakan, and because he could not carry the Mahamuni image he took away the frontlet together with the gold and silver images of the Lord that were in Arakan. How these two statements conflict is thus explained: The *nalata* relic is taken to mean the forehead-relic, the *unhissa* relic to be the frontlet-relic. So the scholars have agreed that the relic mentioned in the Nalatadhatuvamsa is the forehead-relic, and that the one mentioned in the Arakan and Burmese Chronicles is the frontlet-relic. But the Old Chronicle, the Great Chronicle, and others agree in saying that king Dwattabaung brought the frontlet-relic from the Kanyan country and enshrined it; whereas the Arakan *thamaing* say that it was not taken till the reign of Anawrahtaminsaw. Howbeit, the Burmese Chronicles based on lines of tradition, should alone be trusted rather than foreign sources, where it is a point of Burmese history concerned with Burmese names and kings.

Anawrahtaminsaw destroyed the city of Tharehkittara, fearing lest rebels should occupy it in time to come. He dug up the *nawarat* boat of the nine gems, used by king Dwattabaung and buried by his son Dwattaran, and having beheld it he buried it again. Thence he returned and came to the homeland, Pugarama.

[*He builds Shwezigon Pagoda.*] Then he consulted the noble saint Ashin Arahan, desiring that the religion should last full five thousand years for the benefit of all beings; and setting the frontlet-relic on a jewelled white elephant he made a solemn vow, and said: 'Let the white elephant kneel in the place where the holy relic is fain to rest!' And he set it free. And the white elephant knelt on a sandbank, the site of the Shwezigon pagoda. When the king saw that it knelt upon a sandbank, he was sorry, for he had thought the religion would last full five thousand years. His heart was ill content that the white elephant knelt not upon natural soil, but on shifting sand. That night Sakra appeared to him in a dream, and said, 'O king, at the spot where the white elephant knelt, the religion will last full five thousand years. Be not thou afraid!' And the king was glad, and made ready to build a pagoda. And Sakra strengthened the ground with solid rock, two hundred and forty thousand times thicker than before, and clamped it all round with iron plates. And Anawrahtaminsaw, seeing that the religion would stand firm for five thousand years, dwelt in five *pyatthad* south of Shwezigon, and in the year 421 he built the Shwezigon pagoda.

When the relic-chamber was ready, the Lord's frontlet-relic adorned itself with the greater and the lesser signs and the six rays, and rose all-glorious with grace transcendent, and shouldering the eight priestly requisites ascended the sky and prophesied, saying, 'In days of yore this king was a Pulali elephant, and during the three months of rains once ministered to me. Now also he hath exalted my religion. In time to come he shall be Lord like me!' And the king swooned with joy ineffable and pure, like cotton, teased an hundred times, soaked in oil an hundred times strained; and he abode sobbing, embracing the gem-embroidered casket where the relic lay. And Shin Arahan said

to the king, 'Much yet remaineth to uphold the Lord's religion.
Cast in gold the likeness of one embracing the gem-embroidered
casket, and enshrine it.' And the king, according as Shin Arahan
had said, cast the golden image and enshrined it.

Concerning the building of Shwezigon there are the *thamaing*
and the inscriptions. The sandbank which is the site of Shwezigon
is the sandbank where Pyuminhti met his royal mother. It is
called Zeyagon, and so Sigon, the *S* being pronounced as *Z*. And
all *zedi* after its likeness are called Zigon—so the New Chronicle
says. The Ekakkhara Kosa sub-commentary speaks of the en-
shrinement of the tooth, collarbone, and frontlet in Shwezigon;
and thus Nawadegyi has written in the *yadu* in honour of
Shwezigon pagoda:

> 'The sacred relics,
> The tooth, collarbone, and frontlet,
> All-glorious and richly dight.'

[*He obtains the tooth-relic from Ceylon.*] When he had built
Shwezigon pagoda and finished the three terraces, he thought,
'I am one to whom the Lord's prophecy hath been vouchsafed.
Though I entreated the holy tooth from the Tarop country, I gat
it not. Sakra told me there was a prophecy, and gave me the
emerald image and the frontlet-relic, and he hath given me them to
worship. If now I might get the holy tooth in the island of
Ceylon and enshrine it in this pagoda, all beings will have great
benefit for full five thousand years.' Thus he prayed. Early that
night Sakra, seeing that the Lord's religion would be clearly manifest, sent the king a dream that he should get the holy tooth from
Ceylon. When the king awoke he was of good cheer and joyful,
and calling his four generals and the host of ministers he consulted
them saying, 'I purpose to cross over to the island of Ceylon and
bring the sacred tooth ever worshipped by Ceylon kings. Ministers,
how think ye?' Then spake Kyanzittha: 'Great lord! If we four
horsemen go with thee and march to attack—not Ceylon island only,
but all the umbrella-holding kings of the whole island of Jambudipa
confederate against us, they cannot resist our hand!' And the
king hearing the words spoken by the four generals was glad, and
calling his servants the Kala footrunners and the four riders on
demon horses, he went to the port Pava to the end that he might
cross over to the island of Ceylon.

Now when they reached the port, Bandhukampala, the seat of
Sakra, hardened.   And he said, 'What ado is there in the world
of men?'   And he looked and saw Anawrahtaminsaw going to
bring the sacred tooth from the island of Ceylon.   He saw that
when the king reached the island of Ceylon, the two founders of
empire would wage a mighty war and bring destruction on the
whole island.   So he took the guise of a captain and said to
king Anawrahta, ' I cross to the island of Ceylon this day.   Come
thou in my ship!'   In happy hour he spake, and it liked the king
well, and he followed with the four riders on demon horses.   That
night Sakra gave them to eat the food of spirits and to sleep in
mansions spread for spirits, insomuch that Anawrahtaminsaw and the
host of his attendants tasted the bliss of spirits and slept heavily
and waked not.   And Sakra brought them that night to the port
of Lokananda.

And king Anawrahta awoke, and lo! he was at Lokananda, and
his heart was displeased, and he said, ' Sakra hath done this thing,
not wishing me to go to the island of Ceylon!'   And when he came
to the palace Sakra gave him a dream that night, saying, ' Send an
embassy and ask the sacred tooth, O king, and thou shalt get it!'
So the king consulted Shin Arahan, and he sent a white elephant
as a present and asked the holy tooth, instructing an able minister
to use seemly words.   Meanwhile to Dhatusena, king of Ceylon,
Sakra had given a dream that Anawrahtaminsaw, ruler of the great
country of Arimaddana Pugarama, endued with glory, might of
arm, and dominion, came with four riders on demon horses, fastened
a rope round the spirit image of laterite, as large as four men with
joined hands might embrace—the image which for benefits in this
world was reverently worshipped by the whole island of Ceylon—
and bare it away; moreover he took the holy tooth also.   When
he awoke, Dhatusena, king of Ceylon, trembled exceedingly with
great fear and dread.   And the ship sent by Anawrahtaminsaw,
because it was helped by Sakra, reached Ceylon island in seven
days.   And the envoys offered the Ceylon king their presents
together with the white elephant sent by Anawrahtaminsaw, and
spake the reason of their coming.

The Great Chronicle says the Ceylon king was Sirisanghabodhi.
But king Sirisanghabodhi, eighty-seventh in descent from king
Vijaya, became king only in the 107th year of the religion, or 541 ;

that is, in the time of Narapatisithu, donor of the nine *saga* images. This strongly conflicts with the date given in the Great Chronicle itself, which states that Anawrahtaminsaw, who became king in 379, died in 392 (abolishing *khachapañca*). This date in the Great Chronicle conflicts not only with the Dipavamsa and Culavamsa and others, but also with the scribes of the Kalyani inscriptions, &c. When Anawrahtaminsaw became king in the year 379, it was contemporary with the sixth year of prosperity of king Dhatusena of Ceylon.

When the king of Ceylon heard all the charge of Anawrahtaminsaw his heart was full of joy and tenderness, and he went to the *pyatthad* where the holy relic lay, saying, ' As my friend hath charged me, I will make request, that he may worship it '; and he pleaded with great honour and reverence. And the holy tooth adorned itself with the thirty-two greater and eighty lesser signs and the six rays of noble men, and rose all-glorious with grace transcendent shouldering all the eight priestly requisites, and abode passing to and fro in the sky. And the Ceylon king setting upon his head a gem-embroidered casket fraught with the nine jewels, pleaded with reverence devoutly. And lo! from the holy tooth proceeded yet another tooth, and they passed to and fro in the sky as if two Lords had appeared. When he saw it the Ceylon king made long entreaty that the tooth which had proceeded should settle on his head; and it descended from the sky and settled on the top of the gem-embroidered casket on the king's head. And the king bare it on his head to the harbour and descending neck-deep into the water set it on the ship. Moreover he charged them saying, ' Let my friend Anawrahtaminsaw descend, as I have done, neck-deep into the water and bear it on his head.' And the envoys set it in a *pyatthad* richly fraught with gems, and conveyed it reverently and well. Then they sailed with the help of Sakra from the island of Ceylon and reached the port of Lokananda in seven days.

Anawrahtaminsaw, hearing that they had come bringing the holy tooth in the ship he sent to the island of Ceylon, was glad, and he mounted the white elephant called Pulèpyon, and went forth to meet the tooth as far as the port Swèdawkyo. And because king Anawrahta met it not as the Ceylon king had charged, but met it riding an elephant, the ship whereon the tooth was laid returned and stood in the sea. Some records state that the ship returned as far as Ceylon. When the ship returned Anawrahtaminsaw was sore perplexed, and pleaded with great honour and reverence. Then at last the ship whereon the tooth was laid came near, and the king descended neck-deep into the water, and setting the gem-embroidered casket on his head, surrounded with an innumerable host of ministers, fighting men, and followers, he bare it to the golden throne. And when he reached the golden palace he caused it to rest before the palace in a *pyatthad* richly overlaid with jewels, and paid great honour and reverence.

[*Anawrahta's pagodas.*] But Shin Arahan spake on this wise to the king : ' Far better will it be to build a *zedi* where all beings may worship during the full five thousand years of the religion, than to keep the holy tooth within the palace and worship it there.' So Anawrahtaminsaw for the benefit of all beings set the holy tooth in a jewelled *pyatthad* on a jewelled white elephant and set it free, saying, ' Kneel wheresoever it be pleased to rest ! ' And the white elephant ascended and knelt at Shwezigon where the frontlet-relic was enshrined. So Anawrahtaminsaw enshrined the holy tooth in Shwezigon. And the king made a solemn vow and said : ' If verily I am to attain Buddhahood, let another holy tooth proceed from the first.' And lo ! another tooth proceeded ; and he laid it on the white elephant and set it free again, and made a solemn vow, saying, ' Kneel wheresoever it be pleased to rest ! ' And the white elephant ascended and knelt at the top of Mt. Tangyi. There he built a *zedi* and enshrined it. Yet again the king made a solemn vow, and set it free, that it might kneel wheresoever the holy tooth was fain to rest. The white elephant knelt at Lokananda where the ship from Ceylon had put in. There he built a *zedi* and enshrined it. Yet again he made a solemn vow, and yet another tooth proceeded. He laid it on the white elephant once more and set it free, and the white elephant knelt on the top of Mt. Tuywin. Thereon he built a *zedi* and enshrined it. Yet again he made a solemn vow, and yet another tooth proceeded. He laid it on the white elephant once more and set it free ; and the white elephant went eastwards, and having lain for a while on Mt. Thalyaung went thence and ascended Mt. Hkaywe, and went thence and knelt on Mt. Pyek. There Anawrahtaminsaw built a *zedi* and enshrined it. Moreover thinking that on Mt. Thalyaung and Mt. Hkaywe also

he should build *zedi*, he built one on each and enshrined many
relics of the sacred body. Thus desiring that the religion might
endure full five thousand years for the benefit of all creatures, he
built *zedi* to enshrine five holy teeth, and with great honour and
reverence called his blessing upon them.

136. *Of the sending of Kyanzittha, Nga Htweyu, Nga Lonlephpè, and
Nyaung-u Hpi to Ussa Pegu to help in the war.*

[*Kyanzittha saves Pegu.*] One day it was reported : ' An host of
Gywan warriors hath marched on Ussa Pegu. Send us help to
fight them ! ' Said Anawrahtaminsaw, ' Good horsemen, four
hundred thousand, shall be sent to succour you ! ' So the messengers
returned. And the king caused his four captains—Kyanzittha,
Nga Htweyu, Nga Lonlephpè, and Nyaung-u Hpi—to disguise
them in the garb of spirits, and with their followers and fourscore
Kala footrunners go to help in the war. Now when they came
the king of Ussa Pegu spake words of dudgeon : ' Horsemen four
hundred thousand were to be sent ; and forsooth four horsemen
come ! ' But the four riders on demon horses said, ' Speaketh he thus
about us ? ' ; and they discovered divers feats of skill and prowess
in such places as cucumber plantations. And the king of Ussa
Pegu and all the people marvelled and extolled them saying,
' They are not men but spirits. We have never seen—nay, we
have never heard of their like.' And the king was glad and offered
store of presents. Now when the Gywan warriors came up with
a great host of horse and elephants, the demon horsemen charged
into their midst, splitting the Gywan army into four divisions ;
and the generals of those four divisions—Aukbraran, Aukbrarè,
Aukbrabon, and Aukbrapaik—they captured alive. And the
Gywan warriors dropped their arms and weapons from their hands
and fled with naught but a loin-cloth. The four demon horsemen
presented the four generals they had captured to the Ussa king ;
and he was exceeding glad and gave them great rewards.

[*Princess Manisanda.*] Now the Ussa king sent to Anawrahtaminsaw his daughter as a gift. Her name was Manisanda.
She was his favourite daughter, and of golden colour, and her
weight was just that of an image of a lion. Moreover he sent
the sacred relic worshipped by the line of Ussa kings, who kept
it in a golden casket. And the four demon horsemen took each

their turn to convey the princess Manisanda. One day when it
was Kyanzittha's turn to watch, he lay with her, and lo! when
they weighed her against the lion-image, the lion-weight was light,
and the body of the princess heavy. And the three captains when
they knew it told Anawrahtaminsaw that so it was while Kyanzittha took his turn to watch.

[*Kyanzittha's flight.*] Anawrahtaminsaw waxed exceeding wroth
and cried: ' Did he so? Showed he no reverence to such a king
as I ?' And he glowered on him and bound him with ropes, and
hurled at him the Areindama lance. But Kyanzittha's *karma* was
not yet fulfilled, and he escaped, for the blow fell upon the rope
that bound him, that it snapped. And Kyanzittha caught up the
Areindama lance and fled. He went out by the Nyaungzi gate
and reached the Myitnasokkate landing-place, and seeing the boat
of a fisherman in mid-river he sought conveyance to the farther
shore; but the boatman abode feigning not to hear him; wherefore
he thrust at the boat with his lance, and lo! when it felt the lance,
the boat came up to the bank and he crossed over to the *kalagyaung*
on Aungtha shore.

But the king sent seven Kala footrunners to pursue and slay
him. And as they pursued they said, ' Kyanzittha is a man of
glory. While he seeth us, we may not catch him. We must catch
him while he is asleep.' Now Kyanzittha was faint with weariness
and hunger; and when he reached the forest he drave the Areindama
lance into the ground and set himself to sleep. But how often
soever he planted it, the lance fell. And Kyanzittha was wroth,
and he flung it into the forest. And lo! .the seven Kala footrunners lay in wait peeping from a bush to catch him; and the
lance pierced them, and laced them, as it were, upon a string.
And Kyanzittha slept. When he awoke he entered the forest to
pick up the lance, and behold, the lance had laced the seven Kala
footrunners, as it were upon a string. Seeing it he thought,
' Verily the king, the lord of my food, desireth my death and from
his heart hath purposed it!' So he picked up the lance and went
north to Kyaungbyu.

[*Thambula.*] In that place there dwelt the niece of a *mahti* saint,
and she was very beautiful .with all the signs of royalty, great and
small. And the monk, her uncle, was skilled in the Vedas, and he
took his niece's horoscope and looking at it said, ' My sister and my

brother-in-law once spake to me on this wise: " Our daughter was dressing cotton and she fell asleep, and as she slept bees clave to the hem of her skirt. Surely a man of glory shall visit her!" Know therefore that thou shalt have him do thee obeisance. On such a day thy future husband shall come from the south-west and ask for water. He who asketh water is thy future husband. On such a day be ready with good food and drink!'

When the day spoken of by the *mahti* was come, Kyanzittha visited that place. He came trifling his lance, and seeing the *mahti's* niece that she was goodly to look upon, he said, 'Prithee, give water!' and plucking a lime from a sour lime tree in the monastery, he peeled it with the Areindama lance and began to eat it; and it tasted sweet and delectable. When the *mahti* saw him eating thus with relish, he asked for it and ate it, and lo! it tasted sweet and delectable as the food of spirits. And he thought, 'When this stranger plucketh and giveth it, the sour lime hath a sweet and luscious taste. He is no common man, but a man of glory!' So he bade his niece and caused her to offer him water. And the niece, Thambula, came softly and gave him water and offered him the good food she had made ready. And when he had partaken of the food and drink she offered him, Kyanzittha said, 'Minister to me! I trust my life to thee!' And the *mahti's* niece Thambula consented and ministered to him well.

[*The hair relics.*] Anawrahtaminsaw built a *zigon* pagoda over the sacred hair-relic presented by the Ussa king, and worshipped it. That pagoda he named Mahapeinnè. This is the history of the sacred hairs presented by the Ussa king. King Dwattabaung destroyed the *zedi* built by Balika—one of the two built by the brothers Taphussa and Balika—and taking the four hairs built a *zedi* at Tharehkittara and worshipped it. On the destruction of Tharehkittara the Talaing kings destroyed that *zedi* and removed once more the four hairs. Two hairs they enshrined in the Shwemawdaw pagoda, and one at Kyaikko. One hair was that which the succession of Talaing kings worshipped, keeping it in a gem-embroidered casket in the palace. But it is said in the Nalatadhatuvamsa that Jeyasena the Naga king stole two sacred hairs and that Taphussa and Balika noticed it not, and that while king Kakavanna reigned in the island of Ceylon certain noble saints took them from the place where they lay, hidden in a casket in the belly of the Naga, and enshrined them in the Mahamangala pagoda in lake Seru.

[*Manuha.*] Moreover Anawrahta dedicated Manuha the Talaing king with all his family attendants to the Shwezigon pagoda, his work of merit. Manuha was their head.

[*Anawrahta's women.*] Sawlu was the only son born of Aggamahesi, chief queen of king Anawrahta. The handmaids of queen Aggamahesi were five hundred daughters of chief ministers wearing livery crowned with ruby, and hair done in the *suli* style; five hundred daughters of ministers wearing livery crowned with emerald, and hair done in the *yakin-uyit* style; five hundred daughters of ministers wearing livery crowned with diamond, and hair done in the *yakin-ucha* style. The four daughters of rich men wearing livery crowned with pearl, the fifty humpbacked women, the fifty bandy-legged women, who served the king, all wore necklaces crowned with gold. Moreover he had women as harpists, women to blow trumpets and sound drums, tabors, and castanets; only women might play music before him. Manisanda, daughter of the Ussa king, he named Thirisandadevi and kept her in a jewelled *pyatthad.* The handmaids that surrounded queen Thirisandadevi were three hundred daughters of ministers wearing livery crowned with ruby, and hair done in the *suli* style; three hundred daughters of ministers wearing livery crowned with emerald, and hair done in the *yakin-uyit* style; three hundred daughters of ministers wearing livery crowned with diamond, and hair done in the *yakin-ucha* style. Thirty humpbacked, thirty bandy-legged women wearing livery crowned with gold, women to sound tabors, together with women-drummers, women-harpists, and women-trumpeters, had daily to make music before her.

137. *Of the pahto, gu, and monasteries, dams, channels, reservoirs, and canals, which he wrought and finished wheresoever he went roaming the country with his host of followers.*

[*Anawrahta's forces.*] The host that followed Anawrahtaminsaw, it is said, were thirty and eight white elephants, eight hundred thousand black elephants, eight million horses, one hundred and eighty million fighting men, eight hundred thousand *kyaw* boats, *hlawga, tha* boats, and *hngek* boats. In going the circuit of his country with his followers and visiting the Kala country of Bengal,

he left human images of stone, as well as many figures of tabors,
harps, trumpets, cymbals, tambours, castanets, *muyo* drums, horns
and bugles, flutes and clarinets, with dancers, saying, ' Hereafter
when my great and glorious sons, grandsons, and great-grandsons
come this way, let music be performed !' Thence going throughout
all the parts of Burma he built in every quarter pagodas, *gu*,
monasteries, *tazaung*, and rest-houses, and returned home to
Pugarama. When he arrived, being very faithful in the Lord's
religion, he had the thirty sets of Pitakas copied from the Mun
character into the Burmese character, appealed to noble saints and
had them oftentimes collated, and placed them in a *pyatthad* richly
fraught with gems, and caused them to be taught the noble Order.

[*Dams.*] Moreover, throughout all the parts of Burma, wheresoever
they were needed, he made dams, channels, reservoirs, and canals.
Coming to Lèdwin in the south, he ascended Mt. Thalyaung and
looked, and seeing that it would be a great benefit to all beings for
full five thousand years of the religion to dam up at divers stages
the water falling from the top of Mt. Kayut and make the fields
drink thereof, he and his seventy-two million fighting men made four
dams near the Panyaung river—Kinta, Nganaingthin, Pyaungbya,
and Gumè. These dams together with Nwatek, Kunhse, and
Gutaw on the river Mekhkara, seven in all, Anawrahtaminsaw
made, creating eight hundred thousand *pè* of royal measure.
Kyaussè was made by Narapatisithu of Pagan ; Thintwè dam in
the reign of Shwenanshin of Myinzaing when the Tarops came
to Myinzaing. Hsitaw dam was made by king Swasawkè of
Ava. Ngakyi dam was made later when Myobyè Narapati reigned
in Ava.

[*Frontier towns and fortresses.*] King Anuruddhadeva, having
ascended the throne in the year 379, in his sixteenth year, 395, on
Friday the twelfth waxing of Tabaung, began to build at the self-
same hour these forty-three towns, to prevent mixture with the
Shan Yuns, who dwelt with the Burmese kingdom of Tampadipa
and Kamboja kingdom ruled by Maw kings of the Shan country
of Maw : Kaungsin, Kaungton, Ngayon, Ngayin, Shwegu, Yinhkè,
Mota, Katha, Htikyin, Myataung, Tagaung, Hinmamaw, Kyan-
hnyap, Sampanago, Ngasingu, Konthaya, Magwe, Taya-aung, Ot,
Yenantha, Nagamauk, Yinmatè, Sonmyo, Tonpon, Mattaya,
Thekkèkyin, Wayindot, Taungbyongyi, Myotin, Lahe, Shinmatek,

Mekhkara, Taon, Myinzaing, Myittha, Haingtek, Thagara,
Nyaungyan, Shwemyopeppa, Myohla, Kèlin, Hswa, Baranathi.
Moreover in his own country of Burma he built fortified towns,
chief of which was Theinpya, supplying each a levy of one thousand,
eight hundred, four hundred, three hundred, two hundred, one
hundred, eighty, fifty, thirty or twenty men. When the captain
of the Law made the circuit of the country, a troop of armed
soldiers must follow him, according to the number assigned them.

[*Kalaminyèsishsin builds Haingtek.*] The minister Kalaminyèsishsin was charged to build the forty-three towns beginning with
Kaungsin, Kaungton and ending Taung-u, Kèlin, Hswa, Baranathi.
He was clearing the surface of the ground to build a town, when,
from the north, a tuskless elephant came up and passed along eastward. That day he began to build the town, and because of the
upcoming of the tuskless elephant he named it Haingtek. Later
this minister Myinyèsishsin, builder of the town Haingtek, devised
evil against king Anawrahta and met his punishment and died,
and became a spirit.

[*Anawrahta's pagodas.*] In the year 401, on his return from building the Pawrithat pagoda in Nyaungshwe Intein, king Nawrahta
found that the mot-htaw *zedi*, built by king Dhammasoka over the
relic of the Lord's eye-socket, was in ruins and covered with jungle,
underwood, and thicket. From within the *zedi* a golden fly, as
large as a peafowl, took on radiant colours and wrought miracles;
and the king was glad and built it up again and called it Shweyin-
myaw pagoda. When he returned, his masters of white magic and
learned brahmans, his masters of black magic and learned men
entreated him to enter Haingtek town, and Nawrahtaminsaw
entered it. Therein he built a *zedi* and called it Payahla. Moreover the handmaidens built Yinhla *gu*, Hkankyi *gu*, and Hpaya *gu*.
He built a *gu* and called it Minyè after Minyèsishsin his minister,
founder of towns, who died and became a spirit. North of the
town, moreover, he built a spirit-house for the people to worship.
He kept twenty headmen in twenty villages within the area. The
eleven Lèdwin villages built by Anawrahtaminsaw are these : Pinlè,
Myitmana, Myittha, Myinhkontaing, Yamon, Panan, Mekhkara,
Tabyettha, Thintaung, Tamoshso, and Hkanlu. When thus he
had finished all his dams, channels, reservoirs, and canals, he called
the spirits of trees and of the earth to witness, and planted a palmyra

H

tree at the foot of Mt. Pyek saying 'When I become king once more in Pugarama, let the palmyra seed sprout!'

[*Death of Anawrahta.*] Now a small frog one day croaked under the lodge where the king abode. And king Anawrahta questioned his masters of white magic and black, saying 'What meaneth it, this frog's croaking?' His masters of white magic and black made answer 'The male frog is dead, and the young female frog lamenteth, bearing her husband's corpse upon her back.' And the king questioned them yet again saying 'What meaneth it?' They said 'Great Lord! Verily it means thy ruin at the hands of an enemy! Ere thou enter the homeland of Arimaddana Pugarama, thou shalt enter the happiness of the world of spirits!' Said Anawrahtaminsaw 'Ye utter such words to such a king as I? Ho! minions, make search and see if there be verily a young female frog bearing her husband's corpse upon her back!' So his minions dug up the earth and looked, and lo! there was a female frog bearing her husband's corpse upon her back, and they presented it to the king. But the king waxed exceeding wroth and swelled with royal pride, and he locked iron fetters on his masters of white magic and black and cast them into prison.

Thereafter he mounted the white elephant Thanmyinzwa, and surrounded by seven thousand ministers he returned with his fourfold army to the homeland Pugarama. He reached Pugarama and entered the Tharapaka gate when an hunter came and reported: 'A wild buffalo called Cakkhupala is ravaging Aungtha Myicche, so that the people dare not go abroad.' And the moral *karma* of the king's former acts was exhausted; and having entered the Tharapaka gate so far as the elephant's right foot, yet he entered not the palace, but turned back with his followers, to the end that he might charge and kill the buffalo with his elephant, and so he marched to Myicche Aungtha. When he came and saw the buffalo, he opened the goad and let loose Thanmyinzwa upon whose back he was riding. But that buffalo was not of natural kind, but because of the evil *karma* of his past acts had become a buffalo; wherefore he charged and reached over the back of the royal elephant and gored the king to death. The seven thousand ministers and the host of fighting men that followed after, broke up and scattered in confusion.

This is the story of that wild buffalo. It was an enemy in

a previous life, and had become a *lein* tree-spirit dwelling in a *lein* tree. Anawrahtaminsaw marching to the Tarop country came to the *lein* tree, and said, 'Lo! I, the king, have come. Yet this *lein* tree-spirit cometh not down from the *lein* tree, but behold, there he is, abiding therein! Shall it be ever so?' And he made Kyanzittha strike him with the Areindama cane. Now the spirit had not the power to defend himself, for it was a cane given by Sakra, but he trembled and came down and fled. From that day forth he plotted only evil against Anawrahta. While the king's moral *karma* was strong his plots availed not, but when the king's evil *karma* gave him occasion they availed him, insomuch that the king died.

Now the *lein* tree-spirit and the Naga snatched the king's body, and there was war. Then Sakra took and buried it on Mt. Gandhamadana. Elsewhere it is written that it was buried on Mt. Vepula. The place on the hill-top east of Mt. Tangyi, where the Naga and the spirit snatched the royal corpse, is still known as Mt. Lu.

[*Extent of his kingdom.*] Anawrahtaminsaw was a king full of glory, might of arm, and dominion, and these were the boundaries of his kingdom: westward, the Kala country Pateikkara; in the north-west corner, Kadu-nganagyi-yedwinmi; northward, the Tarop country, also called Gandhala; in the north-east corner, the Panthe country, also called Kavanti; eastward, the Pinka country known as Sadeittha; in the south-east corner the country of the Gywans, also known as Arawsa. When he wished to march upon another country he marshalled his four hundred thousand *kattu* and *lunkyin* boats, and his four million *hlawga* and *kyaw* boats. He marshalled the latter east and west towards the upper country. On the east side of the river, it is said, they reached from Pugarama to the site of Ava. Moreover, when he marshalled them on the west side of the river it is said they reached from Taungponnyaunghla to Sagaing. His four hundred thousand *kattu* and *lunkyin* boats of war he marshalled east and west towards the lower country. When he marshalled them on the east side from Pugarama it is said they reached even to Tharehkittara. When he marshalled them on the west side also from Taungponnyaunghla it is said they reached even to Prome Hpo-u-maw.

Thus this noble king, full of glory, might of arm, and dominion, who for full thirty-three years of royal prosperity had advanced the welfare of the religion, his own welfare, and that of the generations of his sons, grandsons, and great-grandsons, died at the age of seventy-five. Thirty-three years he was in the nether house; he flourished for forty-two. About the time of his death bees clave to the throne door of the palace; an ogre laughed from the top of the Tharaba gate; the lustre of the royal sword faded; a vulture alighted on the palace; the *deinnetthè* coincided with the *thingyan*. The day of his birth was Tuesday.

138. *Of king Sawlu.*

[*Sawlu's infancy.*] In the year 421 his son Sawlu became king. When he was a babe, and the feeding ceremony was held, Sawlu ate not the egg made ready at the head of the repast, but ate one placed beneath it. When the wise saw it, they said, 'During his reign the royal line will break!'

[*His queens.*] Soon after king Sawlu ascended the throne the queen Uhsauppan ended her *karma*; so to Thirisandadevi, daughter of the Ussa king, he gave the name Hkin-u and the place of Uhsauppan.

[*His treatment of Kyanzittha.*] Now Shin Arahan and all the ministers and headmen of villages and circles spake unto the king, saying, 'Kyanzittha is one who should not be parted from thy side. Recall him from hiding and wandering as the wind!' So king Sawlu sent for him. Now Kyanzittha commanded Thambula, niece of the *mahti*, who was with child, saying, 'When the child within thee is born, if it be a girl, sell this ring and nourish her with the price thereof. If a boy is born, bring the son and the ring.' And he came to Pugarama and attached himself to king Sawlu. One day because the concubines said that he had speech once more with queen Hkin-u, his provincial prosperity was forfeited, and he was sent back to Dala in the lower country. And the ministers said, 'Great king! when once thy father was wroth with him and he hid, thou wast fain to recall him. Now that thou, great king, art wroth with him and he is kept in Dala, it is not meet that he be parted from thy side. Let him be recalled forthwith!' So king Sawlu was mindful of the government of villages and the kingdom, and recalled him, and when he returned he gave him his old provincial prosperity.

[*Nga Ramankan's Revolt.*] Moreover, he gave the town of Ussa

Pegu to Nga Ramankan, his tutor's son. One day the king and
Nga Ramankan played at dice, and Nga Ramankan won, and
he rose up and clapped his elbows. Said king Sawlu, 'Thou hast
won a mere game of dice, and dost thou arise and clap thine
elbows? If thou art a man, rebel with Pegu thy province!' 'In
sooth?' asked Nga Ramankan. 'We kings,' quoth the king,
'should we utter aught but sooth?'

[*The Battle of Pyedawtha.*] Now Nga Ramankan had been
plotting already, and he went to Pegu his province and collecting
a force of soldiers and an host of elephants and horses he advanced
on Pugarama by water and land. Before he reached it he abode
encamped at the island of Pyedawtha. When king Sawlu heard
that Nga Ramankan had marched as far as the island of Pyedawtha
he straightway sent forth Kyanzittha with a large force of soldiers
and an host of elephants and horses, and the king marched after
with the rearguard. Now Nga Ramankan thought: 'Kyanzittha
is skilful in war. Victory will not be easy save by crooked ways
and stratagems.' Thus laying it to heart, with strips of bamboo he
fashioned false arrays of elephants and horses, and placed them
in swampy and muddy places, and set howdahs thereon, and framed
also human figures to hold ·shields of every kind, round and
embossed, oblong and convex.

King Sawlu and Kyanzittha encamped when they reached the
island of Pyedawtha, saying, 'It is too late to-day. To-morrow we
shall fight.' Then in the dim moonlight Nga Ramankan came
forth and provoked them to do battle; so they followed and fought
without heed or observation. And the king, thinking that an
elephant-figure set in the mud was a real elephant, set forth to
fight, and Thanmyinzwa, the royal elephant he was riding, fell into
the mud and stuck. And king Sawlu climbed down from his back
and ran, and entering a hole in a banyan tree in the forest abode
there. And Thanmyinzwa was captured, and the whole army was
despoiled and fled; there was none to stop them.

[*Kyanzittha's flight.*] Now Kyanzittha rode all night on horseback from Taungkwin and reached Pugarama early in the morning.
And the chief ministers and councillors who abode in Pugarama
said to Kyanzittha, 'When our lord king Sawlu is not, there is no
other king to reign over us than thou!' And they opened him
the gate and gave him the five royal emblems. But Kyanzittha

said, ' I will see first whether my lord the king is or is not. If my lord liveth I will take and set him on the throne.' So he placed the royal emblems which the ministers had offered him in front of the Shwezigon.

[*Capture of Sawlu.*] Now Nga Ramankan said, 'I must not slacken till I seize Sawlu and Kyanzittha!' So he mustered his forces and tarried awhile, securely building up a great army. Meantime the king Sawlu had eaten nothing for three meals and was exceeding hungry; and he came out of the hole in the banyan and met a soldier of Nga Ramankan gathering fuel, and lo! he was eating his rice. 'Take thou this priceless ring', said the king, 'and give me thy rice bundle. But tell none that thou hast found me!' So shut he his mouth, and the fuel-gatherer gave him his rice bundle and said, 'Eat!' King Sawlu ate and abode there, entering the hole in the banyan. And the fuel-gatherer went away with the ring in his waistband. When he reached the army he could not refrain from showing it to his comrades, asking ' Of what value is it?' Now it was a priceless ring; so at last Nga Raman came to hear thereof, and when he had taken and looked at it he knew it to be Sawlu's ring; and he examined the fuel-gatherer by torture, placing him in a press. And the fuel-gatherer was in grievous pain and answered according to the truth, and thus Sawlu was captured and kept in bonds.

[*Kyanzittha tries to rescue him.*] Then Nga Raman took Sawlu and came up by water and land and abode encamped with a great army at Myinkaba. And Kyanzittha said, 'I will steal my lord and set him on the throne!' And he stole him from the place where he was kept. Now while Kyanzittha bare him on his shoulder Sawlu thought, ' Kyanzittha is one whom my father hath injured, whom I have injured. Methinks he stealeth me to kill me! But Nga Raman is son of my tutor and with me hath sucked together the same breasts. Surely he will not kill me!' And he cried aloud, ' Kyanzittha is stealing me!' And Kyanzittha forsook him, saying, ' Vile king! Foul king! Stay then to die at the hands of the Talaings a dog's death, a pig's death!'

[*Kyanzittha's escape.*] Now the soldiers of Nga Raman followed quickly and surrounded him, and he went down into the water and swam westward. And seeing him aweary, the Mahagiri spirit created him an island and cried with the voice of a *myittwe* bird.

And when Kyanzittha ascended the islet and rested, the Mahagiri
spirit took the guise of fishermen, father and son, and conveyed
him in a small *tanswek* boat to the bank at Aungtha. When he
reached the farther bank at Aungtha he crossed to Kyahkapwara
and went north to seek for the hunter Nga Sin.

[*The headman of Ngahtihlaing.*] When he came to Ngahtihlaing
he asked for cucumber from the plantation worked by the village-
headman of Ngahtihlaing. Now the Htihlaing headman was a
man of great strength; he had no door to his garden but a fence
of thorns as high as an elephant, and he went in and out by leaping it. Said he to Kyanzittha, 'If thou canst enter like me by
leaping, thou mayest eat my cucumber!' And Kyanzittha entered
leaping with the help of his lance and plucked and ate of the
cucumber and strung some together with a creeper and came out
leaping over the thorn-fence, as high as an elephant. Seeing it,
the village-headman of Ngahtihlaing thought, 'This is no common
man. He is one great and glorious. It were well surely to trust
my life to him!' And he offered him his daughter; she had
beauty and the signs great and small; and he himself served him
as his slave. Thenceforth Kyanzittha was known as Htihlaingshin.

[*The hunter Nga Sin.*] So he abode at Htihlaing village and
mustered his forces and sought for the hunter Nga Sin. And the
hunter Nga Sin, hearing that Kyanzittha sought for him, was
afraid, and he crossed to Ngasinku and fled. The place is still
known as Ngasinku. The place where he split the cutch and made
himself a bow is still known as Shahkwe. The place where Kyanzittha made search for him is still known as Sheinpaka. The place
where Nga Sin, the hunter, was caught is still known as Ngasinkaing. Htihlaingshin Kyanzittha, when he had won the Htihlaing
headman and the hunter Nga Sin, mustered his forces and held court
in eleven villages in the south. Nga Htihlaing held court at Ngahtihlaing; the place is still known as Ngahtihlaing. The place in
the south where Nga Sin the hunter held court with his army is
still known as Ngasinkaing.

[*Magic rites at Lèdwin.*] Now all the horsemen and footmen
and elephantry approached Kyanzittha because of the prophecy
made of old by the wise that Kyanzittha would be king. And the
Htihlaing monk Shin Poppa performed many magical rites. This
is how he performed them. He recited charms over minium and

cinnabar and drew figures of the sun and moon on the frontlets of
elephants, on saddle pommels, on shields of every kind, round and
embossed, oblong and convex, and on standards of war, and surrounded them with magic charms and sorceries. When he had
prepared them he piled them in rows at Lèdwin.

[*Nga Ramankan kills Sawlu.*]   Now when Nga Ramankan found
Sawlu after Kyanzittha had forsaken him, he put him to death at
Anuradha, where the head of Pyuminhti's great bird was buried.
Thereafter he advanced by water and land, thinking, ' Now I shall
rule in the city of Pugarama ! '   But the ministers and headmen of
villages had spoken : ' Lo ! Kyanzittha ruleth the eleven Lèdwin
villages. We may not yet open the gate. It will be like two
buffaloes wallowing in one pond. Let him not be king till he hath
fought and conquered Kyanzittha ! '   So they abode in security
and opened not the city gate.

[*His defeat and death.*]   Then Nga Raman came up country by
water and land, saying, ' I must first compass the ruin of Kyanzittha ! '   He abode at the site of Ava and built up a great army
on water and land.   And Kyanzittha, when he had performed divers
rites of magic, fought with all his host; and the soldiers of Nga
Raman were sore afraid, as though he would eat their flesh ; and
the mighty battle was broken. Nga Raman mounted the golden
raft of the nine gems and fled. And all Kyanzittha's fighting men
pursued him. When he reached Myinkaba south of Pugarama, he
encamped and made another stand. And Htihlaingshin Kyanzittha abode on the hill of Shwezigon and built up a mighty army.
Therefore Nga Ramankan durst not stand longer at Myinkaba, but
fled down country with the golden raft of the nine gems. And
when Kyanzittha knew it he sent Nga Sin the hunter to follow and
dispatch him. And Nga Sin the hunter caught him up below
Ywatha ; and he climbed a fig-tree and uttered lovely notes like the
voice of a bird. When Nga Raman heard that sound he opened
the window of the golden raft and looked saying, ' What bird is
that, uttering notes so sweet and wonderful ? '   Now he had but
one good eye ; and Nga Sin the hunter, from the place where he
waited peeping, drew his bow and shot. And it hit the eye of
Nga Raman, and he died. The place is still known as Ngasinku.

[*Sawlu*, fl. A.D. 1059–1064.]   King Sawlu had the power neither
to devise a thing nor to perform it. It was his wont to act so as

to grieve the hearts of his ministers and councillors. The Shwezigon, which his father left unfinished, he builded not. He hearkened
not to the words of the wise, but lived only for enjoyment. Forty-
one years in the nether house, five years he flourished ; he passed at
the age of forty-six. About the time of his death smoke issued
from the Pahtodawgyi ; the Thursday star fought with the Saturday star. The day of his birth was Wednesday.

139. *Of king Htihlaingshin Kyanzittha.*

[*Kyanzittha's palace.*]   In the year 426 Htihlaingshin Kyanzittha
became king. When he had become king he built a palace and
dwelt there, deeming the site a fair one, with Anawrahtaminsaw's
palace on the east, on the north the grave of the skull of the great
bird that lived in the time of Pyuminhti, on the west the *moth-taw*.
When he ascended the throne he worshipped the spirits.]

[*His queens.*]   His queens were these : first, Apèyatana ; second,
Hkin-u, daughter of the Ussa king ; third, Hkintan, daughter of
Htihlaing, village-headman ; fourth, Thambula, niece of the *mahti*.
She came to him later and he gave her the title Uhsauppan and
made her queen. Of these queens, Apèyatana, the chief queen,
gave birth to a daughter Shwe-einthi, queen Uhsauppan to a son.

[*Shwe-einthi and the prince of Pateikkara.*]   Now the king loved
his daughter Shwe-einthi and he kept her in a palace with a single
post. When the prince of Pateikkara heard thereof, he set in his
mouth a live gem and came through the sky : and when he had
come he gave the Kyanthaing ministers who guarded her a bribe of
ten baskets of silver, and became familiar with Shwe-einthi. And
Htihlaingshin heard thereof and he called his ministers and consulted them, saying, ' Whether should I marry my daughter to the
prince of Pateikkara or to Sawyun, my master's grandson ? '   Thus
made he comparisons. And his ministers answered, ' Great king !
If thy daughter wed the prince of Pateikkara, ere-long this will be
nought but a Kala country ! '   And the king said, ' Sawlu's son
Sawyun is halt in his feet and cannot walk ! '   Nevertheless he
gave him her in marriage and made him heir.

Thereafter as Shin Arahan was going to worship at Mahabodhi
he met the prince of Pateikkara coming through the sky with the
live gem in his mouth, and he accosted him saying, ' Prince, thou
shouldest not go. Shwe-einthi hath been given in marriage to

Sawyun!' 'Ha!' quoth the prince, opening his mouth; and the live gem slipped out of his mouth, and he fell from the sky and perished. Some chronicles say that he came through the sky by means of a ruby-ring, and meeting Shin Arahan and hearing that Shwe-einthi was married to Sawyun he starved himself and died saying, ' Let me die if I cannot get her whom I love!' And Shin Arahan, who had been his fellow-worshipper in a former life, gathered and kept the bones of the prince of Pateikkara at the place called Wa.

[*Birth of Alaungsithu.*] Soon after his death the womb of Shwe-einthi conceived, and when the tale of months and days were fulfilled a prince was born; and lo! the throne-door opened and the great Einshin drum sounded of itself without any one striking it. From the day of his birth the prince cried violently and would not hold his peace. And king Htihlaing questioned his masters of white magic and black, saying, ' What meaneth my grandson's crying?' And they answered, ' O king, he crieth because he is fain to know the boundaries of the kingdom.' When he heard their words of answer, he wrote thus on gold palmyra : ' Eastward the Panthe country, also called Sateittha; south-eastward the country of the Gywans, also called Ayoja; southward Nagapat Island in mid-ocean; south-westward the Kala country, also known as Pateikkara; in the north-west corner Katu-nganagyi-yepawmi; northward the Tarop country, also called Gandhala.' The prince, it is said, ceased not his crying until they read aloud in his presence the writing on the gold palmyra. And when his grandsire saw the miracle, he said, ' Let me wait as an heir for my grandson's palace!' And he took the babe in his bosom and ascended the throne and anointed him king with the title Thirizeyathura.

[*Kala captives.*] At the time of his anointing the king's generals brought him Kyikala prisoners of war, saying, ' We have conquered the Kala country with Thandaung and Ngathonpinlè.' And he made the Kalas live in quarters at Singu.

[*The fellow-worshippers.*] In a former life the future Htihlaing-shin was a king, the future Thirizeyathu, the king's grandson, was a prince, the future Shin Arahan was a brahman, the future Mahagiri spirit was a rich man's son, and the future Thekminkaton was a general. While the future Htihlaingshin was king, these five all went to the pagoda and worshipped. And the prince

prayed thus : ' In a future life may I be a glorious king ! '   And
the son of the brahman prayed : ' May I be a monk whom kings
shall worship ! '   And the son of the rich man prayed : ' May I be
a spirit whom kings shall worship ! '   The general prayed : ' May
I be a king, a fellow-builder of empire ! '   And the future Htihlaingshin prayed : ' May I be the lord and governor of these four,
wheresoever they be born ! '   And according as these five had
prayed, even so it came to pass : the king became king Htihlaingshin,
the prince Thirizeyathura, the brahman Shin Arahan, the rich
man's son the Mahagiri spirit, the general Thekminkaton.

[*Thekminkaton.*]   One day it was told king Htihlaingshin that
Thekminkaton was come troubling the border villages.   And the
king set apart a great number of fighting men and elephants and
horses to hunt Thekminkaton until they caught him.   Then Shin
Arahan preached before the king and told him of what had been of
yore, and he said, ' O king, sin not against thy friend who prayed
with thee in thy former life ! '

[*The Mahagiri spirit.*]   Likewise the Mahagiri spirit showed
himself and forbade the king.   Then said king Htihlaingshin,
' If the Mahagiri spirit prayed with me of yore, why helped he me
not when I was in misery ? '   And the Mahagiri spirit answered :
' O king, when Anawrahtaminsaw tied thee with a rope and thrust
at thee with his spear, and by my help the blow fell on the rope
that bound thee and it snapped and thou, O king, went free, who
helped thee but I ? '   ' True ! ' said Htihlaing Kyanzittha, ' I knew
not that the spirit helped me.'   Said the Mahagiri spirit : ' When
the battle brake in Taunghkwin and thou, O king, didst flee in the
darkness of the night, who but I went before thee on a striped
horse, dressed in a monitor skin, and shewed thee the way ? '
' True ! ' said the king, ' I knew not that it was the spirit.'   Said
the Mahagiri spirit : ' When thou stolest Sawlu and men pursued
thee, and thou wast aweary and couldst swim no longer, who but
I created an islet and cried like the *myittwe* bird ?   Who but I, in
the guise of fishermen, father and son, conveyed thee to the farther
bank at Aungtha in a small *tanswek* boat ? '   ' True ! ' said the
king, ' I knew not that it was the spirit.'   So Shin Arahan
admonished Thekminkaton and stilled the war.

[*The coming of Thambula.*]   Now Thambula, niece of the *mahti*,
had of old been warned by the king : ' If a son be born, come

bringing me the son and the ring.' When the king had reigned
two years she came leading her son by the hand ; and he was seven
years old. When she came to Pugarama king Htihlaingshin had
his marshalls of war in audience, and she durst not go up into the
palace but abode before it and walked up and down, north and
south, holding her son by the hand. And the king's minions
sought to drive her away, saying, ' Woman ! Our Lord the king
cometh forth. Tarry not here, but begone ! ' But Thambula said,
' I have need to speak unto the king. First let me speak ! ' and
she abode and departed not. And the king's minions spoke of it to
the king. So he called her in ; and when he saw Thambula and
her son he spake in the midst of his ministers saying, ' Great
favour, verily, hath this lady shewn me ! ' And he called his son
and took him to his bosom, and he said, ' Men say that the
son cometh first and the grandson last. Yet but now I have
anointed my grandson king, and lo ! the grandson is first and
the son last ! ' Thereafter he appointed Thambula, niece of the
mahti, his queen with the title Uhsauppan, and gave her son
the name of Zeyahkittara and made him ruler of Dhaññavati and
the seven hill-tracts.

[*Nagayon and Apèyatana pagodas.*] Once when Sawlu was wroth
with him, and his prosperity and followers were forfeited, king
Htihlaingshin slept alone in a grazing-ground for horses; and
while he slept a young Naga came and watched over him. At
that place, when he became king, he built the Nagayon pagoda.
At the place called Apèyatana he built a *gu* and called it Apèyatana.

[*Shin Arahan and Kyanzittha.*] In a former life Shin Arahan
was a monk, and king Htihlaingshin a puppy who followed the
monk wheresoever he went. One day the puppy died, and the
monk in pity gathered the bones and kept them in an heap. At
the place where the heap of bones lay a tree had grown, and whenever the tree shook in the breeze the king's head suffered pain.
Though all his masters of magic treated him with medicine he
might not be relieved. When Shin Arahan heard of it he preached
before the king and told him of what had been of yore; and he
took the bones and gave them to the king, who buried them well.

140. *Of the rebuilding of Shwezigon pagoda, Anawrahtaminsaw's work
of merit, by king Htihlaingshin Kyanzittha.*

[*Shin Arahan's remonstrance.*] Now Shin Arahan spake thus to the king: 'O king, Anawrahtaminsaw built the *zigon* over the relics of the Lord's frontlet and the tooth. He finished not the work wholly, but he finished only the three terraces. His son Sawlu became king and lived only in the enjoyment of worldly pleasures; he furthered not his father's work of merit. And now thou hast become king and received the heritage of Anawrahtaminsaw; and thou too delightest only in pleasures, and takest no thought to finish Anawrahtaminsaw's work of merit!' Thus he derided him.

[*The completion of Shwezigon pagoda.*] So Htihlaingshin made promise to finish the king's work of merit. This is how he strove to build Shwezigon pagoda. First, he had the rocks of Mt. Tuywin hewn and split into blocks three spans in length, one span in breadth. Then he assembled all his soldiers throughout the kingdom and drew them up in two lines opposite each other from Shwezigon pagoda even to Mt. Tuywin; and thus they passed from hand to hand the rocks which had been split and hewn. Now in passing them the men were sorely troubled by the sun's heat; and when the king saw it he planted tamarind seeds, on each side a row, from Shwezigon even to Mt. Tuywin; and he made a solemn vow, and said: 'If I am a king worthy to receive the Lord's inheritance, let this tamarind seed sprout even here and give shelter to men!' And lo! in one night the tamarind seeds grew so high that men could take shelter.

Sakra in the guise of a master mason hewed and split the rocks. And when they made mud into mortar and it did not set, Sakra made ready mortar of lime and fresh cow's milk, and at last it set. The king, it is said, gave silver and bought milk, one thousand pails a day, from the rich men throughout all the kingdom. During the daytime only, men worked and finished just one circle of the spire; and at night the spirits worked, it is said, and finished two circles. Sakra with his own hand began and finished the lion figure at the south-east corner; with his own hand he overlaid the pagoda with plaster, and that plaster was eight hands in thickness.

Htihlaingshin Kyanzittha is said to have rebuilt and finished Shwezigon pagoda in seven months and seven days. When it was finished he was rapt with joy and gladness, and he said, 'I have received the Lord's inheritance!'; and he boasted, 'The prayer

I have uttered shall verily be fulfilled!' Shwezigon pagoda is famous in the world of men and the world of spirits as far as the world of Brahmas. After it was finished, Sakra, it is said, was ever wont to come down on the *pavarana* day and visit it.

[*Building of the Ananda.*] One day eight noble saints stood for alms at the king's palace. And the king took the bowl and fed them with food, and asked, 'Whence come ye?' And they said, 'From Mt. Gandhamadana.' Now king Htihlaingshin was full of faith, and he built and offered the saints a monastery for the rainy season. He invited them to the palace and fed them with food continually during the three months of rain. Once he entreated them to call up by their power the likeness of Nandamula grotto on Mt. Gandhamadana. And they did so. And king Htihlaingshin made a great *gu* after the likeness of Nandamula grotto, and called it Nanda. The Nanda Mawgun tells how the Nanda pagoda was designed and built.

[*Other pagodas of Kyanzittha.*] When he had built the works of merit above recorded, nine sacred relics of the Lord's body arrived from the Ceylon king. He built a *pahto* and called it Minochantha. Moreover, he built a *gu* at each of the places where the lance fell when he played with it, while he was in hiding in the north. At Ngasinkaing also he built pagodas, one at the top and one at the foot of the mountain; the pagoda at the foot was called Hseippauk because there he threw his lance and it reached even to the landing-place; the pagoda at the top was known as Mingyaung. At the site of Ava also he built a *zigon* and called it Htihlaingshin. Moreover, he built a *zigon* in Pareimma his birthplace. He played with his lance at the place where he had converse with the Mahagiri spirit, and also to the south and the west, and wherever the lance fell he built a *gu*. Many were the pagodas, *gu*, monasteries, *tazaung*, resthouses, and ordination halls besides, which he built throughout all the kingdom. Furthermore, he dedicated five great bells cast in solid copper, each one thousand *adula* in weight: three at Shwezigon pagoda, one at Nanda pagoda, one at Minochantha pagoda.

[*His death.*] Such works of merit he amassed, and passed at the age of seventy-two. Forty-four years in the nether house, twenty-eight years he flourished; he passed at the age of seventy-two. About the time of his death three ogres appeared on the top of the *pyatthad*. The Tuesday star fought with the Saturday star. The day of his birth was Tuesday.

141. *Of king Alaungsithu.*

[*Alaungsithu's birth.*] In the year 454 his grandson Alaungsithu became king. He was born on a Thursday. At the time of his birth the great Einshin drum gave forth sounds of itself without any one striking it: the throne-door opened of itself without any one opening it. King Htihlaingshin, the grandsire, taking the grandson to his bosom, said, ' I wait as an heir for my grandson's palace, meet only for an Alaung ! ' And he anointed and raised him to be king with the name Thirizeyathu.

[*His names and titles.*] Thus on account of the sounds issuing from the great Einshin drum, some chronicles call him Alaungsishu. Moreover they call him Shwegudayaka, because he first built the Shwegu pagoda after he became king. And they call him Thirizeyathura, the name given him by his grandsire. They also call him Chettawshi, because his navel issued about a span when he cried as a babe. They call him too by the title Siritaribhavanadityapavarapanditasudhammarajamahadhipatinarapatisithu, given by Sakra at the foot of the rose-apple tree. They call him in *thamaing* and *mawgun* Narapatisithu, taking the final syllables in the original name given by Sakra. They call him Alaungsithu in some chronicles because of the words spoken by the Shinbyu image when it fell into Balavamukkha and exclaimed ' Alaungsithu, take me ! '

[*His queens.*] The king had four wives, Yadanabon, Tilawkasanda, Razakommari, and Taungpyinthi ; these four were anointed queens. Queen Yadanabon gave birth to Minshinsaw. Queen Tilawkasanda, who afterwards was given the title Uhsauppan, gave birth to Htaukhlega. Queen Razakommari had no son nor daughter. Two daughters were born of queen Taungpyinthi, the elder called Taunghpya and the younger Shwekyu. The sister of queen Taungpyinthi had had four husbands ; because her husbands failed not ere long to die, she was raised to be queen with the name Hkin-u. She had four daughters by her late husbands. Sawnan, daughter of the first husband, was Rajathu's wife. Eindawthi, daughter of the second husband, was Kinkathu's wife. Sigon, daughter of the third husband, was Narathu's wife.

Kyaungdawthi, daughter of the youngest husband, ended her *karma* before marriage. The mother, when Alaungsithu raised her to be queen, again gave birth to Chit-u and Kyaungdawthi. The king gave his four daughters each a sea-shell full of dust of gold, and they dissolved it in ointment of sandalwood and fragrant perfumes and anointed themselves.

[*Mahathaman.*] One day the king's brother-in-law Mahathaman rode his elephant up to the palace and brought it along the stairway and was mounting up when the Mahagiri spirit saw him and threatened him saying, ' Durst thou in my presence bring dishonour and reproach upon my friend ? ' Mahathaman trembled when the spirit threatened him, and he and the elephant were flung afar. Now when they knew of it the wise said, ' In the reign of this king there shall be many rebels in divers parts of the country '.

[*Decoits in the palace.*] In the year 456, while he was reigning, more than an hundred thieves and cut-throats entered the palace, and peace was not restored until the people of the inner palace and the chamberlains, hearing of it, came to the rescue and smote and thrust with spear and cutlass. At the very door leading to the royal throne three men were slain, and with the filth and bloodshed the palace was not fit to behold. Some of the thieves and cut-throats fled and escaped, and the ghosts of their dead appeared thereafter and affrighted the people at night. It is said they threw dry dung, made water on them, forced the Tharaba gate, and opened the door of the south airy palace and affrighted the people. This has been told in accordance with the chronicle prepared by the famous Shin Godhavara, who was the first to ascend Hngeppyittaung.

[*The king's teachers.*] There were four teachers to instruct the king—Shin Arahan, the elder the son of Seinnyekmin, Shin Ananda, and the Mahagiri spirit.

[*The queens' handmaids.*] The handmaids that surrounded each of the four wives of Alaungsithu were these : three hundred daughters of ministers wearing livery crowned with emerald, their hair done in the *suli* style ; three hundred daughters of ministers wearing livery crowned with diamond, their hair done in the *uyit* style ; three hundred daughters of ministers wearing livery crowned with ruby, their hair done in *ucha* style ; three hundred daughters of ministers wearing livery crowned with pearl, their hair done in the *yakin* style ; thirty hump-backed, thirty bandy-

legged women; four witty maids, daughters of rich men, together
with women-drummers, women-harpists, and women-trumpeters,
whom he caused continually to make music before the four queens.

[*The king's armies and boats.*] King Alaungsithu's armies, it is
said, were these: threescore thousand captains, thirty-two white
elephants, eight hundred thousand black elephants, eight million
horses, eight million boats, one hundred and sixty million soldiers.
These are the names of the twelve royal boats for making the
circuit of the kingdom with his armies: Thonlupuzaw, Thonlukya-
hngan, Pyigyinaung, Vazirathinhka, Aungthatago, Moaukkyè,
Swèle-yathit, Nawarat, Pyigyiwun, Tinyapyizon, Linzin, and
Nagakye.

[*His public works.*] The king, surrounded by his queens and concubines and an host of ministers, visited the south and north of
Burma. He made reservoirs, canals, dams, and channels. He fixed
the measure of the cubit and the *ta*. He marked off fields with
the *pè* measure. Wherever food availed he settled his soldiers and
the host of elephants and horses. Having thus joined up the
divers parts of his territory he made a colony and fortress wherever
they were needed. Moreover, desiring that the colonies and forts
throughout the country should use in merchandise one standard of
weights and measures, he fixed the standard of the tical, two anna,
and one anna weights, and others, as well as the measures of *tin*,
hkwè, seit, sayut, pyi, hkwek, and *salè*. Thus dealt he with the forts
and colonies. And that the religion might last five thousand years
for the benefit of all beings, he built many ordination halls and
pagodas, monasteries and *zigon, pahto, gu*, &c. Furthermore, he
planted outposts far and near wherever his country adjoined other
countries.

[*His journey to the coast.*] Then longed he to behold the divers
marvels of the great deep; and, having appointed guards to watch
the homeland Pugarama, he took an image of the Lord cast in gold
of his own weight, together with queen and concubine, and went
down to the coast by water and land. When he reached the
Talaing country he entered the Kyelaung stream, and having
built a royal refectory at Bassein and left queen and concubine
therein, he embarked upon a ship and sailed, surrounded by eight
million boats.

[*The glass-image of the Naga.*] And he came to the end of

Mt. Tangyi: and there, on a rock-mat as large as a *pè* of land, was an image of the Naga king made of glass, which appeared to human eyes like the sun-king. For when the rays of the sun were bright upon it, the glass reflected the rays until it seemed a second sun, and the lustre of the glass threw a white shimmering radiance over the whole ocean. And the king lifted up his hand to screen his eyes. Now he wore on his forefinger a ring of live emerald given by Sakra, and lo! the radiance of the emerald quenched the radiance of the glass and overspread it, so that the host of ministers that followed might see the image of the serpent king of the Nagas. He called the *thingyan* at that place, and thence he passed towards the golden rose-apple tree.

[*The stone musicians.*] Now when he saw the stone images with the five instruments of music slung about them, which his deceased great-grandsire Anawrahtaminsaw had left behind him in his wanderings over the country, he asked what images they were. His masters of white magic and black made answer: 'They are stone images, O king, which thy great-grandsire Anawrahtaminsaw left behind him saying "When my sons and grandsons roam over the country and visit this place, strike ye the drums and harps and tambours, and blow ye the trumpets!"' So the king commanded them saying 'Lo! I have come. Why strike ye not nor blow?' Thereupon the stone images struck and blew as if they were alive.

[*Visit to Ceylon.*] Thence he passed and came to the island of Ceylon. The Ceylon king offered him his daughter Saw-uhtwe together with a great *thinkanek* boat that held eight hundred thousand men. Moreover, he offered for the king to worship an image ever worshipped by Ceylon kings, in the likeness of Shin Mahakassapa practising ascetic attitudes.

[*The golden rose-apple tree.*] He put the image that was offered him on the *thinkanek* boat, and embarked, and came to the golden rose-apple tree. When he reached it he saw, at the foot of the rose-apple tree, the rock-mat whereon the Buddhas sate, fair as a shell new polished. He longed in his heart to sit thereon, and sought counsel of his masters of white magic and black. But they made answer, 'It is not meet to sit there. Peradventure it is the seat of Buddhas. Place thereon thine headdress; but first make this solemn vow—If this be verily the seat of Buddhas, may the headdress which I set thereon be consumed like a fowl's feather

cast upon a fire!' And the king did even as his masters of white
magic and black had told him, and lo! in a moment the headdress was consumed like cotton cast upon a fire. And when he
saw it he was of good cheer and tarried, holding a great festival
for full seven months.

[*Gifts of Sakra.*] Then Sakra said, 'This king is one who
upholdeth the Lord's religion'; and he anointed him king and
bestowed a title also, to wit, Siritaribhavanadityapavarapanditasudhammarajamahadhipatinarapatisithu. Moreover, he gave him
the *hmyauk* drum used by kings, and small cymbals and articles
of royal pomp and splendour. Furthermore, he wrought and offered
him an image of the Lord made from the rock-mat, seat of
Buddhas, shaped like the prow of the *thekkatan*; the image was
known as Shinbyu. He also offered a dexter branch of the golden
rose-apple tree, and carved an image of the Lord out of the stump
of the branch and offered it; the image was called Shinhla.

[*The king may not go to Mt. Meru.*] Now the king desired to go
thence and visit Mt. Meru; he made all things ready. When
Sakra knew of it he beset the king with divers lets and winding
words, saying, 'The king thinketh to reach a place that none can
reach!' Therefore he offered him six relics of the Lord's body,
and appeared visibly before him, and he said, 'Much yet remaineth
for thee to do, O king, to fulfil the great religion. It is not meet
for thee to go to Mt. Meru.' So king Alaungsithu left that place
and returned homewards.

[*Balavamukkha.*] And as he voyaged, he came upon the Balavamukkha, and suddenly the *thinkanek* boat whereon he sate shivered
as though about to break in sunder, insomuch that the Shinbyu
image offered by Sakra was thrown off and fell into the water.
Then king Alaungsithu made a solemn vow, and said, 'If I am
verily to gain the noble boon I ask, may Manimekhala and the
other spirits take my boat out of danger to a place of refuge!'
Thereupon all the spirits and ogres bare the royal boat and brought
it from Balavamukkha to a place of refuge. But the king was
sorry because the Shinbyu image was thrown out. Now a pair
of Brahmani ducks joined their wings and caught it as it fell,
and there it abode in pious attitude, and cried, 'Alaungsithu, take
me!' So the king took the Shinbyu image and worshipped it.
Thereafter he was known as Alaungsithu.

[*The Ogress of Mallayu Island.*] Thence he passed to Mallayu Island. And all the spirits and ogres watched him, in host so many that the shore bent beneath their weight. And an ogress also watched him, holding her comely son. So intently did she watch him that her son slipped from her hand and fell. And the ogress entreated him, saying, ' Surely in looking at thee, O king, my son slipped from my hand and fell. Oh! save my son and restore him!' And the king said, ' Lo! I, the king, have come. The son of the ogress fell as she watched my coming. Yet Manimekhala and the other spirits have not saved nor restored him. Shall it be ever so?' And he struck the water with his cane. Then the spirit Manimekhala took him from the water and offered him to the king, and he restored him to his mother. She was right fain to have her son restored, and she took divers kinds of perfumes and presented them. And Sakra offered perfumes of *tharekhkan* sandalwood and a dexter branch of the great Wisdom Tree.

[*The rock of the white elephant.*] The white elephant Gandha-laraja, which the king of Dagon rode, had died in the sky, and, falling into the ocean, become a rock. On that isle, rock-model of the elephant, the noble saint called Shin Mahinda, son of king Siridhammasoka, was wont to walk to and fro. The king when he reached that place paid great worship and reverence.

[*The king of Manaung.*] Now the ministers of the king who ruled the island of Manaung spake into his ear, saying, ' To-morrow the king called Siritaribhavanadityapavarapanditasudhammaraja-mahadhipatinarapatisithu, ruler of the great kingdom of Arimad-dana Pugarama, cometh. It were meet, we think, to make ready presents for offering, worthy of that king.' And the king of Manaung asked his ministers, ' Must I bow down and worship the king who cometh?' His ministers answered, ' Yea. He is a great and glorious king. Thou must needs bow down.' And the king of Manaung said, ' Better it were to die than to do obeisance to him ', and he hung an earthen pot around his neck, and descended into the water and died.

It came to pass that king Alaungsithu stayed his boat at the place where the Manaung king descended into the water and died. And the ministers great and small of the king of Manaung prepared great store of gifts and presents and offered them. And

king Alaungsithu asked them, saying, 'Lo! I have come. Why
cometh not my friend, the king of Manaung, to greet me?' And
the ministers spake into his ear, and said, 'Great and glorious
king! He feared that he must bow down and worship thee when
thou camest, and hath descended into the water and died!'
'What!' quoth king Alaungsithu, 'died he fearing he must
worship such a king as I? Booted it him aught to die?' And
he stood at the prow of his boat, and pointing with his finger
cried, 'Lo! I have come. King of Manaung, my friend, why
comest thou not forth to greet me?' Then the king rose up as
if he were alive, and the earthen pot was hung about his neck,
and he bowed down and worshipped. When the people of Manaung
saw it they were sore afraid.

[*The great scorpion.*] And so he came to Jambudipa. Now
there was in the forest a huge scorpion which had killed and eaten
an elephant, and lived and made a nest of the tusk thereof. When
he saw the elephant-tusk, he said, 'What meaneth it?' His
masters of white magic and black made answer, 'It is the nest
of a great scorpion.' So when the scorpion had gone in search
of food the king took the tusks of the elephant and set them
aboard his boat and bare them away. And when the great scorpion
returned from pasture and saw not his nest, he followed swimming
after the boat of king Alaungsithu. But the king was a king
great and glorious, and he might not overtake him. Therefore he
lifted up his head and tail, signifying this : 'He who hath taken
my nest is not a common man, but great and glorious. Let him
make a boat like me, and ride it!' So when the king came home
to Pugarama he made a boat after the likeness of the scorpion.

[*The tharekhkan images.*] He carved five images of the Lord out
of the *tharekhkan* offered by Sakra, and enshrined the six sacred
relics offered by Sakra in the Myappaungmyizzu, which he fashioned
with fragments of the *tharekhkan*, enclosing the dexter branch of
the Wisdom Tree. And he bowed down and worshipped. Then
Shin Arahan exhorted him, 'Place the relics of the Lord's body
where they are fain to dwell, for the benefit of all beings throughout
the five thousand years of the religion. Place them not, O king,
for thine own worship in the palace.' So Alaungsithu placed the
six images on the royal boat and went up by land and water.
Thereto he made a solemn vow and said, 'At the place where the

six images of the Lord are fain to dwell, let a clear sign be
revealed!' And when he came to Kunywa, lo! flocks of birds
were flying in the sky. And when he saw it he questioned his
masters of white magic and black, and they replied, 'Hereafter
this place will be the Mahanagararachinna country. Here the
images of the Lord are fain to dwell.' So the king set the images
of the Lord on five white elephants, and he made a solemn vow and
said, 'Let the white elephant stand at the place where they are
fain to dwell!' And he loosed the white elephant, and it stood
at the place where the future Buddhas resorted. There the king
built four pagodas—Kunywa, Pahkan, Shintaungma, and Hsingyo,
and they practised piety. One pagoda, Myappaungmyizzu, he gave
for worship to the noble masters filled with virtue and merit, who
practised piety in Pahkangyi.

Now when he assayed to set on a white elephant the Lord's
image carved from the topmost of the five parts of the *tharekhkan*,
it would not be lifted, neither would it follow. And the king asked
the reason of the wise. His masters of white magic and black
made answer: 'Great and glorious king! When thou journeyedst
downcountry, a wild fowl dwelling in Thiha forest flew up to the
raft and laid an egg. They durst not tell thee of it, for thou didst
not ask. There the image of the Lord is fain to practise piety.'
So the king went up again and built a *zedi* on the mid island in
the parts of Thiha forest, and there the image of the Lord practised
piety. From the *thamaing* of the five parts of the *tharekhkan*, it
would appear that the king built it in his journeying downcountry.

[*The rebels.*] King Alaungsithu abode not long in the homeland.
Because he often made the circuit of his kingdom, his men who
served in the cavalry, elephantry, and the other parts of his army,
suffered much ado. Bassein, the Talaing country, was in anarchy.
Nga Thit in Tetthit Island showed discourtesy. In Mt. Hketthin
Nga Hnwè rebelled. Zeyyamingala, who dwelt on a hill com-
manding the Theks, was insolent. The Kala appointed in the
island of Ceylon was corrupt in his allegiance. Tenasserim brought
not tribute as he was wont. And Thekminkaton strayed from
gratitude and truth.

The generals Nga Yèdaing and Nga Yènaing were sent with
a great host of elephants and horses, and they marched and came to
Ngasinkaing. Thekminkaton advanced to meet them; and they

defeated him and returned presenting many prisoners of war. The
king went forth with a great army as far as Lanhpya and there he
made a village and a home for the captured prisoners of war and
caused them to dwell there. Because he held whatsoever he got,
the place is still known as Yahkaing.

[*The head of Thekminkaton.*] When they had caught Thekminkaton, the two generals cut off his head and came and presented it.
But the Mahagiri spirit appeared and said, ' O king, why hast thou
killed thy fellow-worshipper ? ' And the king replied, ' Fellow-
worshipper though he be, he hath disquieted the border villages
and purlieux. Therefore I have but punished him. I desired not
his death.' And the Mahagiri spirit said, ' Place the head of
Thekminkaton in a gem-embroidered casket and worship it, with
gold and silver chandeliers, gold and silver flowers.' So the king
placed the head in a gem-embroidered casket and made as if to
worship it, as the Mahagiri had said. But when he placed it face
to face in front of him, the head straightway turned about. And
the king said, ' Friend, I gave not the order to kill thee. I desired
not thy death. It was only the error of my generals. I did but
cause them, according to the wont of kings, to see to the cleansing
of the country and extend the boundaries of the kingdom. If
I speak truth, let this wood-oil tree that I plant, live ! ' And
he took a large wood-oil tree at Lanhpya and turned it upside
down and planted it. During the night it put forth leaves and
branches and it lived. And the king brought the head of Thekminkaton and came to Pugarama and he gave it a fair burial upon
Mt. Tuywin and all the people worshipped it once a year.

[*The king subdues Tenasserim.*] The towns and villages that
rebelled and were in anarchy he assailed, sending many chosen
hosts of elephants and horses. He marched by water and land
with queen and concubine to the mutinous parts of Tenasserim and
turned not back until he had mastered it.

[*Death of Shin Arahan.*] When he returned home Shin Arahan
made *parinirvana*. Thereafter the place of Shin Arahan was given
to the elder, son of Seinnyekmin, who became primate and was
borne in a golden palanquin wheresoever he went. Moreover, the
king presented the elder Ananda and the elder Bodhi, both men
fulfilled with all virtuous qualities, with golden litters-of-state and
pole and awning.

[*Bones of the prince of Pateikkara.*] In a former life in the flesh king Alaungsithu was son of the Pateikkara king; and when he heard of the union of Shwe-einthi with Sawyun he fell from the sky at the place called Wa, and died. Accompanied by his fourfold army he took the bones which Shin Arahan had gathered, and dropped them in water at Nyaung-u shore; and he made a solemn vow and said, 'If they are verily my bones, let them float on water!' And behold, the bones swam, and he took them out and treasured them in Shwegu pagoda in the land of conquest.

[*Shinbyu and Shinhla images.*] Then he thought: 'It were better for the benefit of all beings to set the images of the Lord, Shinbyu and Shinhla, where the Lord is fain to dwell than to keep them in the palace and worship them.' So he set the two images of the Lord upon a raft and went upcountry attended by an host of fighting men, thirty-six million by land and thirty-six million by water. Moreover, he made a solemn vow and said : 'Let the mouth of the Lord speak at the place where his image is fain to dwell!' When they reached Pyatthadhla-amaw at Sagaing, the ogre Ngawek spurned the royal raft with his foot, and the *pyatthad tupika* of the raft fell. The place was called Pyatthakkya, but long afterwards it came to be known as Pyatthadhla. Thence he went up and reached Gyaukma above Sagaing, when the Shinbyu image spake, 'Let me ever abide in this chasm!' So king Alaungsithu set the Lord's image on a white elephant and made a solemn vow saying, 'Kneel wheresoever it be pleased to rest!' And he set it free. And the elephant entered Gyaukma and knelt on the side of the riverbank. Therefore the king again made a solemn vow and said, 'It is not meet to build a pagoda on the side of the riverbank and worship it. Let it ascend to a high place and kneel!' So the white elephant ascended to the top of the bank and knelt. There the king built *gu* for the two images Shinbyu and Shinhla, and there they practised piety.

[*Dying charge of Minyèbaya.*] In Arakan the minister Thinhkaya, the Wayaunghngessani, rose up against Minbilu, tenth in descent from Thekminkaton, and became king; and Minyèbaya, son of Minbilu, with his wife Sawpauknyo, came to Paukkarama. But though he waited continually on the king he might not regain Arakan, the inheritance of his ancestors, but sojourned in sorrow with his son Lek-yaminnan and his daughter Shwegutha. Now at

last he fell sick, and when his sickness lay sore upon him he called
his son and charged him saying: 'Ever since the reign of the
king's grandfather we have waited upon him faithfully and sought
access, hoping that we might yet rule over our father's heritage;
but our wish is not fulfilled. Now I must die. But do thou
remain and strive to return to the home and village of thine
ancestors. If thou canst not return during this king's reign, thou
shalt not in the reign of his successors. For why? This righteous
king alone hath many elephants, horses, chariots, and fighting
men. He excels in action, plan, wisdom, foreknowledge, foresight.
Thou must needs contrive that this righteous king put forth his
strength. Therefore do this. When the king observes the head-
washing ceremony, tie thine hair so that it hangs at the back after
the Arakanese fashion, and stand where the king may see thee!'

[*Lek-yaminnan is restored to the throne of Arakan.*] Thus he
spake, and died. And his son did as his father charged him. And
when the king saw it he said, 'Scantest thou ceremony at a time
of ceremony?'; and he dragged him forth to slay him. Then
answered Lek-yaminnan, 'If thou slayest me, I must die. But
first, hear me!' And he spake even as his father charged him.
And the king took pity on his minister Lek-ya and appointed him
commander-in-chief, and made his Burmese army march under
Theinpyissi by land and his Talaing army under Lek-yaminnan by
water. When Minpati, grandson of king Wayaunghngessani,
heard that they came marching against him, he made ready his
fleet and met and fought with them at Pateikkara Taungnyo, where
the Talaings on the water perished. Therefore the Burmese host
on land turned back. But when he heard of it the king was wroth,
and he reinforced and made them march again. And they slew
Minpati and put Lek-yaminnan on the throne with his sister
Shwegutha. Thus Aduminnyo hath written in the Yakhaing
Minthami Egyin:

Sing we again!—This time of Minbilu, the last,
Tenth in the great glorious kingly line in Sampawek:
He was entrapped and slain by guileful plot and rebellion;
His minister Thinhkaya reigned, also called Wayaunghngek;
To the third generation his line dwelt long in Pyinsa Mro-
   haung.
Minyèbaya, the good king's clotted blood,

With Pauknyomya came to the Golden Kingdom.
Lek-yaminnan and Shwegutha
Their own children of true royal bone,
Laungsithu vested in royal pomp and splendour;
And with ten myriad Talaings, ten myriad Pyus,
At the moment of victory reckoned by the calendar
They built afresh the new city of Parein.
All the people loved and adored them . . . .

Twinthinhmu Mahasithu seems to say that it was in the reign
of the king's grandson Narapatisithu that Lek-yaminnan was put
on the throne of Arakan.   But after studying the line of kings in
the Arakan Chronicle and noting that the reign of king Alaungsithu outlasted the year 480, we should not accept the word of
Twinthinhmu.

[*Alaungsithu's visit to Gandhala.*] Thereafter the king marched by
water and land to the Tarop country to ask the sacred tooth.   And
when he came the Utibwa, ruler of the great Tarop kingdom of
Gandhala, went forth to greet him with store of gifts and presents.
And the two kings spake graciously together.   The Utibwa asked
him, 'Why hath my royal friend visited my kingdom?'   And
king Alaungsithu answered, 'I have not come for the sake of
worldly prosperity.   I have come to entreat the holy tooth, that
thereby I may attain transcendent happiness.'   And the Utibwa
said, 'If the holy tooth is fain to practise piety with thee, take it!'
So king Alaungsithu offered divers gold and silver chandeliers, gold
and silver flowers, gold and silver balls of parched rice, and worshipped and made plea at the *pyatthad* where the holy tooth abode.
And lo! the tooth adorned itself with the thirty-two greater and
eighty lesser signs and the six rays, and shouldering the eight
things needful ascended the sky and went passing to and fro.
Then the two kings did obeisance and pleaded with great reverence
and honour.   But albeit they pleaded after this wise the holy
tooth remained and descended not from the sky.   So at last the
Utibwa spake, 'Of old thy great-grandsire my friend Anawrahtaminsaw entreated the holy tooth, but it would not practise piety
with him.   Now also it happens even as of old in the reign of thy
great-grandsire.'   But king Alaungsithu was distraught in soul and
ceased not, but pleaded still.   Therefore the Utibwa, seeing that he
pleaded thus but the tooth would not practise piety with him,

spake these words: ' Friend, howsoever thou entreat it, the Lord's
holy tooth will not practise piety with thee.   And why?   There
is the Lord's prophecy that it shall remain in the kingdom of
Gandhala the full five thousand years of the religion.'   And he
gave him store of gifts and presents.

[*Alaungsithu's pagodas.*]   So king Alaungsithu knew he might
not have the holy thing to worship because there was no prophecy of the Lord allowing it, and he returned to Pugarama by
water and land.   When he reached the homeland he built the nine
mot-htaw in the north.   He heaped up many works of merit
throughout the whole of Burma, to wit, Inhkayu, Hlèdauk,
Mweandaw, Shwebawgyun in Kyawzin.   Thereafter he built Thabbyinnyu pagoda in Paukkarama, and offered two great bells, one at
Thabbyinnyu, one at Shwegu pagoda: they were cast of pure
copper, ten thousand *adula* in weight, larger by far and nobler than
the five great bells offered by his grandfather, king Htihlaingshin.

[*The thief on the striped horse.*]   One day, while he had his
councillors in audience, he stretched forth his arm and boasted in
his pride.   But he was old in years, and the flesh hung loose upon
his arm, and when the ministers saw it they laughed.   And the
king was ware of it and said, ' My ministers laugh, for they think
my strength is gone from me!'   So he called his ministers one day
and cried: ' Ho! ministers on my left hand and on my right!
Hear ye not that a wight wearing a striped headdress and riding
a striped horse, robbeth folk by violence at sundown near the foot
of Mt. Tuywin?   Up! ye four, and rest not till ye catch him, or
my wrath be upon ye!'   So the four generals took four good horses
from the stable and hied them forth, for they were minded to rest
not till they had caught him.

Then the king took his horse Shwepansabwin and wrapped a white
cloth about its belly and tightened the girths; and at dusk, leaving
one he trusted at the gate and saying, ' Shut not the gate until I
come!' he spurred amain to the slopes of Mt. Tuywin.   From his
shoulder hung a scabbard and a sword, and on his head he wore a
striped headdress.   And the four generals thought, ' Verily it is the
thief!' and they gave chase, for they were minded to rest not till they
had caught him.   But the king escaped and rode away from them,
and again he turned and rode towards them; so did he many times,
till his horse grew weary, then he plunged down the sheer cliff at

Nyaung-u and watered his horse. Now the four generals thought
among themselves, 'The thief feareth us, and lo! he hath plunged
over the cliff and perished!' But the king, when he had watered
and breathed his horse, came up out of the chasm and charged and
pierced through the line of the four horsemen surrounding him
and shook off their pursuit. Then he turned and rode towards
them, and again he turned and rode away from them; and so he
made sport of them upon the broad acres of Hpo-u. And now the
four generals were sore afraid and said, 'This is no man, but
a spirit, a devil!' And thrice the king drave them before him;
he appeared in front of them, he appeared at the back of them;
he appeared on their left hand, he appeared on their right; and so
he returned to his royal city.

In the morning early he came forth to audience, and called the
four generals into his presence and asked them, 'Ho! ministers,
found ye the thief who rideth the striped horse?' 'Sire,' said they,
'may we be bold to speak into thine ear, to bow our heads beneath
the golden sole of thy foot! He who rideth the striped horse is no
man, but a spirit, a devil. But and if he be a man, he is no common man; surely he is a lord of glory fulfilled with majesty and
power. For not alone we four, thy servants: if all the horsemen
in thy kingdom pursued him they could not catch him, no, not if
they compassed him in on every side.' Thus spake they into the
king's ear, and he said, 'Ministers! Ye thought I was old. I am
not old yet!' All the host of ministers who heard it were sore
afraid and trembled.

[*Alaungsithu's elephant-hunting.*] King Alaungsithu was full of
glory, dominion, and power. He was perfect in all the lore
of elephants and horses and the art of archery. Once he had sport
with his ministers in Mahton forest, coursing elephants. He
caught more than a thousand elephants unblemished—some with
one tusk, some without tusks, some with straight tusks, some
with tusks bent downward, together with young she-elephants.
Moreover, when he had sport in Pantaung forest he caught more
than seven hundred young she-elephants unblemished. In Talop
forest he mounted the royal elephant by climbing the tusk, and
caught with a noose of Thintwè rope more than seven hundred
young she-elephants. And when he had sport with elephants in
Ngahsaunggyan forest, he caught more than an hundred young

male elephants. This is the record of his sport with multitudes.
And oftentimes beside he sported all over the country.

[*Rubies at Mt. Mali.*] Once it was reported that the whole
ground shone with jewels at the foot of Mt. Mali. So the king
went up by water and land and gathered rubies there. He filled
one boat withal, a boat six cubits in beam. These rubies he made
like balls of parched rice and enshrined them in Shwegu pagoda
and Thabbyinnyu pagoda, and worshipped them.

[*Alaungsithu's boasting.*] One day king Alaungsithu pondered
saying, ' I am a great king and glorious. I have reached the foot
of the rose-apple tree. I have received the title given by Sakra.
Moreover, I have carved images of the Lord from the five parts of
the *tharekhkan* and the dexter branch of the Wisdom Tree, and
worshipped them. I have visited the islands of Ceylon, Mallayu,
and Manaung, and seen divers sights and marvels. Surely my
ancestors were not so great, so glorious and powerful as I ! '

Thus he committed a sin in thought and speech. At that
moment the sight of both his eyes vanished. When thus he could
not see he sought counsel of the wise, and his masters of white
magic and black spake into his ear, saying, ' Thou hast sinned
against thy royal grandsire and great-grandsire. Therefore hath
thine eyesight vanished. Worship them with gold and silver
chandeliers, gold and silver flowers, gold and silver balls of parched
rice, and thine eyes shall see ! ' So the king cast in gold the
images of the forty-four generations of kings from king Thamoddarit, first founder of Pugarama, to his father Sawyun ; and he set
them on a golden table and worshipped them with gold and silver
chandeliers, gold and silver garlands, and gold and silver balls of
parched rice. When thus he worshipped, the three images of
Pyuminhti, Anawrahtaminsaw his great-grandsire, and Kyanzittha
his grandsire alone remained seated as before ; the images of the
kings of other generations fell and lay strewn on this side and that.
At the same moment when he worshipped the king's eyes saw.

[*His splendour.*] The king was very beautiful to look upon ; his
voice was melodious. Song he loved, and the sound of harp and
horn. He had great store of goodly elephants and horses, maga-
zines, treasures, chattels, gold, and silver. Within these leaden
halls and treasuries his clerks and scriveners had daily to indite and
copy, it is said. Moreover, he caused cunning workmen to cast

images of pure copper in the likeness of his great-grandsire Anawrahtaminsaw, his grandsire Sawlu, his grandsire Htihlaingshin
Kyanzittha, his father Sawyun, together with Nyaung-u Hpi,
Nga Htweyu, and Nga Lonlephpè, his great-grandsire's paladins ;
and of the chief circle-collectors of revenue, the petty circle-collectors of revenue, the chief Tanhsaung minister, and the petty
Tanhsaung minister ; and he kept them all, together with the
inscription, inside the Shwegu.   Furthermore, on the inscription
within the Shwegu he noted down the number of his young white
she-elephants, of his young black she-elephants ; the number of his
hlawga boats, his *kyaw* boats, his *kattu*, his *lunkyin* ; the number of
his soldiers, his aldermen, and scriveners.

[*Minshinsaw and Pabhavati.*]   Once the king of Pateikkara
offered him his daughter.   And king Alaungsithu had great compassion on her and gave her the name Pabhavati and an host of
handmaids and attendants.   And ever she waited on the king and
ministered to him.   One day his three sons came up to do homage
to their father.   At that moment Pabhavati, daughter of the Kala
king, was at the king's side upon the royal couch.   When the
king's sons drew nigh she abode there and descended not from
the couch.   Now when Minshinsaw, the king's son, saw that she
descended not, he turned away his face and paid no homage to his
father, saying, ' I am the eldest son.   Shall this Kala wench abide
on the couch in my presence, before all the ministers and councillors ? '   And he tarried a little while and departed saying, ' I am
not well.'

[*Minshinsaw and Anantathuriya.*]   Now king Alaungsithu had
compassion on Anantathuriya, son of the royal usher, and gave him
a robe with the *tuyin* skirt fastened beneath it, worthy to be worn
by princes only.   One day a council was held, and Anantathuriya
arrayed himself in the robe and attended the council.   But when
Minshinsaw the king's son saw it, he stripped Anantathuriya and
gave him a robe fit for him and made him wear it, saying, ' This
garment is not for a king's usher or nurse to wear.   Only the
king's brother and son are worthy to wear it.   Let it not be worn
thus by each and every one ! '

[*Minshinsaw in exile.*]   But the king heard it and he said,
' I gave the garment and suffered it to be worn.   Shall he act
thus while I live ?   When I am dead and he is king, how will he

trouble and oppress my sons and daughters, councillors and captains! He will be like a cat among a brood of chickens!' He
spake, and stripped him of his provincial revenues, his bodyguard,
his estates, his gold and silver, and cast him into prison. Now his
mother, queen Yadanabon, entreated the chief ministers and councillors and caused them to speak unto the king, that he might
show mercy. Many times they besought him, and at last the king
took pity and restored him all his elephants, horses, and estates, but
drave him out, saying, ' Because thou hast once shown a sullen face
in my presence, abide not in my city ! '

So the king's son Minshinsaw took all his elephants and horses
and his bodyguard and dwelt at Htuntonputek toward the east,
founding a village and domain. There he dammed Aungpinlè lake,
three thousand *ta* in length and breadth ; moreover, he dammed
the lake at Tamoshso. He built three canals, creating thirty
thousand *pè* of cultivated land. He ate three crops a year; so rich
was the land and fertile. Because he ordered things on this wise
he filled many granaries and treasuries of gold and silver, goods
and grain. Moreover, he had great hosts of elephants, horses, and
followers. He invited certain of the noble Order, scholars of Pali,
commentaries and subcommentaries, and caused them to write many
books and teach them. He succoured them with the four things
needful and caused the religion to shine.

[*Narathu.*] When king Alaungsithu had banished his son Minshinsaw from the city, he thought, ' Narathu, my middle son, is
able both to devise a thing and to perform it.' So he caused him
to direct and govern the affairs of the kingdom. Narathu's mother
was the daughter of Dhammakyin, minister to Htihlaingshin Kyanzittha. That minister's daughter the king raised to the throne as
a maid of honour, in rank less than a queen and more than a
concubine.

[*Death of Alaungsithu.*] Thus the king called Siritaribhavanadityapavarapanditasudhammarajamahadhipatinarapatisithu, fulfilled
with glory, majesty, dominion, and power, had for over threescore
and ten years of kingly prosperity advanced the welfare of the
great religion and the welfare of the generations of his sons, grandsons, and great-grandsons after him. Now when he reached the
age of an hundred and one he fell grievously sick. His son
Narathu removed him from the throne and kept him within

Shwegu pagoda. And the king recovered consciousness awhile and said, 'This is not my palace, surely!' And the handmaid spake into his ear saying, 'Not thy palace, but thy work of merit!' 'Whose trickery is this?' he cried. She answered, 'Thy son Narathu decreed it.' And the king was convulsed with anger; his whole body burned like fire. Then his son Narathu bethought him: 'If the king ariseth from his sickness I shall be utterly destroyed!' So with clothes and garments he pressed down the king until he died. Some chronicles say that he was placed beneath a pergola of gourds, and that it fell on him and so he died.

Twenty-six years in the nether house, seventy-five years he flourished; he passed at the age of an hundred and one. About the time of his death the Saturday star fought with the Thursday star; the *deinnetthè* coincided with the *thingyan*; light streamed from the earth. The day of his birth was Thursday.

[*Alaungsithu or Narapatisithu?*] The Great Chronicle states that it was Alaungsithu who used the *thinkanek* boat to roam the country; who reached the rose-apple tree at the head of the Island; who was given by Sakra the name Siritaribhavanadityapavarapanditasudhammarajamahadhipatinarapatisithu at the foot of the rose-apple tree; who built images of the five parts of the *tharekhkan*, and the Shinbyu and Shinhla, the nine *saga* and nine *mot-htaw* pagodas. But the New Chronicle says it was his grandson Narapatisithu. Thus the statements of the two Chronicles differ; and the New Chronicle has quoted reasons and produced allusions in support, such as the subcommentary on the Bodhivamsa, the Kalyani inscriptions, and the Pwinlin *gu*.

We have consulted the subcommentary on the Bodhivamsa and the various inscriptions mentioned in the New Chronicle. The subcommentary on the Bodhivamsa, speaking of the power and glory of the grandson Narapatisithu, only states that he possessed a boat that obeyed his every wish, and a white elephant, and that he was the father of king Zeyatheinhka; it does not state that he reached the rose-apple tree at the head of the Island. The Kalyani inscription only mentions the coming of the elder Chapata and others from the island of Ceylon in the reign of the Pagan king called Narapatisithu in the year 543.

[*Nagagyaung inscription.*] Moreover we have taken out the various inscriptions with dates of the time of Narapatisithu the grandson. The Pagan Nagagyaung inscription only mentions the noble king, lord of the great kingdom of Arimaddana, bearing the name Siritaribhavanadityapavarapanditasudhammarajamahadhipatinarapatisithu, and the date—the fourteenth waxing of Tawthalin in the *kyataik* year 540; it does not state that he reached the rose-apple tree at the head of the Island.

[*Shwedaungmè inscription.*] The Shwedaungmè inscription only states that Min Zeyathura became king in the year 536, receiving the name Narapatisithu: that desirous of building many works of merit, such as the nine *Saga* and thirty red *gu*, he went roaming over the north of his kingdom : and that when he came to Ngasinku town he built and offered a pagoda and called it Shwedaungmè, being one amongst the nine *saga* pagodas; it does not state that he reached the rose-apple tree at the head of the Island. Not a shadow, not a hint appears in all these many inscriptions that the grandson, king Narapatisithu, reached the rose-apple tree at the head of the Island.

[*Pada zedi inscription.*] Now turn we to the inscriptions, *thanbaing,* and old writings and records with dates of the time of king Alaungsithu the grandfather, and take out those that accord with the statement of the Great Chronicle. The Pada *zedi* inscription states that king Siritaribhavanadityapavarapanditasudhammarajamahadhipatinarapatisithu was born on Friday the first waning of Thantu in the year 512 : that he was exceeding glorious and powerful, without a rival in Jambudipa : that he exercised his limbs by visiting the rose-apple tree at the head of Jambudipa Island; that he made matchless prayer; that in order that the religion might last five thousand years, he dutifully gave oil-lights and offerings at the sacred footprint left for the sake of Nampadana, the Naga king who dwelt by Nampada river, and at the sacred footprint left on the top of Mt. Saccabandha at the suit of Saccabandha the elder. Here there is plain evidence that king Alaungsithu the grandfather reached the rose-apple tree at the head of the Island.

[*Thihataw inscription.*] The inscription in the Thiha forest pagoda gives the limits of the glebelands at its site, and states that it was dedicated on Saturday the full moon of Tabaung in the year 477 : and that king Alaungsithu built it and hollowed out a cave in it and placed therein the *zedi* made by king

Dhammasoka and the image, measuring four hands, of pure *tharek-hkan*, being the fifth and topmost part. Now the phrase in this inscription, 'four hands of pure *tharekhkan*', makes it proper to believe that only king Alaungsithu the grandfather reached the rose-apple tree at the head of the Island; for the tale is plain that Sakra gave the king the five *tharekhkan* and the Shinbyu and Shinhla images when he reached the rose-apple tree at the head of the Island.

[*Lèkaing Kyauttaga Thamaing.*] And it is stated clearly in the Lèkaing Kyauttaga Thamaing that there has been a prophecy on this wise: 'In time to come Alaungsithu, donor of Shwegu in Pagan called Arimaddana, roaming the kingdom in his magic boat, shall visit this place and build a *zedi* at the site of my *tharekhkan* monastery'; and that when king Alaungsithu came roaming the kingdom, he was shown by Sakra the copper *parabaik*, as large as a wool-dressing basket, which had been inscribed by Mahapunna the elder and kept in the *zedi*.

[*Shwekunop inscription.*] The inscription in the Htilin Shwekunop pagoda states that Alaungsithu, ruler of the great kingdom of Pagan called Arimaddana, went roaming his kingdom in the year 453: that he stopped awhile for refection at a place which was called Htilin because there the white umbrella opened of its own accord; that a sacred relic assumed the likeness of a gold mahseer; that the king took it to be a mahseer indeed in the fishery, and tried but could not catch it; that at last he caught it by covering it in a golden net, and enshrined the relic and offered it to the pagoda known thereafter as Shwekunop. This shows that king Alaungsithu went roaming his kingdom.

[*Shwemot-htaw inscription.*] And the inscription in the Shwemot-htaw pagoda states that king Alaungsithu, lord of thirty-six white elephants, resplendent with the rays of glory, might and dominion, offered land to the Shwemot-htaw pagoda on Saturday in the *maga* year 457. This shows that king Alaungsithu was the donor of Shwemot-htaw pagoda.

[*Thamaing of the five tharekhkan.*] In the *thamaing* of the five *tharekhkan*, the Shinbyu and Shinhla, it appears that king Narapatisithu, spirit of the world, ruler of the great Arimaddana Paukkan country, went roaming his kingdom: that he was attended by eighty-four thousand ministers, one crore and sixteen lakhs

of followers, the magic boat, the *thinkanek* boat, and eight million
boats in all; that at that time he was anointed king in the shade
of the rose-apple tree: and that in the year 457 king Narapatisithu
received the *tharekhkan* images.   This leaves matter for doubt and
misbelief, for men may say, ' Since the *thamaing* mentions king
Narapatisithu, it must be the grandson Narapatisithu.   There must
be a corruption in the writing of the date.'   But if we compare the
various *thamaing* we find they agree; and this is the right view—
that both *thamaing* and inscription refer to the grandfather king
Alaungsithu, also by the name of Narapatisithu, that both *thamaing*
and inscription refer to the grandson also as Narapatisithu, and the
grandson in turn received the name of the grandfather.

Conclusion.   Therefore, from consideration of the reasonable
accounts that are found in various inscriptions and *thamaing*, it
should be held and remembered that it was the grandfather, king
Alaungsithu, who alone reached the rose-apple at the head of the
Island.   As for the grandson, king Narapatisithu, he continued to
enjoy during his reign the *thinkanek* boat, first obtained in the
reign of his grandfather, king Alaungsithu; he roamed the kingdom
and received the seal and name of Siritaribhavana, &c.; thereafter
he carved and built nine images of the Lord from the *saga* post at
the prow of the raft, and worshipped them.   This much alone
should be taken as true.   It should not be held that he reached the
rose-apple tree at the head of the Island, nor that he was the donor
of the five *tharekhkan*, the Shinbyu and Shinhla images.   Therefore
we must resolutely affirm that only the grandfather, king Alaungsithu, was lord of the magic boat and reached the rose-apple tree
and was donor of the five *Tharekhkan*, the Shinbyu and Shinhla
images; therewithal the various inscriptions and *thamaing* agree.

Epilogue.   Here endeth the fourth part of the Great Royal
Chronicle, sifted and prepared in accordance with all credible
records in the books, after consulting learned monks, learned
brahmans, and learned ministers: written in the sacred chamber
in front of the royal Palace of Glass and divers-coloured jewels,
beginning from the first waxing of Nayon in 1191, in the reign
of His Majesty, sovereign of umbrella-holding kings of divers
great kingdoms and countries, master of mines of gold and silver,
ruby, amber, and all other gems, builder of the fourth city of
Ratanapura and the palace, lord of the *hsaddan* king of elephants,

lord and master of white elephants, lord of the universe, and great captain of the Law.

The fourth part of the Great Royal Chronicle is ended.

PART V

Honour be to Him, the Blessed One, the Saint, the Lord Buddha!

142. *Of king Narathu.*

[*Murder of Minshinsaw.*] In the year 529 his son Narathu became king. It was on this wise. When it was known to Minshinsaw that his royal father was no more, he gathered together all his men and prepared to march by land and water. Now Panthagu the elder was the son of a dealer in alms bowls; he was worshipped like the Lord by the whole country of Pagan. And Narathu spake into his ear saying, ' I hear that my brother Minshinsaw, learning that our father is no more, is marching by land and water to seize the golden umbrella and the golden throne of our father. It will take long if thus he marcheth with his army, and the home affairs of the kingdom will suffer. Lo! I, thy servant, am here already. Call my brother, and let him come speedily with a sword and a horse only and ascend the throne!' But the elder Panthagu replied : ' If I call him and he come, and thou abide without raising him to be king, I have sinned against the saintly Law.' So Narathu sware a mighty oath that he would shoulder his brother's sword and set him on the throne. And Panthagu the elder believed the oath sworn by Kalagya and went to the place of Minshinsaw and told him all. And Minshinsaw, hearing the words of the elder, trusted them, and he set him on a single barge of gold and came downstream. When he reached Leppan port, Narathu, according to the oath he had sworn, went down to the boat and, shouldering his brother's sword, he raised and set him on the throne. After his anointing his food was poisoned and that night he died.

[*Wrath of Panthagu.*] When Minshinsaw was dead, in the same year Narathu became king. But when Panthagu the elder heard that he was poisoned and dead, he went to the palace and cried : ' Thou vile king! Thou foul king! Thou fearest not the woe

thou shalt suffer in *samsara*. Though now thou reignest, thinkest
thou that thy body shall not grow old, not die? A king more
damned than thou there is not in all the world!' 'Nay, master,'
said Narathu, 'I acted according to the oath I sware to thee.
I shouldered my brother's sword and set him on the throne.' But
the noble master made reply: 'A man more vile and foul than thou
there is not in the world of men!' And he departed and went to
the island of Ceylon.

[*Cruelty of Narathu.*] King Narathu had once been the demon-
guardian of a mountain who had shaded the Lord with three *in*
leaves what time he made his prophecy on the summit of Mt.
Tangyi. So he was great in glory, might, and dominion. His
ministers, both great and small, his followers and all the people
stood in fear and awe of him. He raged furiously with wrath and
pride. When he became king he slew his bride called Kyaban,
whom Alaungsithu had given him. He also slew her son Ottarathu
and his uncle Mahabo the scribe. Powerful monks he constrained
to become laymen, insomuch that certain noble monks, fearing to
become laymen, escaped to the island of Ceylon. The king was
brutal and savage. His queens, concubines, and handmaids stood
in fear and awe of him and loved him not, but hated him and
cursed him in their hearts. All the inhabitants of the kingdom
starved in toil and sweat, and many forts, villages, and domains
were ruined. The people completed not the Dhammayan, his work
of merit, for they were sore afraid and toiled with too great
heedfulness and rigour.

[*He murders his wife.*] Now the daughter of the Kala king, who
was offered during his father's reign, ministered to him continually
after he came to the throne. One day she learned that when he
entered the closet he took not with him water for washing. So she
abode afar off and came not nigh him, in disgust that he took not
water for washing at his times of making water, easing, and sexual
intercourse. Thereupon the king was wroth, and with the sword
that was in his hand he smote her that she died.

[*Revenge of the king of Pateikkara.*] But when her father the
Kala king heard thereof, he chose eight from among his eight
hundred mighty men of valour and spake on this wise: 'Comrades!
Go ye, wearing the garb of brahmans, to where the king is who
slew my daughter, and slay him. And when the king is dead, die

ye, piercing your own bodies with the sword. I will provide your families with bounties, food and drink.' His eight mighty men of valour made reply : ' Provide our families with bounties, food and drink throughout their lifetime, and we will kill that king till he be dead ! ' So the king of Pateikkara gave them great rewards and caused the eight to wear the garb of brahmans and sent them away. They carried each a conch at the waist, and each a sword; and so they came to Pugarama.

[*Death of Narathu*, fl. 1167-71.] They ascended the palace and drew nigh the king, encircling him under guise of presenting the conch and *neza* grass. And they pointed the finger straight at the minister Theiddikagyi, and cried: ' Minister! Of old ye all took many bribes and so our master's son perished. Now too, because ye prevented it not, our master's daughter hath perished.' And they pierced the king with the sword until he died. Thereafter they pursued the minister Theiddika to pierce him, but they caught him not. Then they pierced their own bodies with the sword and died, all the eight of them. Because the king was pierced to death by the Kalas he was afterwards known as Kalagya.

King Kalagya heeded not the sense of shame nor the fear of reproach; he spake not the words of truth. It was his wont to treat chief ministers, high councillors, and people within and without the palace with cruelty and roughness; he regarded not faces. He ground down and oppressed the folk and the villagers. Because he acted on this wise his ministers and councillors and all the people, both laymen and monks, cursed him in their hearts. Forty-five years in the nether house, four years he flourished; he passed at the age of forty-nine. About the time of his death the moon and the Thursday star fought; the *deinnetthè* coincided with the *thingyan*; cucumber came to fruit upon the top of Shwezigon. The day of his birth was Saturday.

143. *Of king Minyin Naratheinhka*.

[*Naratheinhka*, fl. 1171-74.] In the year 533 his son Minyin Naratheinhka became king. When he ascended the throne he made his younger brother heir and gave him the title Narapatisithu. In the reign of this king there was abundance of rain and water. Far inland the country was fat, pleasant, and fertile, and all the people living in ease and happiness blessed the king right gladly in their hearts.

[*His queens.*]   His queen was Minaungmyat, eldest of the three
daughters — Minaungmyat, Minlat, and Minsawhti — born of
Kyaungdawthi, daughter of Alaungsithu.   While the grandfather
Alaungsithu was still alive he had joined his two grandchildren in
wedlock.   The king also took the two daughters of Eindawthi, wife
of Yazathu, nephew and son-in-law of Hkinon, Alaungsithu's consort,
and raised them to be queens.   He also raised his middle sister-in-
law and made her queen.   He named his chief queen Taungpyinthi ;
the elder daughter of Yazathu he named Alèpyinthi ; his middle
sister-in-law he named Myauppyinthi.

Whenever the king went riding his elephant he caused his three
queens to follow after on three elephants in pomp equal to each
other.   Whenever they sate in a palanquin, or bier with canopy,
a sedan or a litter, he caused them to follow after him, equal in
pomp, not one excelling or less than another.   They were equal in
betel cups, betel covers, basons, spittoons, jugs and pipkins.   Each
was attended by handmaids equally attired in bracelets, necklaces,
rings, earrings, and apparel.   Because he loved them equally, one
not more nor less than another, they were content and felt no envy
nor eyed each other askance.

[*Veluvati, bride of Narapatisithu.*]   One day they entered a forest of
the Pyaws in Myinzaing Wek-win, and there they found in a giant
bamboo a little daughter born of heat and moisture, having great
beauty and the signs great and small.   When she came of age she
was like the colour of new-burnished gold, and they presented her
to Minyin Naratheinhka.   But at the time when the king saw the
girl, her hour of glory was not yet, and he exclaimed ' Vast ears !
Alack-a-day ! '   And he gave her to his brother Narapatisithu.

Now the king's queen-mother lived with her younger son Narapatisithu, and when she saw the woman born of moisture, in her
wisdom she took thought and cut the damsel's ear till it was just
as it should be, and offered her to him.   When her ear was cut
aright she bore a marvellous beauty insomuch that all men seeing
her were dazed and could not stand upright.   And the great queen-
mother schooled her and taught her the arts that all princesses
should know, and so she became fulfilled with all womanly graces.
And because she was conceived and born of moisture her colour and
beauty resembled not those of any other woman.

[*The king plots to take Veluvati.*]   One day the great queen-mother called her daughter-in-law, consort of the heir-apparent, and they entered the palace. And when the king saw his brother's wife, how fair she was to look upon, his soul was dazed and he could not stand upright. And he thought on this wise: ' I will cause mine heir to march, telling him that war hath broken out in Ngahsaung-gyan. When he hath set forth I will take my brother's wife and raise her to the throne ! ' So he prompted the mouth of a minister and caused him to come, saying, 'War hath broken out in Nga-hsaunggyan ! ' And the king called Narapatisithu and ordered him to march to Ngahsaunggyan.

[*Narapatisithu is sent to Ngahsaunggyan.*] Now his brother Nara-patisithu was a prince of nimble wit and discernment, and he com-manded Nga Pyi his equerry, saying, 'If any ado arise in mine house, take the horse Thudaw and come quickly ! ' Then he mar-shalled his troops by land and water, and went up-country with his councillors and captains, circle and village headmen, and all his host. When he reached Thishsein, lo ! there was no trouble soever at Ngahsaunggyan ; and he weighed the matter in his heart, saying, ' My brother hath duped me with a false excuse ! ' And he gathered and conferred with his councillors and captains, his circle and village headmen, and bound them with a solemn oath. And his councillors and captains said, 'In verity Minyin Naratheinhka hath made his brother Narapatisithu heir, for he hath no son.' The more gladly, therefore, with one heart they leagued with Narapatisithu.

[*The horse of Nga Pyi.*] When Minyin Naratheinhka heard that his brother had reached Thishsein, he took his sister-in-law and raised her to the throne. Nga Pyi the equerry crossed over to Aungtha at the stroke of the morning bell and rode his horse at a soft and easy pace. It was not yet noon, they say, when he reached Chindwin Pareimma. Crossing the Pareimma, he made straight for Hanlin and reached the stream of Ngapat at sunset. And because night 'was drawing on and the royal horse was tired, he watered it and fed it with grass and slept that night at Mt. Myinhli.

Now when the horse Thudawzin had rested, he neighed loudly, for he scented his master. And the prince knew his horse's neigh and could not sleep, saying, 'Verily it is the sound of mine horse, neighing ! ' Then he made a solemn vow and said, ' If it is indeed the sound of mine horse neighing, may this pillow be pierced with

a hole, and fail not ! ' And he struck the royal pillow with his
hand, and lo ! a hole was pierced. The place is still known as
Malwèonpauk; and the place where Nga Pyi slept is Mt. Myinhli.

[*Narapatisithu kills Nga Pyi.*] When Nga Pyi the equerry had
slept and it was early morning, he came at the stroke of the morning bell and told all his tale. And when he heard that matter
prince Narapatisithu was in high dudgeon and waxed wroth and
cried, ' My beloved queen Veluvati ! My brother hath taken and
raised her to the throne ! ' Then he asked Nga Pyi the equerry,
' Where didst thou sleep yesternight ? ' ' I slept ', said Nga Pyi,
' at the stream at Ngapat, for the horse was tired and I replenished
it.' ' What ! ' said prince Narapatisithu, ' Not near, not far thou
hast slept from the place where I lay. Didst thou well to sleep ?
We princes might accomplish much, had we an hour to plan it.'
And in his royal pride he slew Nga Pyi. The place is still known
as Kuttawya.

[*Mission of Aungswangè.*] Then the prince cried, ' Our enemy is
behind us ! ' And he called his minister Aungswangè and commanded him saying, ' Bear my yoke though it cost thee thy life !
See that thou catch my brother unawares and slay him. When
that is done I will make thee great, and give thee whom thou wilt
of my three sisters-in-law.' So Aungswangè chose fourscore mighty
men of valour and took them in a fast *hlawga* boat and went in
furious haste, not knowing day nor night.

[*Narapatisithu at Kyek-yek.*] Prince Narapatisithu marshalled
his troops by land and water and came downstream. When he
reached Kyek-yek he made a solemn vow and said : ' If my brother
shall verily be slain, at the moment I spread this cloth at the
pagoda in the south, may the Lord himself bow down and take it ! '
And when he spread the cloth, behold ! the Lord himself bowed
down and took it. When he saw that thing he came downstream,
marshalling his troops by land and water.

[*Burial of Nga Pyi.*] But the body of Nga Pyi, whom he had
slain, floated not near nor far from the royal raft. And the prince
saw it and asked, ' Whose body is it ? ' His ministers answered,
' The body of Nga Pyi whom thou hast slain.' And he commanded
them saying, ' Bury the body at the head of yon island, and let it
be worshipped by all people in this place. See that ye build a
goodly spirit-house.' So the ministers did as the prince com-

manded, and built a spirit-house. The isle where Nga Pyi was
buried is still known as the isle of Shwepyishin. Even the village-
headmen were fain to worship there.

[*Aungswangè kills Naratheinhka.*] When Nga Aungswangè,
the royal servant, sent by prince Narapatisithu, reached the palace,
he entered with his fourscore mighty men of valour hugging sword
in scabbard. Now it so befel that Minyin Naratheinhka was
entering the closet, and they followed after as far as the closet.
And the king asked him, ' Who art thou ? ' He replied, ' Thy
servant, Nga Aungswangè. O king, thy brother sent me ! ' And
the king looked, and lo ! he was hemmed in by white and gleaming blades. And he besought them saying, ' Slay me not ! Let
me only serve my brother as his watcher of crows, his scarer of
fowl ! ' But Aungswangè replied, ' O king, my lord thy brother
hath not so ordained it.' And he slew him even in the closet, and
he died. A ruby earring that he wore fell from the closet to the
ground.

Thirty-two years in the nether house, three years he flourished ;
he passed at the age of thirty-five. About the time of his quarrel
with his brother a two-headed horse was born ; a tiger and leopard
fought with teeth, and the leopard won ; the Thursday star and
the Tuesday star touched. About the time of his death a vulture
alighted on the door of the palace ; the Saturday star crossed the
disc of the moon ; bees clave to the main cross-beam of the palace;
smoke issued from Shwegu pagoda. The day of his birth was
Monday.

[*Narapatisithu*, fl. 1174–1211. *He kills Aungswangè.*] In the
year 536 his younger brother Narapatisithu became king. He was
anointed with his queen Veluvati.

When his sisters-in-law heard that he would give them to
Aungswangè, they clasped his knees and besought him with meek
and piteous words : ' O king, are we women known to covet so
many husbands ? We have done no sin. We are not mere sisters-
in-law. We are all daughters of thine aunts, Chit-on and
Eindawthi. We are all wives of a king. Though thou pity us
not, yet let us only serve thee in thy royal house as watchers
of crows, as scarers of fowl ! ' So the king called Aungswangè
and commanded him saying, ' Nga Aungswangè, I made thee a
promise indeed ; but if I were to give thee one of my sisters-in-law

it would be held a sin against my grandsires and great-grandsires.
I will make thee great, and give thee a daughter of a great
nobleman.' 'Pish!' said Nga Aungswangè. And the king slew
him, saying, 'He hath braved me to my face!'

Then he seized Anantathuriya, tutor to his brother Minyin
Naratheinhka, and gave him over to the executioners to slay him.
Now Anantathuriya was of a brave and constant heart; about the
time of his death he spake four stanzas of *linka,* and gave them
saying, 'Offer them, I pray thee, to the king!' But the executioners tarried not but slew him, and afterwards gave the writing
to the king.   These are the four verses of that *linka* :

[*Anantathuriya's death-song.*]

When one attains prosperity,
Another is sure to perish.
It is the law of nature.

Happiness of life as king—
Having a golden palace to dwell in,
Court-life, with an host of ministers about one,
Enjoyment—shadow—peace,
No break to felicity—
Is but a bubble mounting for a moment to the surface of
    the ocean.

Though he kill me not,
But in mercy and pity release me,
I shall not escape my *karma.*
Man's stark-seeming body
Lasteth not ever;
Verily it is the nature of every living thing to decay.

Thy slave, I beg
But to bow down in homage and adore thee!
If in the wheel of *samsara*
My past deeds offer me vantage,
I seek not for vengeance.
Nay, master, mine awe of thee is too strong!
If I might, yet I would not touch thee;
I would let thee pass without scathe.
Dissolution lures the elements of my body.

[*The king's remorse.*] Now when these four stanzas were read before the king and he heard them, he commanded, saying, ' Set him free ! ' But the executioners spake into his ear and said, ' The deed is done !' And the king slew those executioners, saying, ' Ye should have offered the writing before ye killed him ; but behold, ye killed him first and offered the writing after.' Now when he had heard the writing the king had great remorse. Again and yet again he gasped and swooned away. Ever afterwards he refrained and checked his anger : and he commanded the chief executioner, kinsman of the king, saying, ' Hereafter when I am wroth, though I give thee the order to slay a man, keep him alive for a month of weeks and look to the matter. Let him die only when he ought to die. If he ought not to die enlarge him.'

[*Narapatisithu's wives and children.*] The queen whom he found in the bamboo he called Veluvati. He also took to himself the three queens of his brother. In his brother's reign Taungpyinthi had given birth to a daughter, Sawpyichantha. Two daughters born of Alèpyinthi and Myauppyinthi ended their *karma* ever in the reign of their father Minyin Naratheinhka. The sons and daughters of king Narapatisithu were these. Queen Veluvati gave birth to Zeyathura. Queen Amyaragan, whose husband had died, was raised to be queen ; she gave birth to a daughter. The history of queen Taungpyinthi is this : Nyaung-u Hpi, comrade and paladin of the king's great-grandfather Htihlaingshin Kyanzittha, had a son Hpothugyi ; his son was Sisse, who had five daughters ; the eldest was the wife of Battara, the second the wife of Pwinhla-u, the third the wife of Sittuyinkabo, the fourth the wife of Minhtihlaing, the youngest daughter was queen Taungpyinthi. She rose into repute only when she had borne three sons. Queen Panyin was of noble race, granddaughter of Sithabin, son of king Htihlaingshin's brother-in-law ; her mother was Taungpyinthi, elder sister of Shwechu, Alaungsithu's daughter. Queen Panyin gave birth to a prince called Myasswashin. Queen Ngè was Thubarit's younger sister, Thubarit being the own grandson of the younger brother of king Kalagya's mother. Thubarit's sister was called Uhsauppan. When she had borne her sons, Yazathu, Pyanchi, and Kinkathu, she ended her *karma*. Moreover, the king took Sawsane, Bwèkya's younger sister, and raised her to be queen. She bare him four daughters : the eldest was called Shwe-einthi,

the second Sigon, the third Kyaungdawthi, the youngest
Shwechu.

[*Zeyyatheinhka.*] Furthermore, the king took a gardener's daughter
fulfilled with beauty and the signs great and small ; and the damsel
ministered to him and bare him a son, Zeyyatheinhka. That prince
spake words that delighted all men ; soft and gentle he was in all
he said and did.   He was perfect in all the arts that every prince
should know.

[*His mother wins him the heirship.*] Once there was a whitlow on
the king's hand, and though medicine was applied, the pain did not
grow less but ached grievously. Only when Zeyyatheinhka's mother
kept it to her mouth did the pain subside.   While thus she did
continually, the humour burst in her mouth ; and she swallowed it,
fearing that if she spued it out the king would awake from sleep.
Now when the king knew of it he laid it to heart and said, 'There
is none to love and cherish me equal to her ! '   And he commanded
her saying, 'I give thee a gift.   Choose thou what thou wilt ! '
Zeyyatheinhka's mother spake into his ear and said, 'O king, thou
hast had compassion on thy servant and given me gold, silver,
elephants and horses, villages, fiefs, and attendants, insomuch that
I am equal to others and lack for nothing.   If now thou pitiest
thy servant's estate, let thy servant Zeyyatheinhka, who is as the
fringe and limit of thy person, stand thine heir in the royal house!'
And the king outspake, 'It is well.   Let him abide his time.   I give
thee the gift thou askest, and my word is sure ! '

[*The king's journeys and works of merit.*]   King Narapatisithu
regarded truth and was master of the ten kingly duties.   Because
he had slain his brother, he, like his great-grandfather Nawrahtasaw,
roamed his kingdom in pomp and beauty with his fourfold army.
North, south, east, and west he wandered all over the land of
Burma, surrounded by his queens, concubines, and handmaids, and
he made many canals and reservoirs and dams and channels.   When
he reached the homeland Pugarama he made nine images of the
Lord out of the *saga*-leaf prow of the *thinkanek* boat ; and in order
that the religion might last five thousand years and all creatures be
profited, he built *gu* for these nine images, one each at the towns of
Kala, Mingin, Myedu, Sipottara, Kyanhnap, Ngasinku, Moshsobo,
Sahmun, and Sagaing ; there they practised piety.   Furthermore,
one plaster pagoda, built with the food of awl and chisel, the

fragments scattered in the carving of these nine images, practised
piety at Amyin town.

[*His bodyguard and revenues.*] The king formed a great bodyguard and escort, for he knew full well the ease with which his
brother was slain.   He made two several companies, the inner
bodyguard and the outer bodyguard, and they kept watch in
ranks around the palace, one behind the other.   Moreover, he
kept around the palace the manifold halls and granaries wherein
he stored his jewels and gold and silver, rice, water, and paddy.
All such goods and treasures an host of clerks and scriveners
checked daily and entered and recorded them ; it is said they failed
not even one day throughout the year.   Six hundred clerks and
scriveners checked, entered, and recorded in the revenues the
gold and silver, ruby and amber, white copper and red copper, tin
ore, iron, satin, *mainglon* carpets, Chinese silks, *kado* perfumes,
elephants and horses ; the whole year round they failed not, it is
said.   The provision made for his bodyguard, elephantry, and
cavalry was this : to every man fifty (baskets) of paddy a month,
and when the year was full a set of raiment each for husband and
wife.   His chiefs and officers he gave an hundred (baskets) of
paddy and sets of raiment, and that continually.   Moreover, he
gave many rewards beside.

[*Sulamani, Kawdawpallin, Dhammayazika pagodas.*] Thus he advanced the welfare of himself and all the people ; and in order that
men might follow the Path and reach fruition in *nirvana*, he built
a great work of merit with two hollow storeys and called it Sulamani.   Likewise, he built a work of merit with two hollow storeys
and an upward winding stair and called it by the name Kawdawpallin.
Moreover, he built at Thamahti a pagoda with five faces and called
it by the name Dhammayazika ; therein he set five images of the
Lord cast in pure copper.   He succoured with the things needful
scholars of the noble Order learned in Pali, in the commentaries
and subcommentaries, who practised piety throughout all the homeland, and they gave instruction in the books.

[*Uttarajiva's visit to Ceylon.*] In the same year, while king
Sirisanghabodhiparakkamabahu ruled over the island of Ceylon,
the religion, which had fallen in that island into soilure and decay,
was purified.   Six years later, in the year 542, Uttarajiva the
elder, chaplain of king Narapati, took many disciples of the Order

and went to worship the Mahazedi pagoda in the island of Ceylon. Among these disciples was a novice of about twenty years of age from the village Chapata, on the outskirts of Bassein town.

[*His lineage.*] This is the history of Uttarajiva the elder. Two hundred and thirty-six years after the Lord made *parinirvana*, Shin Sona the elder and Uttara the elder began to build the religion at the town Taikkala in Suvannabhummi, the Ramañña kingdom. Of the company of these elders was the elder Pyanadasi who dwelt in the town of Thaton ; he acquired mystic powers over things of this world and the higher knowledge, and was wont each morning early to sweep with a broom the site of the great Wisdom Tree and return to Thaton town in time to beg for alms. His pupil was Shin Mahakala the elder, who dwelt at the town of Dagon. His pupil was Shin Ariyavamsa the elder. His pupil was Uttarajiva the elder, chaplain of king Narapatisithu.

[*Chapata stays behind in Ceylon.*] When Uttarajiva the elder, Chapata the novice, and the many disciples of the Order reached the Island of Ceylon, they had converse with the elders of Ceylon concerning the religion, and, inquiring of each other's lineage, they found that the elders in Ceylon island were heirs of Shin Mahinda the noble saint, and that Uttarajiva the elder was of the lineage of Shin Sona the elder and Uttara the elder. Then they ordained Chapata the novice, saying, ' Let us perform a priestly act of pure validity.' Now when Shin Chapata was ordained a monk he followed not his teacher Shin Uttarajiva to Jambudipa, but sojourned in the island of Ceylon advancing his studies. But Shin Uttarajiva the elder with his disciples of the Order crossed over to Jambudipa and returned home; thereafter he was known as the first Pilgrim of Ceylon.

[*His four companions.*] For full ten rainy seasons Chapata studied the Three Pitakas and the commentaries, and when he had mastered them he sought to return home to Pagan. And he thought thus : ' If I return alone and find that my teacher Uttarajiva the elder is no more in the kingdom of Pagan, I shall be constrained to do the duties of the Order with the help of Burmese monks. It were well for five of the Order to go from Ceylon island and so fulfil the perfect ordination.' So he took these four scholars of Pali, commentaries and subcommentaries— Shin Sivali who dwelt at Temalitta village, Shin Tamalinda, son of the king of Kamboja, Shin Ananda, who dwelt at the town of Kiñcipura, and Shin Rahula, who dwelt in the island of Ceylon ; they were five in all, and they embarked upon a ship and crossed to Jambudipa island.

[*Events in Pagan.*] When two *pad* were wanting to complete the twenty-seventh constellation and the year 548 was full, king Narapatisithu was pained by the whitlow aching in his forefinger and slept not full three months. Queen Veluvati died. There was a great quaking of the earth and many pagodas, *gu*, and monasteries came tumbling down. The wise Vajirabuddhi, counsellor of the king, ended his *karma*.

[*Chapata's return.*] In the year 553 Chapata the elder and his fellows came by ship from the island of Ceylon and reached Bassein town. And because the rainy months were nigh, certain rich men built them a monastery with fire-proof walls to the south of Bassein town, and there they recited prayers throughout the rainy season ; the place is still known as Theingoyauk monastery. When the rains were over they observed the *pavarana* and came to the city of Pagan. These five monks of the Order were called the second Pilgrims of Ceylon.

[*Chapata's secession.*] Now the chief Uttarajiva the elder died and was buried before Chapata the elder and his fellows reached Pagan. So when they arrived they went to the chaplain's grave and worshipped there. Thereafter Chapata the elder spake to the elders, his companions, saying, ' Masters, our teacher Uttarajiva the elder visited the island of Ceylon and performed the duties of the Order in one accord with the Ceylonese monks. And now we, too, must perform the duties of the Order in union with the monks dwelling in Pagan city who are of the race and lineage of Ashin Sona and Uttara the elders. Now of old the functions of the Order were controlled by guidance of our teacher, Uttarajiva the elder. But now Burmese monks control them. We will not perform the duties of the Order with these Burmese monks.' So the five monks of the Order who had come from Ceylon performed their duties apart. And king Narapatisithu caressed and regarded beyond measure these five noble elders. He caused a raft of boats to be put together in the river Irrawaddy, and thereon many novices were ordained monks. Thus they multiplied in the course of time till there were many sects of the Order.

[*Rahula turns layman.*] One day king Narapatisithu invited the five elders together with pupils of the Order and held a great almsgiving. Now there was a dancing girl at the festival exceeding fair to look upon, and when Shin Rahula the elder saw her he lusted after her and delighted no more in the law of the clergy but strove to be quit of the Order. The four elders admonished him with words of the Law, but still he could not refrain himself, till at last they drave him out saying, 'Because of thee alone, why should we four be shamed? Though thou desire to quit the Order, do not so in the kingdom of Pagan. Go to Mallayu island from Bassein harbour of ships, and so turn layman.' So Rahula the elder left Pagan and went to Bassein. There he embarked upon a ship and crossed over to Mallayu island. When the king who reigned over Mallayu island heard of his coming, he besought his counsel, for he longed to know the judgements of the Vinaya. So Shin Rahula the elder taught him the Khuddasikkha with the subcommentary and assured him of all the judgements of the Vinaya. And when he heard them the king of Mallayu was full of faith and favour and offered him a bowlful of rubies. So Rahula the elder took the rubies and quitted the Order, and, setting up his house, he dwelt in Mallayu island.

[*Death of Chapata.*] In the kingdom of Pagan, among the four elders who had come from Ceylon, Chapata the elder died; and Sivali the elder, Tamalinda the elder, and Ananda the elder published abroad the books of the Pitaka and caused the religion to shine.

[*Ananda and the elephants.*] One day king Narapatisithu, ruler of the kingdom of Pagan, was moved by faith in these three elders and offered them each a young male elephant. Shin Sivali the elder and Shin Tamalinda the elder took their elephants and set them free in the forest. But Ananda the elder took his elephant to Bassein and set it on shipboard, meaning to send it to his kinsmen at Kiñcipura town. Now when they heard it, Ashin Sivali and Shin Tamalinda the elder spake to him on this wise : 'Master, the elephants which the king of the Law hath offered us, we have made happy by setting them free in the forest. But thou hast made thine elephant unhappy by sending it to thy kinsmen. Thou hast sinned against the Law!' But Shin Ananda the elder made reply : 'In the Law preached by the Lord Omniscient it is written in Pali, Show favour to thy kindred!' But the two elders parted from him saying, ' Because thou hearkenest not to words spoken for thy profit, from this day forth perform the duties of the Order apart from us. Begone, and cleave to us no longer!' From that day forth the elders Shin Sivali and Shin Tamalinda performed apart the duties of the Order. The elder Ananda also performed apart the duties of the Order.

[*Tamalinda quarrels with Sivali.*] A long while thereafter the elder Tamalinda sought to advance the welfare of his pupils who excelled in wisdom, strength, and courage, and by word-suggestion obtained for them the four things needful. For to all who resorted to him, whether councillors, ministers, or rich men, he said : ' Donors, here is one who hath eyes to see and ears to hear, who excelleth in strength and courage. When he hath all the four things needful, he may well study the scriptures and fulfil them. But while he hath not all the four things needful, surely he cannot study the scriptures rightly nor fulfil them.' Now when he heard thereof the elder Sivali spake to the elder Tamalinda saying, ' The Lord hateth and abhorreth the obtaining of aught that is needful by word-suggestion. Why therefore hath my lord obtained the four things needful in this way ? Thou doest not well!' But the elder Tamalinda retorted, ' The Lord hateth and abhorreth the obtaining of things needful by word-suggestion when they are obtained for oneself. As for me I take them not for myself. Nay, I have always known and maintained that no pupil, though he excel in wisdom, strength, and courage, can study the scriptures rightly nor fulfil them, unless he hath all the four things needful; only so will the religion spread and prosper. I have done well.' Then said the elder Shin Sivali : ' If my lord doeth on this wise and will not hearken to the words spoken, we must perform apart the duties of the Order!' So they parted.

[*The four sects in Pagan.*] From that day forth four several sects of the Order were known in the kingdom of Pagan. One sect of the Order was of the race of Shin Arahan, who advanced the religion and brought it from Sudhamma city in Suvanna-bhummi. One sect of the Order was of the race of Sivali the elder; one sect of the race of Tamalinda; one of the race of Ananda. Of these four sects that of the race of Shin Arahan, who first came from Sudhamma city, was called the Former Order. The three

sects who came later from the island of Ceylon were called the
Latter Order. Of the three elders who came from Ceylon, the two
elders Shin Sivali and Shin Tamalinda while they lived caused the
religion to shine, and suffered dissolution according to *karma*. Shin
Ananda the elder advanced the religion in the kingdom of Pagan
full four and fifty years, and suffered dissolution according to *karma*
in the year 596.

[*Sulamani*.] This is the history of the building of the pagoda
Sulamani. When king Narapatisithu returned from climbing
Mt. Tuywin he saw a ruby radiant and shining in a hollow, the
site of Sulamani; and he said, ' It is a sign for me to make a work
of merit here ! ' So he made all the people fill the hollow. Then
spake the elder Panthagu Ngaswèshin, fulfilled with virtues of
omission and commission, unto the king saying, ' The work thou
doest, O king, is not of merit, as thou thinkest, but of demerit ! '
Said he, ❮ I reject the alms offered by the king ! ' Then spake
king Narapatisithu, ' O glorious one ! If thou wilt reject mine
alms, thou canst avoid it only by leaving my kingdom. Is not the
alms offered by the people mine also ? ' ' What ! ' thought Panthagu
the elder, ' Speaketh the king thus to me ? I will cross over to the
island of Ceylon.' And he sojourned in Swègyo practising piety
near Tawgyi.

[*The Ogre on Tharaba gate*.] When the noble master had
departed, an ogre stood astride over the Tharaba gate guarding it,
and moved not when the king would go forth. The king called
his doctors and masters of magic and caused them to prepare divers
charms and medicines. But ever the ogre stood and moved not.
Therefore he called his masters of white magic and black and asked
them, ' Why standeth the ogre thus and will not move ? ' And
they spake into his ear saying, ' Because the noble elder Panthagu
hath gone forth reviled, the ogre standeth and will not move ! ' So
the king called his ministers and sent oftentimes to entreat him ;
but the noble master would not come, but departed saying, ' I cross
to the island of Ceylon.'

[*Mission of Turinkapyissi*.] Now when the king heard that he
had gone, he called his minister Turinkapyissi and sent him saying,
' Entreat the noble master till he follow thee.' Turinkapyissi was
a man full of seeing and hearing, and he set upon the golden boat
Dwalaung an image of the Lord overwrought with gold, and took

L 2

it with him. And the noble master, going to the harbour of ships, met him on the way. And Turinkapyissi said, ' Great master, the Lord Omniscient hath visited this port. I pray thee come ! ' So the monk followed, for it were a sin to disobey the Lord's command. He ascended the boat Dwalaung, and paid all due reverence to the image. But while he worshipped, they carried him away upstream, paddling amain the royal boat Dwalaung. Then the minister Turinkapyissi entreated him in divers ways to uphold the religion. And the noble master was constrained to go with him, for it concerned the religion.

[*Return of Panthagu.*] The king, surrounded by his ministers, went forth to meet him, and raised him by the hand and brought him to the palace. When they reached the gate the ogre descended and bowed down his head before the noble master. Coming to the palace the king with his own hands prepared an alms and ministered to him. ' Great master ! ' said the king, ' henceforth from thee I take my doctrine !'

[*The five pagodas of Beauty.*] Having spoken thus, he offered his five sons—Zeyathura, Zeyatheinhka, Yazathu, Gingathu, and Pyanchi ; and the five princes followed with the noble master. Now when he had gone a mean distance, he drew five circles upon the ground and showed them to the princes and let them return. When the princes came home they told the king thereof, and he said, ' My sons, it is a sign for you to make works of merit.' So he weighed out gold against the weight of their bodies, and with the value thereof he built by Sakra's guidance these five pagodas of Beauty—Sagyo, Myebontha, Kansunbo, Thagyadaung, and Gyauk. Each was called a pagoda of Beauty ; and they were like the work of merit made of *tharekhkan* sandalwood by Pasenadi king of Kosala in the lifetime of the Lord. Sakra himself with his own hand made the plaster for these five pagodas and overlaid it.

[*Nga Swè and Panthagu.*] This is how Panthagu the elder received the name Nga Swèshin. The noble master would not accept *kathina* robes, but it was his wont to go to the place of burial and take only a shroud spread over a dead body and wear it ; and such was called a *panthagu* robe. Now Nga Swèngè was a cowherd, and he spake to the herdsmen his companions saying, ' May it be a merit to you, a merit to me ! I will feign to be dead. Spread ye a cloth, a shroud over my body, and ask the noble

master to pick up the *panthagu*!' His companions did even as
Nga Swè had said; they spake to the noble master, and he went to
the place of burial and picked up the *panthagu*. When he had gone,
lo! Nga Swèngè was dead indeed, and breathed not. And when
his companions saw it they went to his parents' house and told
them all. His parents and their kindred and grandchildren told
the noble master. But he sprinkled and splashed on Nga Swèngè
the holy water of propitiation. Thereupon he suddenly arose and
did obeisance to the noble master. And his parents offered Nga
Swèngè to the noble master, who was known thenceforward as
Nga Swèshin.

[*Thonlu-ahpa, Thanpula, Shwethabeit.*] At Anein town—one of
the three towns, Talop, Amyin, and Anein, governed by queen
Veluvati and her son Zeyathura—king Narapatisithu built a great
pahto and called it Thonlu-ahpa, pagoda of beauty. At Talop town
also, where the likeness of a fire was seen burning in the night, he
made search and found the Mot-htawya, built by king Siridhammasoka, and there he built another great *pahto* and called it
Thanpula. Where Talop town adjoined the land of Pagan, he
made a pleasant cave-temple in a mountain-cliff, and set therein
an image of the Lord as it were walking to and fro. Within the
cliff he enshrined relics of the holy body. The cave-temple he
called after queen Veluvati; the Lord's image, Shwethabeit. Moreover, each of the king's queens made works of merit openly.

[*The comforting of Thubarit.*] Now king Narapatisithu beheld
the wife of Thubarit his brother-in-law; and his heart was bent
towards her, and he raised her to the throne and kept her near him
continually. Her husband Thubarit was as one dazed and lunatic
for full half a month. And when the king heard of it he sought
counsel of his queens, saying, 'What must I do?' And they
answered, 'O king Alaung, how can he be happy when his wife
is taken from him? Let Thubarit choose from among thy women
whom he liketh, and give him her, O king Alaung, instead of his
wife!' So the king gave him a young damsel. And Thubarit
spake into his ear, saying, 'Give me another!' So the king gave
him another damsel. Until he had received the twain, he would
not be comforted.

[*Ranmanngahtwe.*] Once the king went upstream in his golden
raft to crown with *hti* the two Kyek-yek pagodas. Now a huge

crocodile bare the royal raft upon its back and held it fast.
Ranmanngahtwe, a mighty man of valour, went down into the
water and dived, and pierced the crocodile to death with a sword.
Moreover, they made him kill a tiger, and also an elephant, in
single combat. Because he ofttimes vanquished his enemies, the
king gave him the name Anantathuriya. From that day forward
he sent Anantathuriya whenever there were thieves, cutthroats,
rioters, or rebels in border places and purlieux. And wheresoever
he went and assaulted them, he caught great numbers of his foes
alive and brought them to the king.

[*His offerings.*] That minister Anantathuriya made the elder,
Paunglaung, called Mahakassapa, his teacher ; and, building a great
pagoda, ordination hall, and monastery, he held a great festival to
call a blessing thereon. The oblations thus dedicated he recorded
in an inscription, and caused the list to be read aloud before the
king, so that the king might call his blessing. And he said :
'Anantathuriya in his present life hath borne my yoke long and
laboriously. Moreover he hath laid up matter for many benefits
throughout *samsara*. There is none like him so eager to be
blessed !' And he gave him in marriage a princess, Zeyatheinhka's
sister, born of a lesser queen, together with many articles of use
and splendour.

[*Nadaungmya.*] To Nadaungmya, ruler of Nyaungyan, great-
grandson of Nyaung-u Hpi, one of the paladins of his great-grandsire Htihlaingshin Kyanzittha, he gave the office of justiciar, that
he might ordain justice.

[*Character of Narapatisithu.*] King Narapatisithu failed not to
observe the ten duties of a king. He accepted the word spoken by
the wise, whenever there was ado or question in the villages and
kingdom. Because he was able and astute in kingcraft, all the
people loved him. He built pagodas, *gu*, monasteries, *tazaung*, and
resthouses all over Burma, and dedicated glebelands, cultivated
fields and gardens.

[*Zeyatheinhka Nandaungmya.*] He made his son Zeyatheinhka
heir to the palace, and gave great tracts and provinces, with many
articles of use and splendour, to his eldest son Zeyathura and to
Yazathu, Gingathu, and Pyanchi. Now Zeyatheinhka Nandaungmya would ever show honour and reverence to his four
brothers. Every holy day he would visit their houses and failed

not once to pay his duty. And his four brothers were loth that
he should thus come and fail not to pay his duty, and they said,
‘ Brother, build thee a pavilion in the bosom of the palace, and
when we four brothers have ascended it, then come thou and pay
thy duty.’ Even so he ordered it, according to his brothers’ charge,
and failed not once to pay his duty. Because thus he treated his four
brothers with honour and reverence, they loved him exceedingly.

[*His name Htilominlo.*] Their father, king Narapatisithu, set up
the white umbrella in the midst of his five sons and made a solemn
vow and said, ‘ May the white umbrella bend towards him who is
worthy to be king ! ’ And lo ! the white umbrella bent towards
the youngest son Zeyatheinhka. Therefore was Zeyatheinhka
known as Htilominlo.

[*Dying charge of Narapatisithu.*] Thus when the king had
advanced the welfare of the great religion, his own welfare, and
that of the generations of his sons, grandsons, and great-grandsons,
after him, for full seventy-four years of his life, he was taken ill.
He took the hand of each of his five sons in turn and placed them
on his bosom saying, ‘ Ye five dear ones, see that ye break not the
plan I have devised ! Younger and elder, do ye all your business
in concord and lovingkindness. So fair a lot alone is sweet and
comely. One who hath no kith and kindred, how many slaves
soever he may have, is not called happy. Therefore, ye five
brothers, do ye as I bid you, if ye wish the affairs of the kingdom
and the villages to be well ordered and the country quiet. If the
beak is long and ready to fight, cut the beak. If the spur is long
and ready to prick, cut the spur. If the wing is long and ready to
fly, cut the wing. We kings have no love nor hate. We should
give punishment only according to custom. Unless we act on this
wise, our neighbour will not dread nor revere us. Unless he feareth
us, not one of all our divers undertakings can we hope to speed.

‘ Again, men who go forth to fight should be raised to the cavalry
only when they have won ten infantry battles, to the elephantry only
when they have won ten cavalry battles, to the fleet only when they
have won ten elephantry battles. They should be given a town
levying four hundred only when they have won ten naval battles.
Moreover, none should be allowed an host of followers unless he
hath done well and honourably, engaging, as it were, the heart of
all the people. Unless ye give such an one an host of followers,

your neighbour surely will not fear you. Mark ye well these
words of mine. Reject them not nor forsake them, but do ye as
I bid you!'

[*His death.*] Then he charged his five sons to take a solemn
oath; and when they had taken the oath, thereafter he again
exhorted the four queens, royal kinsmen, chief ministers, and
councillors saying, 'If my five sons destroy what I have ordered,
gather in concord around him who doth not reject my words nor
forsake them, and mete ye punishment!' Thus he charged them
under a solemn vow. And when he had assigned to his four queens
and five sons tracts, districts, fiefs, and villages, the noble Alaung
king called Narapatisithu, thus mindful as well of future welfare as
of present, passed at the age of seventy-four. Thirty-seven years
in the nether house, thirty-seven years he flourished. About the
time of his death an ogre showed himself in front of the Mawgun
gate; a comet appeared in the west; the *deinnetthè* coincided with
the *thingyan*. The day of his birth was Tuesday.

144. *Of king Zeyyatheinhka Nandaungmya.*

[*Zeyyatheinhka, fl.* 1211–1234.] On Thursday, the eleventh waxing
of the month Tawthalin, in the year 573, Zeyyatheinhka Nandaungmya, son of king Narapatisithu, came to the throne. The Great
Chronicle and others state that he was king from the year 559.
Thus there is a gap of fourteen years in the reckoning. Whereby,
therefore, do we know that he ascended the throne in 573? We
know it by the Zeyyaput inscription, which says, 'Thursday, the
tenth waxing of the month Tawthalin, in the *athan* year 573, I,
Uzana, ascended the palace.' That same king is called and written
in records Htilominlo or Uzana.

He had four queens: Taungpyinthi, whose name was Hpwadawgyi,
daughter of Ottarathu, son of Thinhkathu, son-in-law of the donor
of Shwegu; Myauppyinthi, daughter of Tharevaddhana; Alèpyinthi called Sawmi, daughter of Myittha headman (so named
because he was born in Myittha village) son of Thanpathin, son of
Alaungsithu, donor of Shwegu; and Eindawthi, born of Theinhkathu,
son of Yazathu, son-in-law of Alaungsithu, donor of Shwegu. Of
these four, queen Taungpyinthi bare two sons, Theinpate and
Taramun. No son or daughter was born of the queens Alèpyinthi
and Myauppyinthi.

[*Zeyyatheinhka's character.*] When Zeyyatheinhka became king he acted righteously, insomuch that he left not void nor wanting one jot of all that his father had ordered and appointed. Humbly and reverently each holy day he failed not to visit his four elder brothers. He made equal division into five parts of all the gifts and chattels, revenues and assessments, whatsoever was yielded by the kingdom and the villages; and according to those portions he offered them, neither less nor more. Because thus he acted right-eously, the ministers and all the people loved him exceedingly; they felt tenderly towards him and blessed him in their hearts. The king was of beautiful complexion; in manner courteous and gentle; fulfilled with virtue, wisdom, and concentration. Because he was at pains alway to acquaint himself with the woes and welfare of his people, both laymen and monks, no region nor village was ever known to be in anarchy or rebellion. The rainfall was good. Far inland there was fatness, prosperity, and abundance.

[*Birth of Kyazwa.*] The king climbed Mt. Tangyi, Mt. Tuywin, and Mt. Poppa. He went downstream to Uyon town and visited the pagodas and *pahto* near the riverbank. Once as he was de-scending to Uyon town on his jewelled golden raft, queen Eindawthi gave birth upon the raft to a son Kyazwa, who received the name **Dhammaraja.** When he was but seven days old, the queen his mother died.

[*Death of Taramun.*] Not long after, when he had returned and reached his kingdom, his son Taramun, born of the chief queen Taungpyinthi, ended his *karma*. The queen his mother and the king were bruised at heart and broken; they would not take food nor water. The two queens Alèpyinthi and Myauppyinthi called the ministers of Theiddika and Kyanthaing, and said ' Loosen the hearts of the king and queen until they be comforted! '

[*The king's comforters.*] So the two great ministers approached the king and spake into his ear: ' O king, the Law teacheth that none of all the conscious beings who traverse the three worlds can escape the law of impermanence; *nirvana* only abideth. All things in the process of becoming are verily impermanent; it is their nature to rise and fall; having arisen they cease, and when they are at peace there is happiness indeed. Thus the Law teacheth; and thou, great king, should take its ordinance to heart! ' But the king spake with his two ministers and said, ' Ministers, I know the law—that it is the nature of all things to rise and fall. But now I cannot know it!' And he gasped and sobbed.

[*Sittana pagoda.*] Thereafter he took counsel with his royal kinsmen and great and trusty ministers, saying, 'Ministers, this misery cometh of the nature of love. Ah! long it needeth to seek *nirvana* free from love, to aspire by prayer to be a Lord Omniscient! May I become a Silent Buddha, and so attain *nirvana*!' And he built and finished a work of merit called Setana; it is now known as Sittana pagoda. From that day forward he went not forth by land nor water, neither to the forest nor to the mountain. He desired only to delight in works of merit.

[*Gawdawpallin.*] He built a *put zedi* at the site of the lodge of his great-grandfather Kyanzittha. He built again and finished Gawdawpallin, which his father Narapati began to build but did not finish.

[*Bodhi, Neraban, Htilominlo.*] He built a pagoda with the likeness of the Lord blossoming under the sacred banyan, the Wisdom Tree; it was called Bodhi pagoda. He made a prayer entreating an easy entry into *nirvana*, and built a pagoda and worshipped it; there was an image of the Lord, as it were, disposed for cremation on a pile of fuel of sandalwood heaped fourscore standard cubits high, what time the Lord attained *nirvana*; it was known as Neraban, which being interpreted is *kusinara*, or the manner of entering *nirvana*. When the king's father made a solemn vow and set the white umbrella in the midst of his five sons, it inclined according to the father's wish; at that place where it inclined the king built a pagoda after the likeness of Sulamani; it was called Htilominlo. The king also was called king Htilominlo. The Great Chronicle mentions the building and rebuilding of the Setana, *put zedi*, and Gawdawpallin pagodas only.

[*Death of Zeyyatheinhka.*] The king was peaceful and deliberate, master of the ten kingly duties. Thirty-seven years in the nether house, twenty-three years he flourished; he passed at the age of sixty. About the time of his death the Saturday star showed a comet; the shadow was reversed. The day of his birth was Tuesday.

145. *Of king Kyazwa.*
    The philosopher, king Kyazwa, fl. 1234–1250.] In the year 596

his son Kyazwa became king, receiving the name Dhammaraja.
He had compassion on all the people, both laymen and monks,
as though they were children of his bosom. He read the Three
Pitakas nine times over. Divers interpretations of the Pali, commentaries and sub-commentaries, he pondered oft; in the mooting
of questions there was none to equal him. Seven times a day he
studied with the noble Order. For the sake of his concubines he
composed the Paramatthabindu, that they might know of mind
and the qualities of mind, matter, *nirvana*, forms of being, and
personality. He would not even lend an ear to affairs of the villages
or kingdom. Whenever there was any inquiry to be made, power
exercised, or point of law determined, he caused his son Uzana, the
heir-apparent, to dispose thereof.

[*The growing of palmyra.*] Anawrahtaminsaw had planted a
palmyra tree at the foot of Mt. Pyekhkaywe, and made a solemn
vow saying, 'When I become king once more in this country, may
the palmyra tree grow!' In this reign, it is said, the tree grew;
and the king, hearing of it, was glad and joyful.

[*Sagu monastery. Date of the king's accession.*] In the year 597
he built at Sagu town a *pyatthad* monastery, and offered it to
Sihamaha-upali the elder. The Great Chronicle does not mention
the building and offering of the monastery; moreover, it gives 581
as the year of the king's accession to the throne. But it was
not in 581, but only in the year 596 that he ascended the throne;
and in 597 he built and offered the *pyatthad* monastery at Sagu
town. Thus there is a gap of fifteen years between the two dates
assigned to his accession. How, therefore, do we know that he
ascended the throne in 596, and built and offered the *pyatthad*
monastery in 597? We know it by the inscription in Hkèdaunggyi
monastery which states that Sihamaha-upali the elder, practising
piety in Sagu town, was invited by king Nandaungmya, and came
and practised piety at Pagan: that in the year 596, when king
Nandaungmya, benefactor of the religion, passed away, his son
Kyazwa ascended the throne; and in the year 597 he built and
offered a *pyatthad* monastery to Sihamaha-upali the elder, together
with seven elders dwelling in separate monasteries—Sarakalyana,
Saradhamma, Kalyanakitti, Nanasiha, Gambhisara, Vajiranana,
and Gunasobha, as well as fifteen of the Order dwelling together
at the chief monastery. Thus we know that he ascended the

throne in the year 596, and that he built and offered a *pyatthad*
monastery at Hkèdaunggyi in Sagu town.

[*The lake near Mt. Tuywin.*] In the year 598 he dammed the
water falling from the foot of Mt. Tuywin, and made a great lake.
He filled it with the five kinds of lotus and caused all manner
of birds, duck, sheldrake, crane, waterfowl, and ruddy goose to
take their joy and pastime therein. Near the lake he laid out
many *ta* of cultivated fields; it is said he ate three crops a year.
Hard by the lake he built a pleasant royal lodge, and took delight
in study seven times a day.

[*Pyatthada pagoda.*] Thus he laboured at the sacred writ of the
religion, and built Pyatthada pagoda, his work of merit, but did
not finish it because the people were ill paid and ill directed. He
bequeathed these words openly in history: ' I care for naught save
the fulfilment of strong virtue ! '

[*Kyazwa's death.*] One day while he was at sword-play the king
gat a wound, and passed at the age of fifty-seven. Forty-one years
in the nether house, sixteen years he flourished. About the time of
his death many vultures alighted on the stable; an ogre showed
himself at the throne-door of the palace. The day of his birth was
Monday.

146. *Of king Uzana.*

[*Uzana*, fl. A.D. 1250–1255.] In the year 612 his son Uzana
became king. His chief queen was a granddaughter of Minshinsaw,
son of the donor of Shwegu. She bare him a son Thihathu.

[*Birth of Minhkweche.*] One day the king went forth to Myittha
village, and found a turner's daughter, exceeding fair to look upon.
When the king saw her, he took and kept her continually near
him, with her hair done in a *suli* knot. Once while she was
fanning the king, on a sudden she fell. And the king asked,
' Was it a fit of epilepsy ? ' The queen replied, ' Nay. It was not
a fit of epilepsy.' So the king thought, ' There must be a reason,'
and he treated her tenderly and cherished her. And when the
months and days of her conception were fulfilled, the girl was
delivered of a male child. When the boy came of age the king
gave him over to his uncle, a monk, that he might study letters
with a noble master, chaplain of the king.

[*Childhood of queen Saw. The hamadryad.*] It came to pass, at

Seit-htein Kanbyu village in the parts of Poppa, that a farmer
in the hills had a little daughter who was just teaching the soles of
her feet to walk. Her father had taken her to the clearing and
left her under a tree, and there she slept, when lo! a great
hamadryad coiled itself around her without touching her body,
and abode covering her head with outspread hood. And when her
father looked up from his tilling and saw the great hamadryad, he
came up running in haste, and the huge snake departed and fled.
He told that matter to a wise man, who said: 'This girl will
enjoy a notable prosperity!' So the girl's parents, being rich in
goods, dressed her in fine clothes and kept her with nurses and
guardians.

[*The myalle plant.*] Now once she had planted a *myalle* plant,
and when she was twelve years old, lo! in a single bush thereof
the *ponnyek*, *saga*, and *chaya* blossomed. When it was told the
wise, they prophesied saying, 'This damsel shall be highly exalted!'
Now it was the custom of all kings to climb Mt. Poppa in the
month of Nadaw, to worship the Mahagiri spirits, brother and
sister. And when king Uzana ascended he heard that in Seit-htein
Kanbyu village three kinds of flowers had blossomed on a single
myalle plant; so he entered the village to behold it. And when he
saw the damsel planting flowers with a bud-stringing stick, he took
her, for she was of an excellent complexion. And the king had compassion on her and kept her continually near him, as a little maid.

[*The royal itch.*] One day the king felt itchy on the back and
asked her to scratch, but without saying where. And the damsel
scratched aright at once, even at the spot where the king felt the
itch. And so she did often, till at last he said, 'Hark ye, miss!
I told thee not where to scratch, but only " Scratch!" Yet thou
dost scratch aright at once. How knowest thou where I am
itchy?' And the young handmaid spake into his ear saying,
'O king Alaung, the body of noble persons is passing soft. Wheresoever a streak appears, there it itches and there I scratch!' The
king hearing the word spoken by the damsel, said, 'This damsel is
full of wit and wisdom'; and he made her great, less than a queen
and more than a concubine, and he caused her alway to minister to
him, wheresoever he went.

[*Uzana's visit to Dala.*] The king was wont to be merry even as
heir-apparent in the reign of his father. He went down the river

to Dala, and built a royal lodge and dwelt there, having sport
with elephants continually.

[*The coming of Minhkweche.*] Now the noble master, chaplain of
the king, took the horoscope of the royal son Minhkweche, and
having looked at it, he called the monk his uncle, and said, ' Thy
nephew's horoscope is clean in lore of astrology. His hour of
greatness is come. Set therefore the prince thy nephew in a small
tanswek boat, and present him at Dala where the king his father is,
ay, and leave him with the king.' So the monk his uncle took
a gift of liquor for the king, and set the prince in a small *tanswek*
boat and went downstream. When he reached Dala he offered the
gift of liquor that he had brought, and delivered to the king
the prince his nephew. And the king was of good cheer and gave
him great regard, and jested with his son, saying, ' Turner's grandson, dog's dung!'

[*The game of gonnyin.*] When Minhkweche was about to become
king, he was playing one day at *gonnyin* with his companions.
And behold, there was lying on the court some dog's dung indeed.
So they took and removed it, and covering it each with an handful
of earth and a bough of a tree they went down flat upon their knees
and worshipped it. When the wise saw the great pile that they
had worshipped, they began to say, ' Erelong this prince shall
become king!'

[*The end of the king's hunting.*] One day the king went riding
on the back of his *katha* elephant, for they would have him see
a goodly elephant caught in the *kheddah*, worthy of a king's regard.
Now the wild elephant was must, and followed the new scent, and
caught in its tusk the girth ropes of the royal elephant; and the
king and the *howdah* fell in a heap, and the elephant touched him.
Thirty-three years in the nether house, five years he flourished; he
passed at the age of thirty-eight. About the time of his death
smoke issued from Thabbyinnyu pagoda; the Thursday star crossed
the disc of the moon; the *deinnetthè* coincided with the *thingyan*;
two crocodiles were seen fighting with teeth on the surface of the
river. The day of his birth was Wednesday.

147. *Of Minhkweche.*

[*Yazathingyan dupes Thihathu.*] The sons of the late king were
Thihathu and Minhkweche only. This is how the younger of these,

Minhkweche, came to kingship. When Thihathu, king Uzana's son whom his father had made heir while yet he was alive, ascended the throne with intent to be king, the chief minister Yazathingyan spake into his ear saying, ' Son of my lord! Thy father hath died at Dala town, a distant village on the borders of the kingdom. There are ministers who have bowed their heads at the royal grave where he is buried; and there are ministers who have not bowed their heads. Tarry thine anointing until all thy servants, ministers, and headmen of villages and circles have returned from bowing their heads at the grave of thy father.' So Thihathu trusted him and said, ' Bow ye your heads at my father's grave and return quickly.'

So the chief minister Yazathingyan departed, and all the ministers and headmen of villages and circles. And when they came and assembled at the grave, Yazathingyan spake on this wise : ' Ministers, if we raise Thihathu to the throne, all the folk and villages will suffer. That prince Thihathu is exceeding proud and wrathful, in envy violent, jealous of another's wife, covetous, ambitious. He regardeth not the words of truth. I speak not of you ministers only : even me, the chief of ministers, he hath treated with contumely and insult. For once it happened that Thihathu came up from behind me, and I saw him not and had not gathered up the lappet of my sleeve, and he spat betel-blood upon the sleeve-lappet ! Though I said, " I chanced not to see my lord's son coming ! " his heart was not appeased.' And he took out of the box where it lay the garment on which the prince spat betel-blood, and showed it to the ministers. And when they saw it they said, ' Even before he is king he hath shent the face of the chief minister and regarded him not. When once he reigneth, where shall we be ? '

[*He makes Narathihapate king*, fl. 1255–1290.] So all the ministers and headmen of villages and circles weie of one mind, one spirit, and, coming to Dala, they seized Thihathu and raised his younger brother Minhkweche to the throne in the year 617. Ascending the throne he received the name Narathihapate. The daughter of the rich man of Seit-htein Kanbyu whom his father took and raised to the throne, he exalted to be his queen. She was known as queen Saw.

[*Rebirths of the Pagan kings.*] The Lord had left a prophecy upon the top of Mt. Tangyi in the country of Pagan that the ogre,

guardian of the mountain, who had once made an umbrella of three
in leaves and screened the Lord from the sun, should become king
thrice in Pagan.   Even so it came to pass; for he became king
once, it is said, as Sale Ngahkwe, once as Kalagya, once as Narathihapate.   Moreover, these three kings of several generations—
king Thamoddarit (who had been Pulèli, king of elephants, one of
the ten ripe future Buddhas), king Nawrahta, and king Kyazwa—
were but one person, who became king thrice in the kingdom of
Pagan.   And these three kings also—Pyuminhti, Thinlikyaung,
Kyanzittha—were one person, it is said, who became king thrice.

It was not until the reign of king Narathihapate that the town
was known as Pagan.   Because he was one who had received the
Lord's prophecy, the king was great in glory and power.   And
because he had become a man from the state of an ogre, he was
violent in envy, proud and wrathful, and gluttonous in eating and
drinking.

This is the tale how Yazathingyan, the chief minister, gave kingship to Narathihapate.   When Narathihapate was a prince, and
his elder brother Thihathu spat the chewed betel upon the sleeve-
lappet of the minister Yazathingyan, it came to pass that Narathihapate came to the house of the chief minister and said, 'Grandfather, be my succour!'   'Son of my lord!' quoth Yazathingyan,
for it was like a hand-touch to one about to weep; 'it is for thee
and for none other!'   Even as he had promised, he failed not to
give the kingship.

[*The king forgets Yazathingyan.*]   But when Narathihapate was
king he forgot and regarded not his chief minister.   So Yazathingyan's heart was straitened, and taking a broken *pankap* he went
into the palace.   And the king asked, 'Grandfather, why dost thou
eat out of a broken *pankap*?'   And Yazathingyan said, 'Son of my
lord!   Ever since the sons and grandsons of a turner have become
great, there is none to mend it; but I must eat out of a broken
pankap!'

Some chronicles write *kunkalap* (betel-stand), and others *pankalap*
(flower-stand).   A *pankalap* is a vessel used by ancient kings and
ministers to hold betel, flowers, or parched rice.   In the dictionary
samuggo and *sammato* are both interpreted as *pankap*, likewise *kuntho*.
Moreover, in the inscription which tells how Narapati, famous lord
of the golden throne, was established king, it is said that he caused

a *pankap* to be placed for holding flowers and parched rice, and
a basket for flowers. For these reasons we must hold it right to
use the word *pankap* in this place.

[*Yazathingyan goes into exile.*] When the king heard the speech
of his minister Yazathingyan, he was sore at heart and asked him,
'Grandfather, when they crown a *gu* with a finial, whereby do they
raise it?' He replied, 'Son of my lord, they make a scaffold first
and so they raise the finial.' Said the king once more, 'When the
finial is set on the top of the *gu*, what do they do with the scaffold?' 'Son of my lord,' he replied, 'when the finial is set on the
top of the *gu*, it is not graceful until the scaffold is destroyed.' So
the king commanded saying, 'I am as the finial, Yazathingyan as
the scaffold! As the finial reaches the top of the *gu*, so I have
reached kingship. And the finial will not appear graceful until
the scaffold, Yazathingyan, be destroyed. Ho! ministers, seize his
office, his elephants, and horses, his minions, and retinue, and off
with him to Dala town!' And they did as the king had ordered
and sent him away.

As Yazathingyan journeyed a great wind arose, and lo! the big
trees brake and split, but the waterplants brake not but only leaned
and swayed. And, seeing it, he was taken with remorse and said,
'I, a servant of the king, have not been as wise even as a waterplant. Because I have acted as a big tree it hath come to this!'
When his escort returned, the king asked what words Yazathingyan
had spoken. So the escort reported them: 'O Lord of glory! A
great wind arose and big trees brake and split, but the waterplants
brake not but only leaned and swayed. And when Yazathingyan
saw it he said, "I have not been as wise even as a waterplant."'
And the king abode in silence.

[*Rebellions of Macchagiri and Martaban.*] Now when Macchagiri
heard that Yazathingyan was gone into exile, he rebelled and was
in anarchy. Nga Shwe also, grandson of Nga Nwè, ruler of
Martaban, was aloof and insolent. When it was reported to the
king he remained downcast, for his wise minister with whom he
aye consulted was not there. Queen Saw spake into his ear,
'O king, how art thou thus downcast? Thou must needs consult
thy councillors and captains. If thou art ill content with them, call
thy chief minister Yazathingyan with whom thou wast wroth, and
seek his counsel. When long days are past, peradventure the rebels

will increase and prosper. Ere they become strong, call thy chief
minister Yazathingyan.'

[*Recall of Yazathingyan.*] So the king sent a minister in a fast
boat and said, 'Call Yazathingyan!' When he reached Dala he
set him aboard the fast boat saying, 'Thy grandson, the lord of
life, calleth thee. Thou must come straightway.' And they
came upstream speedily.

[*The emerald spoon.*] On the way they met fishermen returned
from making an offering of fish. And they saw in the fishermen's
boat an emerald spoon, gotten by casting the net at a venture.
And Yazathingyan asked them, 'Where gat ye the emerald spoon?'
They replied, 'In casting the net we gat it, and now we bring it
for our babes to play with.' Said he, 'Sell it to me!' So the
fishermen took no thought but gave it away in their folly. And
Yazathingyan polished it well, and because it was an emerald
spoon of worth immeasurable it shone with dazzling colours.
Therefore he gave a guerdon to the fishermen and made haste and
came upstream.

This emerald spoon the Great Chronicle and others differ in
calling either an emerald stone or an emerald spoon. But since
the Old Pagan Chronicle and others call it an emerald shell-spoon,
it is better to call it simply an emerald spoon.

When the chief minister Yazathingyan reached Pagan, the king
conveyed him on the back of an elephant. And when he came to
the palace and offered the emerald spoon, the king was exceeding
glad and asked, 'Grandfather, where didst thou get this emerald
spoon?' He spake into his ear, 'O king, because of thy glory
I gat it!' And the king said, 'Grandfather, I was wroth with
thee, but now let not thine heart be troubled!' And he restored
him all his estates, his elephants and horses, his retinue and minions,
whom he had seized. Moreover, he added and gave him to enjoy
new fiefs, both towns and villages, and divers articles of use and
splendour.

[*Tharepyissapate and Yazathingyan.*] Then he purposed to send
two generals to the parts where the rulers of Macchagiri and
Martaban were in anarchy and rebellion. Tharepyissapate, mayor
of the inner palace, he sent against Macchagiri with two hundred
fighting elephants, two thousand horse, and twenty thousand
warriors from the forts, colonies, and border villages along the

upper country north and south. The same day he sent his chief
minister Yazathingyan to march on Martaban by land and water
with two hundred fighting elephants, two thousand horse, and
twenty thousand warriors from the forts, colonies, and border
villages along the nether country east and west.

[*Yazathingyan takes Martaban.*] At Dagon Yazathingyan left
all the boats that followed him, and with great hosts of elephants
and horses he marched by land on Martaban. Nga Shwe, ruler of
Martaban, hearing that the chief minister Yazathingyan was even
now upon him, gathered into the town Taunghteip all those who
dwelt in the border regions and villages, and there awaited his
onslaught. And Yazathingyan, surrounding them on all sides like
cattle enclosed in a pen, strengthened and made whole his own
army and assaulted day and night continually. The folk within
the town, being too dense and many in multitude, shent each other
and were spoiled. The water flowing from the mountain was not
enough for them to drink, and they could not go without the town
to fetch water; therefore the inhabitants were sorely straitened.
When they had stood leaguer for seven days or eight, they were
an-hungry and there was little food. So they all came and made
surrender to the army encompassing them, and thus the whole
town of Martaban was captured. Then Yazathingyan, having won
the town, made all things orderly and secure in Martaban and
appointed ruler of the province a minister called Aleimma, grandson of the old and great Aleimma, minister to king Alaungsithu.
Thereafter he took Nga Shwe, ruler of Marataban, with all his
family, slaves, elephants, and horses, and returned homewards.

[*Rout of Tharepyissapate.*] Meantime Tharepyissapate had set
forth; but before he reached Macchagiri, so slack were the discipline
and strategy, that one night his army was seized with panic and
brake; in hot haste they fled, there was none to stop them.
Yazathingyan met them at Minbu port, and when he heard what
had befallen, said, ' Pyissapate, my friend, this panic of thine army
is a grievous blow.' Let not the king hear of it too soon. After
I have told him of my victory in the war and presented him with
gifts and spoils, then when his heart is merry I will speak soft
words into his ear that his anger may abate.' So Yazathingyan
made haste and came upstream.

[*Ot-hla's mission.*] But the king had heard already that ere he

M 2

met his foe Tharepyissapate had lost his army in a panic, and his
wrath was kindled and he cried, ' Without thrusting or throwing,
without attacking or retreating, lo! he hath lost his army, nor
dealt he blow for blow! Should such a general live?' And he
sent Yazathingyan's son, Nyaung-u Ot-hla, with the order to kill
him. As Yazathingyan came upstream he met his son at the town
Kuhkanngè and questioned him. He said, ' The king's wrath is
kindled against Tharepyissapate, and he hath sent me even to slay
him.' 'Good son,' said Yazathingyan, ' Until thou get a messenger
from me, let not thine hand exceed!'

[*Yazathingyan's return.*] So Yazathingyan came upstream in
haste, and when he arrived he presented Nga Shwe, ruler of
Martaban, with his family and many prisoners of war, elephants,
horses, and all his spoils. And the king was glad and gave him
great rewards. To each of those who had won honour in battle he
gave a guerdon and made them great.

[*His intercession.*] Then while the royal heart was glad and
merry Yazathingyan spake into his ear, ' Great lord of majesty
and glory! All we thy servants have no wish save one—even to
win, at a mere wave of the hand, all the realms and kingdoms on
the surface of the earth in Jambudipa, that thou, O king great
and glorious, mayest rule over them all! But in the Law it is
written : " Whatsoever tends to rise is like to fall. Whatsoever
tends to fall is like to rise. *Nirvana* only abideth, the calming of
this law of rise and fall." It is therefore the nature of battles
that those be lost which one had hoped to win, and those be won
which one had feared to lose. Time and honour, place and position,
discipline and strategy, toil and travail—all depend on these.
Only when thy servant Tharepyissapate is called unto thy feet and
restored to his familiar place, only then, methinks, my service to
my king shall find an end!' ' Tharepyissapatengè!' replied the
king: 'I have sent Nyaung-u Ot-hla with the order to kill him.
If he be yet alive, let him go free!'

[*Tharepyissapate is restored.*] So Yazathingyan sent in haste and
called Tharepyissapate ; and when he came the king sought counsel
of queen Saw, saying, ' Whom must I appoint mayor of the inner
palace?' Queen Saw replied, 'Tharepyissapate is thine own hench-
man, and one whom my lord may trust. Thou hast won great
merit, verily, in saving him alive when he deserved to die. Were

it not well to appoint him mayor in his familiar place ? ' So the king restored him.

[*Surrender of Macchagiri.*] When the king returned from climbing Poppa Nat in the month of Nadaw, he called the four generals, Yazathingyan, Tharevaddana, Sitturinkabo and Sitturinkathu, and commanded them saying, ' Smite ye Macchagiri until ye capture him ! ' So they took four thousand fighting elephants, forty thousand horses, and four hundred thousand mighty men; and when they reached Macchagiri they razed to the dust the outlying villages and purlieux. The Macchagiri king awaited them on the mount of Theks; and they compassed him in on every side, and, making their army whole and strong, barred his escape. The host of warriors who followed them were great in multitude, and soon they were an-hungered, and had naught to eat save fruits and roots only. The inhabitants of the town had not even burnt chaff to eat and were utterly starving. At last the ruler of Macchagiri, being sore afraid, came with his son and brother, and an elder who had visited Ceylon, and uttered words of pleading : ' I dare not again break faith. Spare ye my life ! '

[*Ot-hla is sent with the tidings.*] Ot-hla, son of Yazathingyan, was sent with the first tidings thereof. When he reached Salin he boarded a fast boat and came upstream, dividing not day nor night. Now ere the king went forth in the morning, he opened the palace window and anxiously looked out; for no messenger was come for a long while with tidings of the war. And lo ! he saw a boat with white sails spread coming upstream from Lokananda point. And he thought : ' Peradventure it is the boat of a messenger come upstream from the battle.' And he sent urgently for tidings. Now Ot-hla, servant of the king, would say naught concerning the battle, but said only, ' I am come ! ' And they whom the king had sent spake into his ear the words of Ot-hla. But the king cried : ' So distraught am I that I send urgently for tidings. Yet he will say naught concerning the battle, but saith only, " I am come." Should he answer me thus ? ' And he sent executioners to kill Nga Ot-hlangè.

And Ot-hla looked, and lo ! the executioners came running with gleaming swords and scabbards and ascended the boat. And when he questioned them they said, ' We are come to kill thee ! ' But Ot-hla said, ' First let me tell my lord of the fair event of the battle.' When the executioners reported the words of Ot-hla, the king commanded, 'Let him first come.' So when he entered the king's presence, Ot-hla opened the towel wrapped around his head; and behold, his hair was grievously decayed and fell in shocks, topknot and all. Then he showed the king how the hair thus fallen was full of lice and slimy; and he spake into his ear, 'My lord, I have borne thy yoke till all my hairs are decayed! Without first seeing my lord it irked me to speak. How could I fairly have spoken? Therefore I spake no word.' And the king was glad and praised him saying, 'Good words and true!'

Then he caused his young handmaids to purify Ot-hla's hair, and they cleansed and anointed it with fragrant oil. When his hair was cleansed and the topknot tied, the king caused a barber to attend his beard. And when his body and hands were rubbed with fragrant ointment he robed him in a rich *paso*, and he made ready suckets of delicious flavour, and caused him to eat in the royal presence. He heaped favours upon him.

[*End of the war.*] At the last he said, 'Administer the oath to Macchagiri, the ruler and the whole town. Then bring hither his son Zambuka, his younger sister, his nephew, and his aunt.' Thus he ordered and set Ot-hla free. And Ot-hla hied him forth, dividing not day nor night. When he arrived, the four generals, even as the king commanded, administered the oath to Macchagiri, the ruler, and the whole town, and returned, bringing the best of his elephants and horses and his son and brother.

[*Death of Yazathingyan.*] Now the chief minister Yazathingyan had told king Narathihapate: 'I will not return to the kingdom of Pagan until I have taken captive thy Thek vassal, Macchagiri.' Day and night he had borne the king's yoke and toiled and striven beyond his strength, desiring to reach his end. But he was three-score and two years old, and so decrepit that he could neither sit nor stand nor walk nor lie down. And now he fell sick of a bloody flux, and, though he had physicians to attend him, he could not be cured, but, reaching Dala town, he ended his *karma*. When the lord of life heard thereof, he remembered all that he had done in former and in latter days, and his heart was bruised and broken.

[*Zambuka.*] When Zambuka, son of the ruler of Macchagiri, came, he submitted his neck to the king's golden sole and sware

that he would be steadfast and shoulder the royal yoke. Thereafter
he remained faithful, and the king gave him his daughter born of
a concubine whom he begat in the nether house.

[*The sons of Yazathingyan quarrel.*] Now the two Op-hla brothers,
sons of Yazathingyan, quarrelled over their father's name. And
the king called them, and said : ' For a chief minister, glory, might
of arm, and wisdom, are the root and pith. To have the name
Yazathingyan doth not in itself make one great. In the reigns
of our grandsires and great-grandsires famous generals were of
different names. Whatever be the name of minister or general,
merit and quality alone are the root of all renown. Now ye
ministers quarrel over your father's name. I cannot give you your
father's name. To the elder, Pagan Op-hlagyi, I give the title
Anantapyissi; to the younger, Nyaung-u Op-hlangè, I give the
title Rantapyissi.'

[*The king's rule in the palace.*] Because the king had become
a man from the state of an ogre, he was great in wrath, haughti-
ness, and envy, exceeding covetous and ambitious. He had three
thousand concubines and maids of honour. There were thirty chief
scribes to examine the lists and registers; they failed not day nor
night. The guards of the royal slumbers were staunch and loyal,
and guarded day and night at the inner and the outer wall. Thus
the king's rule was painful to the palace-women, insomuch that
none durst trifle with a single word.

Queen Saw alone was the chief queen. The lesser queens were
five: Sawlon, daughter of a master of white magic; Sawnan,
daughter of queen Hpwasaw's sister; Shinhpa; Shinmauk; and
Shinshwe. These five queens took each their turn to present food
before the king.

The king, being one who had received the Lord's prophecy,
suffered not from any of the ninety-six diseases, and never so much
as sneezed nor yawned; and so none was allowed to sneeze or yawn
in his presence. If any one happened to sneeze or yawn he beheaded
him. One day a young handmaid in the king's presence was
exceeding fain to sneeze, and because she could not refrain it, she
put her face to a great jar and sneezed, hoping that the king would
not hear. But alas! the sound was louder than if she had sneezed
openly. And the king asked : ' What sound is that? ' Queen
Saw spake into his ear, saying, ' A girl was afraid to sneeze openly,

so she put her face to a great jar and sneezed!' And he asked
again, 'How dared she sneeze?' 'O king,' replied queen Saw,
'sneezing and yawning are even as the ninety-six diseases. Only
the king is free from diseases and needeth not to sneeze nor yawn.
But all other folk, who are not free from sneezing and yawning,
cannot refrain themselves, but sneeze!' 'Is it even so?' quoth
the king. 'I knew it not ere this, but aye waxed wroth.' And he
had great remorse.

Now when the king awoke from slumber his mind was not
loosened until he had thrown and hit his handmaids with aught
that was in his reach. So while he was fast asleep queen Saw
removed the weapons that were near him and left only *lompani* and
other fruits. Once when he awoke from sleep he threw the *lompani*
fruit that was near him at a young handmaid; whereby she swelled
at the waist. Therefore the *lompani* fruit was called *hkayan.*

In the hot season the king loved to sport at splashing water. He
made a great shade from the palace to the river wharf and walled
it in so that men might not see, and built a royal lodge for security
thereby; and taking his queens, concubines, and all his women he
was wont to go along a tunnel of cabins and sport in the water.
One day he whispered a young girl and caused her to drench queen
Sawlon with water, so that her eyes and face and hair were wring-
ing wet. Sawlon was chafed at heart, and she put poison in the
king's food and said, 'Sawmauk, I am not well. Prithee, take my
place and offer the king his food!' And Sawmauk thought no ill
but offered the food.

Now, just as he was about to eat, a dog below the table sneezed.
Therefore the king ate not but gave it to the dog; and when the
dog ate, that moment he died. 'What is this?' cried the king,
and Shinmauk spake into his ear, 'Sawlon told me she was ill and
begged me to offer the food in her stead!' So the king called
Sawlon and questioned her and because she could not hide the
matter nor jest it away, she cried, 'Thou grandson of a turner!
I have done thee service and thou hast made me great; and now
that I am exalted to this high degree, lo! thou hast whispered
a young girl and she hath drenched me with water in the eyes of
all, so that my clothes and hair were wet! Therefore my heart was
warped and I plotted against thee.'

Then the king called a thousand smiths and caused them to build

an iron frame and commanded her to be burnt thereon. But
Sawlon gave abundance of gold and silver to the executioners that
they might not finish the iron frame for seven days. Meanwhile
she practised piety and virtue and hearkened to the Law of Abhidhamma night and day for full seven days, and told her beads
recalling the merits of the Three Gems, beginning each with ' Such
is He . . . . .', with ' Well expounded . . . . .', and with ' Well
accomplished . . . . .'.

But when the seventh day was come the executioners called her
with fair and seemly words : ' Wife of a king ! The royal anger
is terrible ! Tarry not, but come !' Then, telling her beads as she
recalled the merits of the Three Gems, Sawlon ascended the blazing
iron frame. And lo ! the fire, they say, was extinguished thrice.
After the third time she prayed, ' May I be burnt and vanish in a
moment ! And may the boon I ask be granted !' So she died.

Not long after Sawlon died the king at his hour of sleep raved
and shrieked aloud, ' Sawlon, come and watch beside me !' Queen
Saw spake into his ear, ' O king, didst thou not put to death thy
slave Sawlon ? ' But the king's heart was bruised and broken and
he could not sleep. When the elder, the king's chaplain, heard of
it he came and admonished him : ' Lo ! thou hast put her to death.
It ill beseems thee, O king, to be broken and bruised therefor. If
other kings, thy fellow builders of empire, hear thereof, they will
laugh thee to scorn. Peradventure they who visit thee hereafter
will scant thee reverence. Publish not thine heart's remorse, O
king, to all the people. Remember the Law of Right Effort
preached by the Lord Omniscient : " Strive to avert the spreading
of evil that hath arisen. Strive to avert the arising of evil that
hath not arisen. Strive to aid the arising of good that hath not
arisen. Strive to aid the spreading of good that hath arisen."

So at last the king was filled with patience and control. From
that day forward he commanded his uncle Theimmazi saying,
' Albeit I am angry, weigh thou and examine every matter. Tarry
for a half month, for a decade of days. Let him die thereafter who
deserveth to die. Who deserveth not to die, let him go free !'
Theimmazi was the younger brother of the king's mother. He
had been a monk, but when the king came to the throne he turned
layman and received the name Theimmazi.

The king's son Uzana was born of Sawnan, a lesser queen,

daughter of queen Saw's elder sister. When he came of age the king gave him Bassein town. The king's son Kyawzwa was born of Shinhpa, a lesser queen. When he came of age the king gave him Dala town. The king's son Thihathu was born of Shinmauk, a lesser queen. When he came of age the king gave him the town of Prome. The king's daughter Misaw-u was born of Shinshwe, a lesser queen; and the king loved her. Now the king feared lest his sons should hearken to the counsels of those who would destroy him, and so make anarchy and rebellion; therefore he suffered them not to sojourn and rule in the fief whose revenues they enjoyed, but bound them to abide by turn both day and night in his presence.

The king was gluttonous in eating; he hankered after curries of meat. Pig's forelegs and hindlegs he would have as meat for his curries. They were first presented before him, and he would give his son Uzana a foreleg, his son Kyawzwa also a foreleg, his son Thihathu a hindleg. One day Thihathu's mother bethought her : ' He giveth forelegs to the sons of others; to my son he giveth but a hindleg!' So she bribed the chief roaster of game and gat for Thihathu, ruler of Prome, the foreleg that was ever given to Kyawzwa of Dala, and for Kyawzwa of Dala the hindleg ever given to Thihathu, ruler of Prome. When the mother of the ruler of Dala knew it, she wove fair words and bewrayed the matter to the king. And the king said, ' I wist it not. Whose trickery is this ? ' And he called the chief roaster of game and questioned him ; who said, ' The mother of the ruler of Prome besought me to give her son the foreleg, and I gave it.' So the king punished the chief roaster of game, and was wont to tease Shinmauk by calling her ' Stealer of pig's trotters !' And when his heart was vexed he would also tease Thihathu, saying, ' Son of a stealer of pig's trotters !' When often thus he teased him, the heart of Thihathu was warped, and he uttered evil words secretly; the which when Uzana ruler of Bassein heard, he laid them to heart and said, ' These twain, mother and son, will certainly assail my lord the king, an if they may !'

[*The king's curries.*] Whensoever the king partook of food, there must always be three hundred dishes, salted and spiced, sweet and sour, bitter and hot, luscious and parching. After he had eaten once or twice of these dishes of curry, he would give them to his cousins and sons, to lesser persons of the royal house, and to his councillors and captains. He would give them also to his queens and concubines, excepting none. It was ever the duty of queen Saw to record these curries and note them down in lists with the stewards. Thus she ordered and appointed them.

[*His places of pastime.*] This is how the king made merry during the three seasons. During the rainy season he took his pastime in a garden close to the royal city. In winter he took his pastime wherever there were flowers and fruits in the upper and nether parts of his kingdom. On the coming of the month of Tabaung he went each year for sport in fishing at Tonhkaung.

[*Building of Mingalazedi.*] On Sunday the sixth waxing of the month of Tabaung in the year 630 he built Mingalazedi pagoda. That was the only year when he failed to go to Tonhkaung. Now in those days a dark prophecy arose : ' The pagoda is finished and the great country ruined ! ' Soothsayers, therefore, and masters of magic said : ' When this *zedi* is finished the kingdom of Pagan will be shattered into dust ! ' Hearing that word, the king tarried and built no more for full six years.

Then Panthagu the reverend elder, fulfilled with piety and virtue, spake : ' O king, thou claimest to have received the Lord's prophecy, but aye thou hast ensued the kingdom of greed, of hate. Thou hast not observed the meditation on Impermanence. Lo ! thou hast built a work of charity and merit, yet now thou tarriest and wilt not finish it fearing lest the country be ruined. Must this country and thou, its king, abide for ever and not die ? ' And the king thought, ' My reverend master ! He hath spoken, seeing that I must long be sunk and drowned in *samsara*. He alone hath saved me from the four places of evil doom. All the Bodhisats of old forsook their families and kingdoms, their towns and villages, praying only that they might be the Lord. I am a king who hath received a prophecy. Who am I that I should tarry and build not the Lord's *zedi*, fearing lest the country come to ruin ? Peradventure, the kings who come hereafter will laugh me to scorn.'

Therefore on Thursday the full moon of Kason in the year 636 he built the *zedi* ; and having cast in pure gold the images of the eight and twenty [Buddhas], of the seven postures, and of the chiefest and the great disciples, all richly fraught with gems and enchased and set with the nine divers-coloured jewels, he enshrined them there. Moreover, he cast in pure silver seated images, one cubit high, of the fifty-one kings who reigned of old in the country of Pagan, together with images of his queens and concubines, sons and daughters, ministers and headmen of villages and circles, and placed them around the sacred reliquary. The relics of the Lord's body he set in a gem-embroidered casket fraught with the nine jewels, and, placing them on the aye-victorious white she-elephant, he bare them, attended by a mighty concourse, from the royal house to the work of merit.

This was the manner of it. He housed the white she-elephant in rich caparisons all overwrought with jewels. Thereon he set the *pyatthad* and within the *pyatthad* a reliquary richly fraught with gems. Within the reliquary were the relics of the sacred body together with a gem-embroidered casket enchased and set with rubies and precious stones of inestimable worth. And so he caused the white she-elephant to pass at a soft and easy pace. The king's family, his kindred, and persons of the blood royal, together with the ministers, followed after, eight hundred in all, adorned with ruby earrings, diadems, and pearls. Moreover, he caused his daughters and the daughters of ministers to do their hair in the *suli* knot and to wear apparel gorgeous with ornaments of rubies, emeralds, and pearls; and they followed after, eight hundred in all.

This is how he decked the path on either hand from the royal house to the work of merit. The road was covered with bamboo flooring. Over the bamboo floor were spread hurdles of bamboo chesses. Above the bamboo chesses mats were placed, and above the mats satin, Chinese silks and woollen tissues. When thus the path was spread, one who went along it was not wetted by the rain, which fell ever before him laying the dust. Such was the manner of it. To left and right along the whole way was bamboo lattice-work, except at the corners, with pots full of lilies, living plantain trees, and living sugar-cane to form a fence. Because the king would have it all designed and built and spread in true and seemly manner, with rigging and hanging of long tapestries and sheets both white and royal, the road was passing fair and pleasant even as the spirits' highway in Sudassana.

After the relics of the sacred body came and were enshrined, the king caused his family and ministers together with the princesses and daughters of ministers, all gorgeously apparelled, to unstring and sever all their ornaments and offer them to the sacred relic-chamber. When the *zedi* pagoda was already built, a relic of the sacred body came from the island of Ceylon, and he enshrined it in Pahtotha at the north-west corner of Mingalazedi. And when his work of merit was complete he held a great festival to call down blessing upon it. We have set forth the year and month and day of the building of the pagoda and the enshrining of the relics in accordance with the *thanbaing* of Mingalazedi, offered by king Narathihapate.

[*Wariru the Talaing revolts.*] In the year 643 Wariru the Talaing killed the minister Aleimma, who ruled Martaban town subject to the king's dominion, and became king.

[*The Tarop ambassadors.*] In the same year the Tarop Utibwa sent ten ministers and a thousand horsemen to demand golden rice-pots, vessels of gold and silver, gold and silver ladles, gold and silver basons, because, said he, they were once offered by Anawra-htaminsaw. Furthermore, some chronicles say that they came demanding a white elephant. The Tarop ambassadors in making demand showed not due respect nor reverence in the king's presence. Therefore the king commanded: ' Slay these ten ministers and thousand horsemen. Let none escape ! ' Then spake the minister Anantapyissi unto his ear saying, ' O lord of glory ! Albeit the ambassadors of the Tarop Utibwa have behaved ill in their ignorance of royal ceremony, it should be noted down, if thou approve, and report sent to the Utibwa. Or again, if thou think fit to be patient, speak thou conciliatory words and so settle the affairs of the villages and kingdom. The kings of old were never wont to kill ambassadors. Be advised, therefore, and endure ! ' But the king commanded saying, ' They have affronted me to my face ! Slay them ! ' So the ministers feared the king's command and put them to death ; they spared not one.

[*Tarop invasion.*] But when the Tarop Utibwa heard that his ambassadors were slain, his wrath was kindled and he mustered all the parts of his army to the number of six million horsemen and two crores of footmen, and they came marching. Narathihapate, hearing that the Tarop Utibwa's fighting men had marched against him, sent forth his generals Anantapyissi and Rantapyissi with four hundred thousand soldiers and great hosts of elephants and horses saying, ' Block ye the road against the coming of the Tarop warriors, and fight them.'

[*Fall of Bhamo and Ngahsaunggyan.*] So the four generals marched, and coming to Ngahsaunggyan town they made it strong and girded it with forts and moats and ditches, and fought in their defence at the river-crossing of Bhamo. For full three months they slew the enemy and spared not even the feeders of elephants and horses, but slew them all. But when ten myriad men were dead, the Tarop Utibwa sent twenty myriad; when twenty myriad were dead, he sent forty myriad; insomuch that the king's men were weary and fordone, and as soon as the Tarops crossed the river Ngahsaunggyan fell.

[*War of Spirits.*] Now there was war between the spirits. Tepathin, guardian spirit of the city-gate of Pagan, Wetthakan, guardian spirit of Salin, the Kanshi guardian spirit, and the Ngatinkyeshin spirit were wounded. (The New Chronicle writes, instead of Tepathin spirit, Thanpathin spirit.) And it came to pass, on the same day when the army at Ngahsaunggyan perished, that the spirit who was ever wont to attend on the king's chaplain returned to Pagan and shook him by the foot and roused him from his sleep saying, ' This day hath Ngahsaunggyan fallen. I have been wounded by an arrow. Likewise the spirits Wetthakan of Salin, Kanshi, and Ngatinkyeshin, are wounded by arrows.' Thus he spake, it is said; and the monk, chaplain of the king, called a young novice and caused him to tell the king that Ngahsaunggyan was destroyed. But the king asked the novice how he knew this thing. And the novice said, ' Tepathin, the guardian spirit of Tharaba gate, hath come from Ngahsaunggyan and brought tidings thereof to the chaplain. Therefore I know that to-day Ngahsaunggyan hath perished.'

[*Despair at Pagan.*] Then the king called his ministers and consulted them saying, ' Pagan town is now too narrow for us, in depth too shallow. It cannot contain the hosts of fighting men, the hosts of elephants and horses. Let us go straightway to the south and establish a strong town from Myitmya Pahtin village in the east, with the town of Ywatha in the midst. This is my purpose. And because at this late hour brick and stone cannot be readily obtained, dispatch we all things quickly and pull down pagodas, *gu*, and monasteries, and take their brick!' Thus by

the king's order, it is said, these buildings were destroyed : one
thousand great *gu*, ten thousand small *gu*, three thousand *Kalagyaung*.

Now while they were destroying them, Anuraja found a
prophecy written on a red copper *parabaik*, and he read the writing,
and it said : 'In the reign of a king who is father of twins, the
country of Pagan will utterly perish at the hands of Tarops.'
And the king made search among his concubines, and lo ! it was
found that twins had verily been born of a young concubine ; and
they told that matter to the king. Then the king said, ' Albeit
I build a town in my defence, I cannot defend it ! '

[*The king's flight to Bassein.*] So he caused them to prepare
a thousand boats of war, *sampan*, and great fighting boats, and
placed therein his gold, silver, and all his treasures. He stored
paddy in a thousand cargo boats. And he set all his ministers on
board a thousand *hlawga* and *kyaw* boats. His concubines and
maids of honour, his royal guards and tutors, he conveyed in
a thousand golden barges. Then because the multitude of slaves,
concubines, and maids of honour was too great, and there was no
room for all of them to embark, the king commanded saying, ' If
the people are too many and there is no room, we cannot leave
behind us and set free the slave-women of the inner palace, for the
Tarops will take them. Bind them, therefore, hand and foot, and
throw them into the water ! '

But the elder, chaplain of the king, said, ' O king, it is hard
indeed for any creature traversing *samsara* to become man. Albeit
he become man, it is still very hard for him to be born in the
dispensation of the Buddha. There is no need for thee, O king,
to suffer the evil that ensueth if thou throw them into the water.
For if thou throw them into the water it will be a theme for future
kings hereafter, tempting them to sing thereof for ever in frenzied
ode and *mawgun*. But if thou grant that any slavewomen of
the inner palace who cannot find a place in the boats, be taken
at will by any, whether monk or layman, it will be accounted thee
as an act of kindness and a giving of life.' ' It is well,' said the
king ; and he set free three hundred slavewomen of the inner
palace, and men and monks made each their choice and took them
away. So the king embarked upon his raft of gold and jewels,
and went down to Bassein in the country of the Talaings.

[Death of Anantapyissi at Mt. Mali.] Now when Ngahsaunggyan
perished, the generals Anantapyissi and Rantapyissi made retreat,
and building two towns to the east of Mt. Mali they renewed the
defence. The two generals put into their mouths dead quicksilver,
and leaping into the sky as high as fifteen or sixteen cubits they
made assault on the Tarops. Thereupon Anantapyissi was smitten
by an arrow shot in the war of spirits, and falling from the sky he
died. Then because the host of the Tarops was very great, they
could not be victorious but were despoiled again. And ever the
Tarops pursued them.

[Pursuit and return of the Tarops.] So the generals gave the
order to retreat that they might save the multitude of the army
from destruction. And when they reached Pagan, lo! the king
and all the inhabitants of the country had departed and fled to
a place of refuge; so they followed after him to Bassein. And
ever the Tarops pursued them; but when they reached Taropmaw
they turned back, for the distance of *ta* by land was very great,
and with the multitude of warring hosts food and drink were
never so scarce.

[Taroppye.] In the year 646, when two *pad* were wanting to
fulfil the twenty-seventh constellation, king Narathihapate fled
through fear of the Tarops. Therefore was that king called
Taroppye. And when he heard that the Tarops had departed, he
tarried five months in Talaing country and purposed to return to
his royal city.

[Uzana and Thihathu.] Now his son Uzana, ruler of Bassein,
spake into the ear of his father, saying, ' All men say it is clear that
when thou, O lord great and glorious, goest upstream, Thihathu,
ruler of Prome, will devise wicked plots and stratagems against
thee. It were wise, methinks, O king, to capture and keep young
Thihathu, ruler of Prome, while he followeth thee now.' The
king said naught in answer to his son but abode silent. So the
elder brother Uzana, ruler of Bassein, seized Thihathu, saying,
' Thou wilt certainly plot a wicked plot against my lord when he
cometh to Prome!' And he locked his feet in iron fetters and
bare him to Bassein.

Then Thihathu, ruler of Prome, cried aloud, ' I am innocent!'
And he wept sore. And when king Narathihapate, his father,
heard the sound of his crying, he took Thihathu, who lay locked

in iron fetters in Uzana's hand, and kept him fettered in a boat close to the royal raft of gold.   Then Nga Thanngè and Thadinngè, two servants of Thihathu ruler of Prome, disguised themselves as fishermen, and feigning to cast their nets in a small boat they stole Thihathu.   So Thihathu escaped, and going up to Prome he made haste and gathered an host of warriors and dwelt there, making all things ready to strengthen and fortify the town.

[*Queen Saw's comforting.*]   Now the king purposed to muster his army at Prome and to go upstream slowly, for his hosts of warriors were scattered.   And his sewers said, ' We cannot find thee three hundred dishes salted and spiced.'   And they served and set around him only an hundred and fifty dishes.   And the king wept, and, covering his face with the lappet of his sleeve, he cried, ' Alas! I am a poor man! '   Then said queen Saw : ' O king Alaung, all suffering creatures who wander in the three worlds must needs endure the eight world-predicaments.   Thine heart will not be comforted until thou weighest these words of the Law : '' Not even the universal monarch, king Mandhata, sovereign ruler of the four great Islands and two thousand lesser isles surrounding them, and of the two limboes of the world of spirits, is free from rise and fall, separations, and the breach of death." '

[*Queen Saw's reproach.*]   So the king's heart was comforted, and he took counsel with queen Saw and others, saying : ' Shall we go up to our royal city of Pagan, or shall we tarry here and collect our armies ? '   Queen Saw spake into his ear, ' 'Tis easy to say, we shall go up : but how are we to go?   Consider the state of the realm.   Thou hast no folk nor people, no host of countrymen and countrywomen around thee.   If thou enter thy city without them, it will go hard with thee if thou fall into the enemy's hand.   Thy countrymen and countrywomen tarry and will not enter thy kingdom.   They fear thy dominion; for thou, O king Alaung, art a hard master.   Therefore I, thy servant, spake to thee of old; but thou wouldst not hearken.   I said : Bore not thy country's belly. Abase not thy country's forehead.   Fell not thy country's banner. Pluck not out thy country's eye.   Break not thy country's tusk. Sully not thy country's face.   Cut not thy country's feet and hands !—But thou wouldst not hearken to my words ; and now it is hard indeed for the realm and villages to prosper! '

Then said the king again, ' What meanest thou ? '   Queen Saw answered : ' Bore not thy country's belly—that is, cast not reproach upon the rich when they are guiltless, for they are as the belly of thy kingdom. Seize not nor spoil them of their goods, and gold and silver. When rich men died, though they had sons and daughters to inherit, they gat not their inheritance. To seize their goods and squander them till all is gone, this it is to bore thy country's belly. Abase not thy country's forehead—that is, deal not harshly in thy reckless choler with thy chief and faithful councillors and captains, who are as thy country's forehead. Fell not thy country's banner—that is, wax not wroth nor rage blindly against the wise men, monks and hermits, who are as thy country's banner. Pluck not out thy country's eye—that is, be not wroth and furious as a devil, without let or thwarting of thine anger, against thy wise chaplains learned in the Pitakas and Vedas, who are as thy country's eye. Break not thy country's tusk—that is, do not chafe and fume, heedless of the future, against the members of thy family, who are as thy country's tusk. Sully not thy country's face—that is, take not by force another's children who are as the mirror of their parents, their husbands, or sons, for such are as thy country's face. Cut not thy country's feet and hands—that is, kill not in anger, regardless of the future and the present, thy soldiers who are as thy country's feet and hands.' And the king said, ' My queen, thou didst not tell me all this tale before ! '

[*The king goes up to Prome.*] And the queen continued, saying, ' O king, this is not all. Even now Thihathu hath reached Prome, his fief. Doubt not but Thihathu will give thee trouble ! ' But the king said, ' Nay. Did not I alone save his life ? When his brother held him in iron fetters and led him away to die, I took and saved him alive. How should he harm me ? ' Said he, ' I will get me to Prome and gather mine army, and thence will I go up to my royal city of Pagan ! '

[*His death.*] So they went upstream in rout and disarray, without union or order. And when they reached the port of Prome, Thihathu stopped the royal raft, and, putting poison in the food, he offered it, and said, ' O king, eat ! ' But the king wist that there was poison in the food, and he would not eat. When Thihathu heard it he caused three thousand soldiers to go and stand around the royal raft with gleaming swords unsheathed within their hands.

And the queen Saw spake into his ear : ' O king Alaung, all this hath befallen because thou wouldst not hearken to my words of old. And now it is nobler for thee to eat of the poisoned dish and die, than to meet a fearful death with thy blood gushing red at point of sword and lance and weapon ! ' Then he took the ring from off his finger, and let fall drops of water over it, and gave it to queen Saw. And he made a solemn vow and said : ' In all the lives wherein I wander throughout *samsara* until I reach *nirvana,* may I never have man child born to me again ! ' And he took the food and ate ; and even as he ate, he died.

Sixteen years in the nether house, thirty-five years he flourished ; he passed at the age of fifty-one. About the time of his death the Pahto pagoda showed a mighty miracle ; smoke issued from the little hills and ridges of the fields ; from within the month of Pyatho the sign of the zodiac passed into Tagu ; the Thursday star alighted on the moon ; the earth quaked with a great echoing sound. He was born on a Sunday.

The Great Chronicle gives the king's birthday as Monday. But in view of the statement—' The wing-broken *garula* takes refuge in a hill '—made in old prophetic writings of Pagan, and of historical glosses which agree in writing Sunday, it is best to regard him as a Sunday child.

[*His children.*] Queen Saw had no son nor daughter. The king's son Uzana of Bassein was born of Sawnan, daughter of Queen Saw's elder sister, chief of the concubines ; he had, moreover, a younger sister, Hpwasawshin (the New Chronicle does not mention her). The king's son Kyawzwa, ruler of Dala, was born of Shinhpa. His son Thihathu, ruler of Prome, was born of Shinmauk. His daughter Misaw-u was born of Shinshwe. The records speak not of any son or daughter of Sawlon.